RAISA,
WHAT HURTS
MY HEART...

Diaries. Interviews. Letters

London
2022

HERTFORDSHIRE PRESS

Published by Hertfordshire Press Ltd © 2022
e-mail: publisher@hertfordshirepress.com
www.hertfordshirepress.com

RAISA, WHAT HURTS MY HEART...

Diaries. Interviews. Letters

Book compiled by **Georgi Pryakhin**

Translated from Russian by **David Floyd, Timur Akhmedjavov**

Edited by **Johnatan Campion**

Typeset by **Alexandra Rey**

British Library Catalogue in Publication Data
A catalogue record for this book is available from the British Library
Library of Congress in Publication Data
A catalogue record for this book has been requested

ISBN: 978-1-913356-54-5

This book was prepared for publication with the participation of President Mikhail Gorbachev, its Russian version was approved by him. Unfortunately, Mikhail Sergeyevich would not see the English edition: on the penultimate day of the summer of 2022, as you know, he had passed away.

The authors, compilers and publishers of the book express their deep condolences to the family of M. S. Gorbachev, the Foundation that bears his name, in connection with the death of this major political figure of modern times, a true peacemaker and reformer: thank you for your help in preparing the publication. We also express gratitude to the Foundation of the first President of Kazakhstan N.A. Nazarbayev, who provided financial assistance in the translation and publication of the book. This publication is dedicated to the blessed memory of Raisa and Mikhail Gorbachev.

On behalf of the authors and publishing teams,
Marat Akhmedjanov

Prologue

From the book by M. S. Gorbachev
"Alone with Myself"

After Raisa's death, I had never felt my loneliness so acutely. For almost 50 years, Raisa and I were together, side by side, and never felt burdened by this. On the contrary, we always felt good together. We loved each other, but even in private we didn't talk much about it. It seemed to us that our main attitude was to save everything that was born in youth. We understood each other and protected our relationship. I can't help feeling guilty about Raisa's death. I try to remember everything and ask myself: why could I not save her? Recently, I saw how worried Raisa was about what was happening to us: how is it that dishonourable people, devoid of conscience, irresponsibility, took over our country? She often talked about it, and when in response I reproached her to stop thinking about the same thing all the time, Raisa would close herself up and fall silent. I felt sorry for her. I painfully experienced her suffering… Again and again, I return to the last night I spent with Raisa – from September 19th to 20th. She died at 2:57am on September 20th, 1999. Raisa died without feeling pain: she was in a coma. We could not say our last parting words to each other. Raisa passed away two days before the scheduled transplantation of stem cells taken from the bone marrow of Raisa's sister Lyudmila. Raisa died five days before the 46th anniversary of the registration of our marriage in the Sokolniki registry office in Moscow.

Until the end, I believed in her salvation and could not accept what had happened. Helpless and confused, Irina and I stood at her head: "Don't leave Zakharka (it's what I called Raisa in our family.) Do you hear me?" I took her hands, hoping that she would at least shake her hands to my prayers. Raisa was silent – she had died... Even before the illness, I talked more than once with Raisa about our future. One day I heard something from her: "I don't want to be without you. I won't be able to live. And you? What about you? Will you marry and continue to live?" I was amazed by her judgement: "What are you talking about?! What are these thoughts that overwhelm you? What kind of death are you talking about? You are young. Look at yourself in the mirror. Listen to what people are saying... You are just tired." – "I don't want to be an old woman," is what often escaped her lips. And when our grandchildren began to appear, the question arose: how should they address her and me? It was she who came up with 'granny'. She explained: a grandmother is something decrepit, and a granny still has energy! She was like that... Raisa loved the parable about the age of women: "A young girl, a mature girl, a young woman, a young woman, a young woman, a young woman – a dying old woman." In the last years of our lives, she often had dreams where we were losing each other. More and more often I saw that Raisa was in a state of anxiety. Sometimes she told me: "Let's drive less." It was already difficult for her to travel long distances with me. But even more difficult – then it seemed to me, I saw it in her sad eyes – the worry of being alone.

One night, Irina and I stood by her bed, wept and could not do anything... It was Raisa's birthday. She would have been 69 years old. In our conversations about the future, she said more than once: if only she could live to see the new century and the new millennium, that's more than enough. She did not live another three months. We had a plan: to meet the onset of the year 2000 in such a way that it would forever remain in our memory. It turned out that Irina and her granddaughters had not yet been to Paris. And an idea was born: to meet the new year, the year 2000, in the most beautiful city in the world, on the Champs Elysees. This is what we planned to do until a terrible grief fell upon us. Nevertheless, the girls and I made a trip to Paris: it was a gift from Raisa to them... Today we were at the Novodevi cemetery. They brought a lot of flowers. It was before Christmas time. Snow fell during the night. I brought Raisa's favourite flowers – red roses. Before my eyes I saw an unforgettable image – red roses against the white snow–covered tombstone. We returned and sat down at the dinner table. On the wall was a large portrait of her, flowers, candles were burning, there was an elegant Christmas tree, the smell of pine needles. On the table was everything that she enjoyed. In one sentence, it was a Russian dinner table with Siberian inclusions – with dumplings and an 'avant-garde' cake. The one that was prepared in the Kremlin confectionery, and which received its name from Raisa. We raised our glasses and stood in silence...

After dinner I went up to the office. Without turning on the light, I stood at the window. The territory of the dacha (a type of Russian holiday home) was illuminated by night lanterns, a dense Russian forest and falling snow, as if you are watching "The Nutcracker" at the Bolshoi Theatre. There was a tradition in the family: to celebrate every New Year with a visit to the Bolshoi Theatre. We watched the Nutcracker ballet and returned home. Then we would say farewell to the old year and then give out gifts, those that Santa Claus, despite the "strengthened security" in the Presidential mansion, managed to bring to our Christmas tree. There was music, there was fun... These are all memories of a past life, of the time when we were all together. Raisa loved the Russian winter and especially liked to walk on wintery days. Once, when we lived in Stavropol, there was a snowstorm and we got lost. Another time when we were in Moscow. Raisa was born in Altai; she spent her childhood and youth in Siberia. For several years her family – who were builders of railways – lived in the Northern Urals, in the taiga. She often recalled sleigh rides, when they, as children – Raisa, Zhenya and Lyudochka – were wrapped in sheepskin coats and taken to a new place of residence. On winter evenings in Siberia, dumplings were traditionally made, then they were frozen and carried out in a bag in the cold. Dumplings were Raisa's favourite food.

I return again to her last days... She courageously fought for her life, patiently endured everything that the doctors did. It was unbearably hard to see. In those difficult, desperate moments, she looked in my eyes, in the eyes of her daughter, for an answer – what will happen to her... On July 22nd, when the doctors at the Central Clinical Hospital made a diagnosis and brought Raisa to the ward, I went to her. She, looking into my eyes, asked: "What did the doctors say?" Understanding her condition, I said: "They are talking about an acute blood disease." – "Is this the end?" Was her question. "No." We had decided to fly to Germany the next day, for additional tests. What hurts my heart... are the examinations to understand the full picture of the disease. There were questions about her treatment… We flew to Munster with the hope of Raisa's recovery. And on September 21st they returned by plane with her, already dead. So, for Raisa, her earthly life had ended.

Moscow, 2012

I HOPE...

Raisa Gorbacheva
tells of herself, of her past and her present in conversation
with writer Georgi Pryakhin

Translator's Note
For the sake of clarity, the words spoken by the interviewer,
Georgi Pryakhin, are printed in italics throughout

To the Soviet Reader

This book was written at the request of foreign publishers. At the very beginning, I speak about the motives that prompted me to respond to these proposals – I will not repeat myself. But, having finished work on the book, I decided to offer it to the Soviet publishing house. And that's why I also receive requests from our publications, television, radio, and journalists for interviews, meetings, and conversations. In numerous letters, addressing me with their thoughts, troubles and wishes, people also ask a lot of questions of a "personal" nature. In addition, a lot of various printed materials related to our family appeared. And I thought: since there is an interest in the family life of the president of the USSR in society, it is better that people learn about it, as they say, through a first-hand account. In addition, for me, this is an opportunity to share with you my pain, my anxieties and hopes, which, I believe, are in tune with the anxieties and hopes of every Soviet family, to everyone who cherishes our common father's house. I am against double standards in anything, including differences in publicity "for export" and publicity within the country, so the book that you, dear reader, are holding in your hands is identical in everything to the one that comes out in the American version published by Harper-Collins.

R. M. Gorbacheva

To the Foreign Reader

I have explained in the first chapter of my book, entitled 'Invitation to an Interview', the motives that prompted me to take up my pen and write this book. I can add to what I have already said only this: for the last few years I have resolutely rejected all the offers I have had to write a book or to give interviews about myself and my family. But now that I have decided to do so my decision is just as firm. This probably happens with many people, and so it has happened with me.

My book *I Hope* had a short gestation – just four months. It is not a book of memoirs or an autobiography with its scrupulous attention to chronology and detail. Still less is it a systematic exposition of my views and beliefs, although they are present in the book. It is a book of straight speaking, probably at times inconsistent, emotional, and patchy. It is a story about myself in the past and in the present, about events and impressions gained on the spot. It is a spontaneous and particularly personal response to what is happening around me and to the dramatic conflicts, shocks and, nevertheless, accomplishments that now distinguish public life in my country.

For me this book provides an opportunity to express myself, to explain certain things and to put to rest certain misunderstandings. It also enables me to share my problems, my anxieties, and my hopes. If that finds a response in your hearts, I will be happy.

As for the form the book takes, it seemed to me that, bearing in mind all the circumstances I have mentioned, the most natural form would be a live conversation.

Raisa Gorbacheva

*"If you think about it – how many good things
in the world rest on one single kind person"*
Raisa Gorbacheva

Raisa, What Hurts My Heart

Invitation to an Interview

I might very well have got to know back in 1964 the wife of the man who was to become the first Soviet President. She was then living near me – a couple of hundred kilometres from the small town where, left at an early age without parents, I was brought up, first in a children's home and later in a school for working-class boys where every other classmate was nearly twice my age and weight. It was there that I began my career as a reporter. At times the future 'first lady' would come a lot closer to our town as she made her way through the daunting sea of mud that the country roads turned into in the autumn. She was then probing into the depths of village life, pursuing her sociological surveys. Like a good agronomist, a real village sociologist has chosen a foot-slogging career. I have before me at the moment a booklet made of poor-quality faded paper published in 1967, on which is written: 'R. M. Gorbacheva. Summary of thesis submitted in support of an application for the degree of Doctor of Philosophy'. It is entitled 'The Development of New Features in the Life of the Peasantry in Collective Farms.' This frail researcher would make her way round the villages in her rubber boots – try to lift your boot out of the mud and your foot in its thick woollen sock comes out of the boot – because at that time there was no other way of getting round the villages as they were then. She would drink tea with the old women and war widows. A truly

17

foot-slogging profession, that of a village sociologist! But she was hardly likely to have used the unfamiliar term 'sociologist' to introduce herself in those days. She probably used other words, more intelligible to the country folk.

It was, however, many years later and a long way from those places that we got to know each other. It was in Moscow that it happened. And now a few days ago I received an unexpected invitation to act as a sort of interviewer for a book largely of a biographical nature. Today I was invited to the president's suburban residence. It turned out not to be a long journey ... Once through the gate the car swept round the driveway, skirting some wood, probably planted many years ago, a 'bright' plantation of trees, as we Russians say. The thick tops of the spruce and firs and the branches of the limes made patterns against the darkening sky, and the older, rugged limes were sunk deep in the undisturbed snow. Beyond the trees I caught sight of a compact yellow two-storey building that reminded me of a country house of the end of the last century. The Volga braked to a halt, and I stepped out and saw Raisa Maksimovna Gorbacheva standing in the wide double glass doors. She was wearing a patterned sweater, probably knitted at home. I had already seen her once in that sweater – at the central republican children's hospital which she supported, and which she had visited some days previously quite informally and had spent more than three hours there. I'd not seen her wearing trousers. The sweater, the trousers and the slippers with cloth tops suited the lady of the house. 'Hello,' she said, stretching out her hand from the threshold. Her look was attentive and welcoming. There was nothing very striking about the hall:

18

indeed, it was rather too functional. To the left, inside the house, was a cloakroom. My overcoat looked rather lonely there. Below the hooks were some house shoes. All the same, I didn't change my shoes. We went up to the first floor by the steep, spotlessly clean stairs. There were some framed pictures hanging on the wall. My hostess pointed to one of them:

— How do you like this owl? People send me as mementoes whatever they can, whatever they can do, especially children. So, they sent me the owl. I asked for it to be hung here. I believe the owl is the symbol of tranquillity and wisdom. Isn't that so?

I was not sure about wisdom, but the owl on the wall was good-natured and anything but grey. It was immediately apparent that the little person who drew it made use of every single colour that came to hand. We went into the library and then into the president's study, which turned out to be much smaller than might have been expected. It was an ordinary room but beautifully panelled in wood. Two things struck me immediately as I crossed the threshold – the bright red, oddly shaped telephone beneath a transparent cover, and an enlarged photograph in a frame standing in a gap between the bookshelves. As for the telephone, I immediately realised, of course, the sort of telephone it was, to judge by its striking colour. As for the large, framed portrait, I could not immediately place it. The president resembles his mother far more than he does his father – that is what I realised a moment later. The enlarged photograph was of a man with a contented smile, as if after long and hard labours, and a thinning tuft of hair. His tunic, open at the neck, was quite worn out – that was clear even in a black-and-white photo. Rows of medals hung on his broad chest. The soldier in the photo had seen life, as they say. He was obviously well over twenty. He was one of the workhorses who had borne the brunt of the war and after. The photo looked as if it had been taken just after the end of the war. The bright red telephone and the enlarged photograph are facing one another. When the president is sitting in his chair at his desk, he probably exchanges glances with his father, now sadly dead. Books in glass-fronted cases covered the walls from top to bottom in the library and the study. I made an effort to remember the titles – perhaps I would have to write about them some day. There were beautiful volumes on Russian history – Solovyev, Karamzin, Klyuchevsky... Through one of the doors, I noticed a strip of paper stuck to a shelf with writing on it: 'Friends – please arrange these alphabetically..." My hostess said with a smile:

— 'In this room I am secretary and librarian and filing clerk all in one. I try to bring some order into things.'

I can't be quite sure, but I was possibly the first member of the Soviet Union of Writers to examine the president's library. In a corner on a shelf behind a pile of books I noticed a postcard in colour with an inscription in French.

— Nikolai Benois. A memento.

The preliminary, improvised excursion was over. If I try hard, I can name only two things that might be called luxuries: the desk in the library with its top made of Karelian birch – very impressive and official-looking – and the cleanliness. It was that zealous, living, almost sweet-smelling cleanliness that hovered in the air and seemed vaguely to recall the cleanliness of the village houses in southern Russia, a resemblance probably evoked also by the photo of the soldier, badly wounded but still returned from the war – it is a rare home in Russia that does not have such a picture. The windows had beautifully hung net curtains. My hostess drew the curtain back for me to look. A little distance from the window, half hidden in the twilight, the trees could be seen in silhouette. The garden?

— The garden... the 10th of March 1985. The day Konstantin Ustinovich Chernenko died. At 10 o'clock in the evening there was a specially summoned meeting of the Politburo. Mikhail Sergeyevich returned home very late – we were then living in the country house near Moscow. We went out into the garden. There was something oppressive in the late-night air, still untouched by the spring. Three deaths in three years. The death of three general secretaries, the country's top leaders, one after the other. Mikhail Sergeyevich was very tired. At first, he remained silent. Then he said: 'Tomorrow there will be a full meeting of the Central Committee. The question may arise of my taking over the leadership of the party.' This was completely unexpected news for me. It was to some degree a shock. More than that. I realised that it was also a surprise for my husband. And we had never previously discussed this subject together. We strolled around the garden where the snow was still lying. My husband again remained silent. Then he appeared quietly to be thinking aloud. 'I worked so many years in Stavropol. This is my seventh year in Moscow. But it is impossible to achieve anything substantial, anything on a large scale, the things the country is waiting for. It's like coming up against a wall.

Yet life demands it and has done for a long time. No!' I heard him say. '**We just can't go on like this.**' That was the first time I heard those words.

We had been sitting for a long time at a small, polished table. The tape recorder was switched on. I had my pen and notebook in my hands. I could see that my interlocutor had undoubtedly been preparing for today's meeting. But those preparations had nothing elaborate about them. She did not have even a notebook, only odd pieces of paper. They were pages pulled out of a notebook and from an ordinary school exercise book, folded in half or quarters with sometimes a complete page of white writing paper mixed up in a bundle. She would take out the next piece of paper which might have just one sentence written on it, glance at it for a moment, as people glance thoughtfully at a playing card, read out the words when she had deciphered them, and, putting her notes aside, develop the thought she had written down. There was nothing zealously methodical about her summary notes or about her reminiscences themselves. It was done and recorded in a hurry. I imagine it works like this: something comes to mind in the course of the day's activities, some thought she has been groping for suddenly comes to the surface, and she quickly makes a note of it on the first thing that comes to hand. If it is true that the style makes the man, then in this case the pieces of paper reflect the style, not just of a way of thinking but of a life far from being without cares.

— So that was the first time I heard those words. Today they are repeated by millions of people and whole legends have grown up around them. I suppose one can say that that night marked the beginning of a new phase that brought radical changes into the life of our country and my life too. The 'Perestroika' years... What have they given us? A great deal. The democratisation of every aspect of our life. The advent of new thinking in international affairs. As I have accompanied the president on trips in this country and abroad, the most important thing I have detected in the sea of human emotions and good wishes is the newly born faith in the possibility of living without war. The 'Perestroika' years have given us much. And at the same time very little. It is hard for our country now, very hard. There are problems that have been building up for decades and maybe for centuries. The difficulty of finding new ways. The shortage of consumer goods. And again, something very important: In the words of Dostoevsky, in a time of troubles and change you always get all sorts of 'dirt' everywhere. Unfortunately, our 'Perestroika' has not been able to avoid that dangerous, destructive and corrosive 'dirt'. How could it be otherwise? On the whole, it is a time of hopes and alarms, of achievements and failures. A time for thoughts and doubts. It is difficult to talk about oneself. It is always difficult, I suppose, for everyone. But today it seems particularly difficult for me to do so.

The telephone rang. I guessed it was not the red one. That probably had a different tone. And in any case, it couldn't ring in the absence of the man in whose study it stood. Its tone certainly followed him around, on his heels wherever he happened to be – in his study, in his car or at some political meeting.

— How are you feeling, Mikhail Sergeyevich? Tired?

I did not hear the reply, if only because I rose and went quietly from the study to the library.

— It is difficult to talk about oneself. I have already had repeated proposals from various newspapers and magazines to give them an interview. And from publishers, including American ones, requests to produce a book about myself. I have not done so. And, to tell you the truth, I never thought of doing it. I neither did it nor thought of doing it. For various reasons, primarily subjective ones. It always seemed to me to be quite unnecessary. I say this quite sincerely. Why should I talk about myself? Just about me? I am not a film star or a writer or an artist or a musician or a fashion designer. And I am not a politician. I am not a statesman who has to take major decisions and be responsible for people's fates. I am the wife of the head of the Soviet state, supporting my husband as far as I can and helping him as I have always done ever since our young days when we linked our lives together. In our family we have always had, and still have, this understanding: the problem of each member of the family is everybody's problem. In 1985, because of Mikhail Sergeyevich's journeys and the visits paid to us by the heads of other states, a problem arose. It is the tradition in other countries for the wives of leaders to take part in various public and formal occasions. This was not the practice of our predecessors. What were we to do? Mikhail Sergeyevich said: 'Let everything happen naturally.' So, quite naturally, we began to adopt the practice, accepted throughout the rest of the world: the wife of the leader of the state began to appear in public. It is just another sign of the 'liberalisation' introduced by 'Perestroika', though it was far from being the most important. The way I behave now and the way my husband and I behave today is the natural continuation of the relationship between us, our careers, and our lives. We have certainly not thought up anything 'special' because of our new duties. So, I ask myself again, is there any need to write about me, or for me to talk about myself? After all, what is most important is the cause for which Mikhail Sergeyevich, his colleagues and supporters are working: that – his cause – is what essentially determines my manner of life today.

And again, it was not the practice in our country for the wives of top leaders to give interviews or write books, especially about themselves. This may appear to a Western reader to be a prejudiced view. But prejudices can also be traditions, and it presumably behoves the wife of the president to observe the traditions to an even greater extent than the president himself, especially in such matters. Nevertheless, I am in this case breaking the sort of 'vow of silence' that I have kept since 1985. I have been brought to this by the logic of life and pushed into it by the meetings and contacts I have had with people, and by the lively and quite genuine, and I would say grateful, interest in our affairs today which are being followed so keenly throughout the world. And finally, the problem of 'Soviet Woman and Perestroika' and the questions put to me, including those in so many letters. Among the innumerable meetings that led me gradually to think about producing a book were those that took place in America. First in 1987 and then in the summer of 1990 when I made a trip with Mrs Barbara Bush to visit a women's college, where the girls showered me with questions. That finally changed my mind. Moreover, it was in those years, around the world and in our own country, that quite a lot of material, articles and even books about me appeared in which goodwill was by no means always accompanied by knowledge of the facts, and on occasion accuracy was totally absent, and invention, myths and even slander became the 'bases' of what was written. Certain authors will forgive me for saying this, but if it had not been for my name appearing in the text, I would never have believed that they were writing about me. It was then that I decided that I would tell my story, about my understanding of life, about what I have lived through, about what was close and dear to me. To speak to those who are willing to listen. To recount and to talk. I have invited you, Georgi Vladimirovich, to be my interviewer.

She put the piece of paper aside. There was a pause. 'Perhaps we should explain why the choice fell on me?' I asked, although I did not know what the reason was – which is why I asked.

— Well, for one reason, because I know you. Because you were born in Stavropol, where Mikhail Sergeyevich was also born. And, finally, because you have four daughters in your family. Therefore, you are a humane and good person. Is that enough?'

'Plenty, in my view.'

— No. The most important thing is that all your children are living with you. That tells me a great deal.

'Thank you,' I said, although I admit it was the first time, I had been praised for that. Truth to tell, the family often criticises me for not improving our lot – seven people in a single flat makes life difficult. A pity they don't hear. My notebook is full. The tape recorder has been switched off. Tea has been drunk. Outside, beyond the net curtains at the window there is complete darkness. We put everything back in its place in the president's study – the table and the two chairs. The cut–glass vase is moved from the president's desk to a low side-table. In parting I glance round the room once more. Next to the photograph of his father is a slightly smaller one of his wife, taken early in their marriage. It is the face of a young girl with a very concentrated, highly attentive expression, looking straight ahead but still seeming to be turned in upon herself.

— That was the year I finished university. Do you know what struck me recently? I am wearing a grey jacket and a dark red blouse. Can you believe it? Yet they still talk of a lack of constancy in women's character.

Grey is one of her favourite colours. The same grey colour that the author Ivan Bunin defined in his elegant way as being not grey at all but 'pearly'. Pearly-grey. But the photograph is a black-and-white one! That means she could remember both the jacket and the blouse. It was what she wore as a student after the war, and like the rest of us she had no difficulty in recalling It. We went downstairs by the same wooden staircase. In the very functional hallway, I notice something I had for some reason not noticed before. It was a little decorated doll's house with a toboggan next to it. It was a very touching reminder of the New Year seen in very official premises.

— That is a completely private house in a state residence. It belongs to the grandchildren. I'm afraid they are both down with colds at the moment.

I left in the same car by the same entrance. The soldier standing beneath the light at the gate saluted as I departed. He was the only soldier I saw at the residence. In fact, I saw only three people altogether: the man on the gate, my hostess, and a charming woman who served the tea and whom the President's wife, with Russian simplicity and friendliness, addressed as 'Shura'. On the way back into Moscow we did not meet a car returning with the president. It was eight o'clock — too early for him to be coming home.

We Were All Children Once

— *Raisa Maksimovna, I have already guessed that you like Antoine de Saint-Exupéry and I have heard you quote more than once passages from Le Petit Prince. I will begin our conversation today with a well-known quotation from Exupéry: 'We were all children once...'*

— Yes, I love him and the little fellow he created, who performed such great and good deeds. Childhood is a world of fantasy and dreams. A time for thousands of questions. And the first attempts to find answers to them. Every one of us had a childhood. And then, when we were children, it seemed as though there could be no other childhood. That is how it remains dear to us. We went to school, then to pioneer groups, and then to young Communist meetings. We were proud of our country's achievements – Magnitka, Dneproges, Komsomolsk on the Amur, the voyage of the Chelyuskin, Valeri Chkalov, Valentina Grizodubova. We admired the heroism of Aleksandr Matrosov, Zoya Kosmodemyanskaya, the Young Guards. We read every book that came to hand. We dreamt about long journeys, faraway countries and cities. My dream was to be the captain of an ocean-going ship... We dreamt of finding treasure. We were always looking for treasure!

— *Today my young ones dream mostly about meeting creatures from other planets.*

— No, we never lost hope and went on stubbornly looking for treasure. Then, of course, we played war games. I know all children

29

play at war in one way or another. But for the children of my generation playing at war had very painful associations – often it was too close to reality. Of course, we played at schools and with our dolls, but what stays in my mind is playing at war. Each of us, of course, wanted to be a partisan, Chapayev or Anka, and, if they weren't given any other 'positive' role, even the little boys were willing to be Anka, the girl from the film Chapayev. No one wanted to be a White, or a German or a Fascist. It didn't occur to us that those same Whites, for example, were also our fellow countrymen. Yes, as I look back now over the years and reflect on my childhood and my generation, and as I study, for example, the photographs I was looking through before you arrived, the most important thing I recall is war. It followed us everywhere. War in Spain. Detachments of volunteers. The Finnish war. The clash with Japanese troops in Khalkin-Gol. And within the country too? The 1930s and the 'enemies of the people'. I remember how, in the first and second grades at school the pictures of Yegorov, Blyukher, Tukhachevsky (military leaders executed in the Purge of 1939) were blotted out in our textbooks. I feel sad, bitter recalling it. And then, finally, the Patriotic War of '41 to '45. Millions of lives lost, millions of lives ruined. Houses laid waste, families orphaned, towns and villages destroyed, scorched earth... Crowds swarming the railway stations. The country was turned into one big railway station. It seemed as though there were only two emotions prevailing – parting and waiting. Faces swollen from hunger. And the feeling of fear – of losing your food ration card or your bread ration. I remember it to this very day. And gleaning the fields for ears of grain and frozen potatoes. That is the way it was. For me and for all my age group. Then came the joy of victory. That had to be experienced.

The happiness of welcoming those close and related to you back home and alive. And, altogether, that overwhelming feeling of the joy of being alive, just, you know, being physically alive. My father was born in 1907 and was a Ukrainian. My mother, born in 1913, is Russian, a native of Siberia. Georgi Vladimirovich, we agreed that there would be no precise or strict logical order in my observations, didn't we? I would rather describe them as a mosaic, spoken on impulse. Things that sprang to mind and fitted in with my current mood. These are not memoirs, isn't that so?

— *That is exactly what I like about them – that they are not memoirs. And I like the fact that you react emotionally when you recall your childhood and those years and do not simply set them out unemotionally on their shelves.*

— My father worked throughout his life on the railway system. Whenever I filled in questionnaires I always wrote: father a railway employee. Non-Party. Oh yes, non-Party. Faith in the Party came to my father along with Mikhail Sergeyevich, my husband. Despite the difference in their ages, my husband became for him a symbol of what a Communist should be. My father arrived in Siberia in the spring of 1929. He was born in Chernigov but came to Siberia in 1929.

— *Where exactly did he move to?*

— He came to work on building the railway. The first railway my father built was the one from Rubtsovsk to Ridder in the Altai. His parents – his father Andrei Filippovich and his mother Maria Maksimovna – abandoned their land in the village and went to live in the town, Chernigov. They left the land because they couldn't feed themselves from it. My father went with his comrades in search of work to the West Siberian region, as it was then called. It is now the Altai region. He found work building the railway, which was actually to run through the village where my mother was born – Veseloyarsk. Oh yes, there is such a village – I just received a letter with New Year greetings from there. Mikhail Sergeyevich said of me in the course of an interview that I was born in Siberia, in the Altai region, in Rubtsovsk. So, the people there began to take an interest in me and my mother. I am touched by that well-meaning interest. And so, it was in Veseloyarsk that my parents linked their lives. My father carried on building the railway and met his wife in the process. Veseloyarsk is a nice name. There aren't so many such names in our country. For some reason we don't like to draw attention to what is best in the character of our towns and villages – is it part of our national character? Sometimes when you are travelling you read the names of the places and can be really put off by them – Gryaznukha, say, or Cherny Yar... But here we have Veseloyarsk. (In Russian, *gryaznukha* means 'dirty place', *cherny yar* means 'black hole', and *veseloyarsk* means 'happy town.')

— *Gogol also pointed that out.*

— I was the first child in the family. I was christened in accordance with the Orthodox tradition. Not in church, of course

– what sort of church could there be then in 1932 at the very height of the struggle against the Church – but in a priest's home. True, my name was not taken from the Church calendar. As you know, the tradition was for the priest to propose a name that he found in the calendar. But it was my parents who chose my name. My father chose it. It is well known how many beautiful national Slavic and Russian names we have. But at that time new names were being invented. New names for new times. Among people of my age lots were called Oktyabrina, referring to the October Revolution, and Vladilena, referring to Vladimir Lenin. And new names were appearing among the better-educated – Nelly, Jeanne, or Alla. But my father named me Raisa – Rayechka. He explained to me later that for him it meant 'rai' – 'paradise'. The apple in the Garden of Eden.

— *It is also used very widely in my part of the country. But I have never heard such an explanation for it. Your father has a good imagination!*

— Don't forget that I was the first child. My father was very fond of all his children but nevertheless he was particularly attached to me throughout his life. To his first child. And he was very proud of me. In the last months of his life, when he lay in hospital here in Moscow, he told me that for some reason he kept thinking of his mother and of me as a little girl. 'I always knew, always felt that you were the one who would save my life,' he told me in hospital. Unfortunately, we did not succeed in saving him for long. He had a complicated operation. In 1986 he died. To recall myself sitting at his bedside in the hospital and to hear him saying what were in fact his parting words to me evokes too many personal emotions. Perhaps there's no need to talk about it? I would rather not.

— *Her voice is quiet. Quiet and at the same time distinct. It is easy to imagine her addressing an audience. I know there was a time in Stavropol when students, including some of my friends, were eager to attend her lectures. They are keen to listen to lecturers like her because they are also pleasant to look at, being more or less the same age as the students themselves. But she now uses a different voice from the one that can be heard from time to time on the television. It is the voice of a daughter whose audience is composed essentially of one person – herself.*

— My mother's parents [she continues, bringing her voice under control] Petr Stepanovich and Anastasia Vasilievna were also from a peasant family. Did they have an easy life? Don't you believe it – as my mother tells me now. Don't you believe that peasants were prosperous in the past. It was hard and hopeless labour. The land, the cattle and little to eat. Your poor grandmother! – my mother Aleksandra Petrovna exclaims every time. It was forced labour and not a normal life that she had. She ploughed, sowed, washed the clothes, and fed six children. And throughout her life not a word of complaint. My mother's sister Vera died when she was sixteen. What of? No one knows for sure. After all, there was no medical attention. The eldest brother Aleksandr died when he was twenty-six. Of what? Again, no one knows. Lenin gave my parents land – that is what my mother always says. Previously they didn't have their own land. They were told, according to my mother, to take as much as they wanted, as much as they could cultivate. But at the beginning of the 1930s my grandfather's family were treated as 'rich peasants', their land and house were taken from them, and they had to make a living by casual work. And later, my mother says, grandfather was accused of Trotskyism. He was arrested and disappeared without trace.

— *Really! Our unpredictable Russian history hangs as heavy as a soldier's greatcoat, soaked in blood. The person sitting opposite me has had a completely different career, a different age and, finally, different 'origins', as they said in olden days. But her grandfather was also ex-propriated. My grandfather was expropriated, and my father shipped from one part of the country to another. Where else can you come across this sort of thing? But in Russia, however painful it may be, you find it at every step.*

— Yes, don't be surprised. My mother still has no idea who Trotsky was, and my grandfather certainly didn't know. And to this very day my mother cannot understand what her father was accused of. We all lived through this common tragedy. That is why today I am so frightened by the appeals you hear on every side to 'seek out the guilty ones'. It would only lead to another round of bloodshed.

My grandmother died of grief and hunger as the wife of an 'enemy of the people'. And the four children she left behind were left to the mercy of fate. My grandfather Petr Stepanovich made sure that his sons had a good education. The eldest, Aleksandr, who died at the age of twenty-six, was trained as an economist. The youngest, Ivan, also had an education. But, in the Russian tradition, no special attention was given to the education of the daughters. In peasant homes the women were practically all illiterate. From the age of eight my mother did the ploughing and spinning. It was only after she was married that she attended courses in reading and writing. She helped her younger sister to be trained as a pharmacist. My mother is a person equipped with natural and very sharp intellectual qualities. All her life she regarded the lack of an education as her tragedy. So, she saw it as her main purpose in life to provide her own children with a proper upbringing. And she did in fact give all her children a good education. My mother did not go out to work: she remained a housewife. The never-ending moves the family had to make in the wake of my father, the railwayman, the trouble that this caused, the various flats we found to live in – goodness knows how many such 'nests' we occupied, and huts and wooden-frame houses. Although we did have one beautiful large wooden house in the Urals. Our family was given it in the war years, by what good luck I no longer remember. And for some time, we had an 'apartment' in the buildings of a former monastery. So, can you imagine what our life was like? That was the war. And even after the war our family lived as before, like birds of passage. It was only after forty years of work that my father and mother were provided with a permanent place to live, and even then with great difficulty. My mother remained a housewife also because by the time she was twenty-five she already had three children. But I can't remember a time, from childhood to the present day, when my mother was not busy at something or other, when she would sit and rest for a while. Throughout her life, her whole life, she was always sewing, mending, darning, knitting, cooking, embroidering, or cleaning. She mended everything herself, kept everything tidy, worked in the garden and, when it was possible, kept a cow or a goat so that the children could have milk. And she is still the same today, despite her years.

In character my mother is strict and demanding. I remember the scene when we accompanied my father off to the front. The overcrowded railway station – I really do recall from childhood so clearly and so sharply the railway stations with that unrepeatable sad atmosphere – women, children and tears. Many women even fainted. And I remember my mother, frozen in her grief. Her words were: 'Who's going to support us? We must hold out.' We saw our father off to the front, but he didn't reach it: he returned home in a military uniform. The whole rail network was put on a military footing. New railway lines had to be constructed in a hurry to serve the front. From our family mother's brother fought at the front and her sister was an army doctor. What did my parents give me? What did my family give? When I ask myself this, do you know what I think of involuntarily? That my parents and all those people who have borne the tragic burden of these years of our history, who have borne on their shoulders that heavy load, did not have an opportunity to realise themselves as they would have wished. That is probably why they made it their aim in life at least to achieve through their children those precious things which were quite out of reach for the overwhelming majority of them. As you know, we

Russians have the expression 'to lift children'. It is in my view a
very instructive metaphor. But I would even say this: our parents
did not give us only an education. By the way they lived their lives
they developed in us a sense of responsibility – for our deeds and
our behaviour. And perhaps the most important thing that my
parents gave me was a capacity to share other people's needs and to
enter into their grief, their pain: the quality of empathy... No, not
a single generation lives in vain on this sinful earth. These pictures
of my childhood lack completeness, they seem to be very sketchy.
One of the reasons, perhaps, is the endless 'moves' we endured. As
a result of our frequent changes of home I had to change schools
many times. And that, of course, created certain difficulties. Each
move meant new teachers, a different level of instruction, different
demands, and different schoolmates. And in general, increased
interest in the new girl, which was inevitable in such cases.

    — *Always the new girl? But does it not seem to you that this
has followed you in your adult life? For about two years I have been
accompanying you and Mikhail Sergeyevich on official trips and I see
how people's interest and journalistic curiosity in you has gradually
increased. Not only in the president – that's normal – but in you too.
When, during the campaign before the Party Congress, he visited the
Second Moscow watch factory, I heard the women in their white coats,
the ones who assemble the watches and who had crowded into the
workshop, asking as they craned their necks: 'Has Raisa come? Where
is she?' You will forgive me for quoting them literally, without your
patronymic. After all, as a woman acquires fame in Russia the first*

thing she loses is her patronymic.

— And what then?

— *I told them No, Raisa Maksimovna had not come along – it was a meeting to deal with strictly Party matters.*

— And what did they say?

— *They were disappointed.*

— Really? Well, the inevitable curiosity and a certain lack of trust in a new girl had an effect, of course, both on my studies and on how I felt. Throughout the years of childhood and youth I have experienced a sort of internal constraint, a feeling of diffidence, sometimes of isolation. After all, children have very odd ways.

— *Have you fully overcome that diffidence?*

— I don't know, any more than I know whether it ought to be 'fully' overcome. But the situation of being 'always the new girl' led me at the same time to develop contact with people. I simply had to become more social. The school of my childhood was not the modern school with all its equipment and furniture. It was completely different. I repeat, the schools varied in a way but were in the most important respects identical. Crudely knocked-together desks, home-made alphabet books, and during the war home-made exercise books, mostly made out of poor-quality paper. And even home-made ink.

— *Home-made ink?*

— Yes – made from soot. There was one textbook to every four or five pupils. During the war a daily bowl of watery soup for lunch. I can remember all of us children at that time, dressed in jerseys, padded jackets or at best in coats and an 'overcoat' out of some homespun or cotton material. There was such material, known as 'serge'. I received my first real overcoat as a present from my mother and father when I was already a university student. It had a small fur collar – a 'Boston', according to my mother. I wore it for a long time. The whole family remembers that coat. My father won a thousand roubles in a draw, and my mother says friends helped them to buy the coat in the village store. Such things were in short supply! Everybody remembers the coat – it really was a milestone in the family history. You know, we all turned up at the university in what we had – one person in her mother's overcoat, another in someone's jacket. That's the way it was.

All the same, it was my school, and, like my childhood, it remains dear to me. I was fond of the teachers. My girlfriends. We sang in the school choir. We produced plays on a stage in the school. The teachers and the head of the school took part in the plays along with us. Such things are now almost impossible, or perhaps that's how it seems to me. At gymnastics we used to construct a human pyramid. I was always lifted up to the very top, probably because I was the lightest. We went on marches. We collected scrap metal and wastepaper, planted out the school yard and published a wall newspaper. We organised school parties. We danced. And we received our first love letters. What else remains in my mind about my school years? We used to help the families who had lost members in the war. We made solemn vows to each other – to be faithful, always to stick together, to help each other and never to conceal anything from each other. We sealed our vows with 'Pioneer's honour' or 'Komsomol's honour'. And we even mixed drops of our blood by making cuts in our fingers. I remember that too. My father and mother did not go to school. In fact, I never called them 'father and mother'. It was 'Mama and Papa'. Neither did I use 'Batyushka and Matushka' – it was not done. Just Papa and Mama. And we always addressed them as 'You – in the second person plural. I can't recall an instance when my parents were summoned to the school. And they never checked on my homework. Only sometimes my father would tell me how he was educated. He was an educated man. He told me about the period of 'school reforms', when pupils moved from class to class according to the votes they received. The 'results' of the ballot were confirmed by the teachers at class meetings. It was up to the children whether they did their exercises or not. 'And look at an impressive product of that system,' my father would conclude, pointing at himself with a grin.

— *Leaving it to the children to decide... Today, at any rate in my home, it would be dangerous even to mention such a thing.*

— I completed the tenth grade in the town of Sterlitamak in Bashkiria. My school-leaving certificate said that I was 'awarded a gold medal for excellent results and exemplary conduct'. That gave me, and I quote from the certificate, 'the right to enter institutes of higher education in the USSR without entry examination'. That was the second year that gold medals were awarded. I chose to enter the Lomonosov State University in Moscow.

— *What year was that?*

— It was 1949. I was seventeen. Like many others, I also realised in childhood the importance of books, that miracle of miracles created by humanity. Books, the great works of literature, were my constant need and love in those years. I was not alone, as I have said, in experiencing this. It was precisely in those years that our country became, as we say today, 'a country of readers'. True, there weren't very many books to be had. No great choice. But we read everything that came our way, everything we could lay our hands on. And every book was a revelation to us. The happiest and brightest pages of my childhood that now float into my memory are of reading books in the family circle. I loved to read aloud. What wonderful evenings they were! The wood would be crackling in the fireplace or the stove. Mama would be cooking supper. My brother and younger sister would snuggle up to me side by side. And I would read. My father was seldom with us, very seldom. In those days you know how people worked – without any days off and without holidays. I remember that my father was 'compensated' for his holiday. That was the expression – 'compensation for holiday not taken'. He never went on holiday, but simply received additional pay and went on working the whole year round. And so, it went on, year after year.

We read everything: Panferov's *Bruski*, Sholokhov's *Quiet Flows the Don*, Tolstoy's *Anna Karenina*, Victor *Hugo's Notre Dame*, Dreiser's *An American Tragedy*, Dumas's *The Three Musketeers*, and his *Count of Monte Cristo*. We read Gogol – *Evenings on a Farm near Dikanka*, Boris Polevoi's *The Story of a Real Man*, Fadeyev's

The Young Guard, and Simonov's poetry. And when my father was with us, I always read Taras Shevchenko, above all his *Thoughts*. For example:

My thoughts, my thoughts, what pain you bring! Why do you rise up at me in such gloomy rows?

Or again:

It is hard, very hard, for a lonely orphan. Bitter yearning and sorrow could make me jump from the bridge. To drown and end this wandering from place to place. Life is unkind, unwelcoming, and I have nowhere to hide...

And again:

What use to me are my dark brows and brown eyes? Or my maidenly chastity that passes so swiftly. My youth is being wasted for nothing. And my dark brows bleached by the wind...

We were very fond of *Katerina* and *The Wide Dnieper*. I have been reading to you in Russian, but my father liked those poems to be read to him in the original Ukrainian – it sounds quite different!

— *The edition of The Kobza-player that she holds in her lap is in some way like a Bible – a very important, beautifully bound volume. She easily finds her way through it. Nevertheless, she has some difficulty switching between the Russian and the Ukrainian: it happens quite often with people who like to listen to Ukrainian and even sing Ukrainian songs. I, for example, cannot say Ukrainian lyrics; I just can't get the pronunciation right.*

— Whenever I pick up a volume of Shevchenko I immediately think of my father. I thought of him when I was last in Ukraine. I had a meeting with some writers in the republic, and we talked about Shevchenko and his Kobza-player. My father was so fond of it! My brother is three years younger than I, and my sister is six years younger. Each of us has, naturally, chosen his or her own way in life, his own career and fate. I always regarded my sister as a child who I, as the older one, took care of. Even today I still call her by the diminutive 'Lyudochka'. When I left home to study in Moscow my sister was only eleven. Of the childhood incidents connected with her and which I recall most often I would like to mention two. She, my brother and I were playing a game we were very fond of: guessing names that each of us had thought of, male or female. It was her turn to think up a name. For a long time, we just couldn't guess what it was. No matter how we tried it was to no avail. It even came to tears. We began to suspect her of cheating us. Then my mother intervened. Finally, my sister revealed the name to us. She said it was a man's name – 'Byvalocha'. We burst out laughing and understood at once who it referred to. At that time, as you know, there were no hotels in the smaller towns and villages. Travellers stayed with friends, and one of my father's colleagues was a frequent visitor in my parents' house. He was a good storyteller, a man who had been around a lot, and all our family loved to listen to him in the evenings. He always started every story with the words 'And so, *byvalocha* (Means 'once upon a time' in Russian), we...' The whole family made fun of his use of the word. But for my little sister it became a proper name, and that was what she had chosen. I can't remember now what the man's proper name was. But I remember very well his invariable *byvalocha*.

— *That is a game that relies on mutual honesty – we used to have something like it in our family.*

— Yes, children's games are all based on playing fair. And here's a second incident. German prisoners of war were brought into railway construction during the war. A fire broke out in the place where we were then living, and several houses were burnt to the ground. Others were partly damaged and needed repair. Among the latter was the house that our family was occupying. The Germans mended the roof of our house and helped us in other ways. My sister – she was very small, with blue eyes and fair hair – continually attracted their attention. On one occasion as I was playing in the courtyard, I saw a German go up to my sister and stretch out a hand to stroke her head. My heart shrank from fear. In a flash I was at her side and dragged her close to me. Only then did I look at the German, and I suddenly realised that he was crying. You know, I was really shaken! And there we stood – the young German weeping, with his head hung low, and I, a young girl, and my young sister clutching me in fright. When I recall that scene today, I think again and again about those feelings that then possessed me and all of us in those frightful days of the German invasion, and I think of the monstrous tragedy that befell millions of totally innocent people.

— *And I now recall seeing you at the cemetery for Soviet prisoners of war in Stukenbrock in West Germany.*

— Yes, I had very mixed feelings when, along with a number of public figures accompanying Mikhail Sergeyevich on his official visit to West Germany, we went to pay our respects at the graves of our unfortunate compatriots. A great number of Germans also arrived at the cemetery on that day. And it seemed to me that the spirit of reconciliation had descended upon that sorrowful place called Stukenbrock for the benefit of all of us, the living, and the dead. Forgiveness. You cannot live hating all the time. I believe that those endless rows of graves – not only in Stukenbrock but in our country too – summon us ultimately not to revenge but to reason... My sister graduated from a medical school. She is a doctor. Her husband is an engineer. She already has a grown-up son and a little granddaughter.

— *And your brother?*

— His life worked out differently. He is a gifted and talented person. But his potential was not fated to be realised. His talents turned out to be unwanted and were ruined. My brother drinks and spends many months in hospital. His fate is a tragedy for our mother and father. For me it is a constant source of pain which I have carried in my heart for more than thirty years now. His tragedy brought me a lot of sorrow, all the more so since we were very close in our childhood: we were always very sincerely attached to one another. It is very hard and painful.

— *Raisa Maksimovna withdrew into herself. And I began to think again about Mother Russia and drink: there are too many very similar, purely Russian disasters in the history of practically every family in the country, irrespective of its position in society. Even today our families are plagued by the same Russian curse.*

— *The time had come to ask a leading question about some other subject. But I just couldn't think of a question. I myself have things to recall on this theme that we touched on by chance.*

— As I looked back on one or the other period of my life, I discovered unexpectedly something surprising! [My host resumed our conversation without any leading questions.] Perhaps not so much surprising as natural. All my memories of my childhood, adolescence, youth, and even adult years are invariably accompanied by some colourful and powerful impression derived from nature. I am convinced that this springs from my childhood. I grew up in the midst of nature. Nature and children constitute in my view a sort of single source. The pure beauty of the natural world has nothing to rival it in this world. I always carry with me the smell of the cherry tree and of pine needles. The joy of hearing the noise of the streams in the Urals in the spring. In the Stavropol region spring passes very quickly; there are no streams; they are in the Urals. It is a real joy. The joy of streams rushing down in the spring and the deep snowdrifts on a frosty, sunny day. And the beauty of the emerald-coloured moss and the patterned embroidery on it – cloudberries, whortleberries, columbines. And all the different kinds of mushrooms hiding themselves away – milk-caps and milk agaric, boletus and Russula. It all belongs back there, to my childhood. And it is from there, I believe, out of my childhood, that springs – for me too – that nostalgia for the silver birch or a field of rye or wheat, edged with cornflowers and camomile, that lives eternally in every Russian's heart. Then later comes the yearning for the scarlet Stavropol steppe in springtime, ablaze with tulips to the horizon. And for the crimsons and violets and greens and yellows of autumn in the North Caucasus. I am convinced that the maltreatment of the natural world and its impoverishment leads to the impoverishment of the human soul. It is related to the outburst of violence in human society. To save the natural world today means to save what is human in humanity. In an interview he once gave, Mikhail Sergeyevich was asked what his favourite leisure occupation was, and he replied: walking on forest paths. Yes, the tracks in the Moscow region, in the Stavropol steppe, the foothills of the Great Caucasus range – he has covered hundreds of kilometres along them. They have provided mental balance, faith, and strength. One of Mikhail Sergeyevich's favourite songs is 'When I go walking near Moscow / 'Where the grass smells of mint / Nature whispers to me lovingly / Her secret words…' Then there's 'The Russian Field' – 'The field, the Russian field, the moon shines down or the snow falls, in joy and pain we are together, I shall never forget.' He is very fond of those songs, and he often sings them. You know [she often begins a new idea with these words – 'you know' – as though she were testing a little bridge before venturing on to it] the philosopher Georg Wilhelm Friedrich Hegel wrote that philosophy is an epoch grasped in thought. What an amazing definition! But what is a song? It is also an epoch, the fate of a nation or of a man. Only it is 'grasped' in music, in a melody and in a word, but ultimately in feeling. The songs of my childhood were: 'Kakhovka, Kakhovka, my very own rifle…' 'The order's given – he

48

to the West, she to the East…', 'The apple and pear trees were in blossom / Mist floated over the river…', 'Dark night, only bullets whistle over the steppe, only the wind hums in the wires, dimly twinkle the stars…', 'The steppe all around / A long road ahead / In that remote steppe, A coachman was dying… 'So very moving in its 'Russianness', the death of that unknown coachman has now lasted longer than any human life, more than a century. 'There is a cliff on the Volga, overgrown with moss from top to bottom…', 'The fire burns briskly in the stove, the sap drops on the logs like tears, and in the dug-out the harmonica sings to me of your smile and your eyes…', 'Arise, vast country! Into battle to the death! With the savage Fascist force, with the cursed horde…'

A song that came later but found a way to our hearts, 'This Victory Day still smells of gunpowder, it's a celebration with greying hair, it is happiness with tears in your eyes…' Yes, although it came a good deal later, it also became inseparable from the songs of my generation. They say the heart sees better than anything. Tell me, whose heart, having lived through all that and having taken it in, will not respond to human grief and human goodness? The voices of Ruslanova, Utesov, Shulzhenko, Bernes, Kozlovsky, Lemeshev – how we came to love their gramophone records! And for how many years have I, like so many others of my generation, preserved those records so carefully. In the same way as I preserve in my memory the inexpressibly sad, although not always sober, voices of the blind and the invalids of the war and post-war years – in the bazaars, in the crowds, the railway stations and in the carriages of the mainline and local trains. Voices singing, not boldly but rather sadly, about battles and attacks, death, and love. The war is over, but it's sad, heart-breaking melody has long been floating around us, like smoke from a passing train. People were singing everywhere, in the trains, in the parks, outside houses, and we the children were the most faithful listeners. Last year, accompanying Mikhail Sergeyevich on a trip, I spent some time in the Sverdlovsk region. It is the region of the semi-precious stones of the Urals, malachite, and rock crystal, and magnificent, severe but at the same time wonderful natural surroundings. It is the country of Bazhov, the author of remarkable stories about the Urals, and of Mamin-Sibiryak, author of *Privalov's Millions*. Then the 'holy place of the Urals' – the town of Verkhoturye, founded in the sixteenth century, through which trade between Europe and Siberia took place along the river Tura. It is a town with unique monuments of the past – a fortress, churches, and monasteries.

There were a great many railways built in the Urals in the war years, and my father was one of those who worked on them. Our family had to move along as the new railroads were built. We travelled as best we could: in railway freight wagons, on trolleys on the temporary railroad, or on sleighs across the trackless taiga. I have particularly vivid memories of the latter. The taiga in winter. A really hard frost. Miles from anywhere. We children in the sleighs, wrapped up in sheepskin coats, the horses sinking up to their stomachs in the snow, snowflakes falling from the shaggy branches of the fir trees and cedars. And occasionally, from above, a penetrating, blinding ray of sunshine. Our stops, to spend the night or to rest, in the godforsaken villages or huts we found along the way, quite cut off from the world. You have to bear in mind that in those war years the taiga was a dangerous place to be, not only in itself, but also because it served as a refuge for all kinds of escaped criminals, deserters and even prisoners of war on the run. It was to the Urals that equipment was evacuated from industrial centres, factories, and workshops in the western Soviet Union. And machinery and weapons were transported from the Urals to the front. I spent a considerable part of my 'Urals' childhood in the Sverdlovsk district. It was there, in the old church that had been turned into a club, that I saw the film Chapayev on innumerable occasions. It was there that we played our girlish games and teased each other. And it was there, in the town of Alapayevsk, that I went to the theatre for the first time in my life. I saw the play *Platon Krechet* – I remember that too.

— *Even now you are involved in the world of children. I have in mind your charitable activities.*

— Yes, we were all children once. Unfortunately, we often forget it. What can be more precious than children's health – physical, moral and intellectual. I think of Armenia and those tragic days following the earthquake. I shall never forget the pitiful ruins where a family house had stood. The faces of the people... The shouts and groans. The shock the people suffered. And the tears. Thousands of people's thoughts and hopes and dreams buried in a moment. Tens and hundreds of tiny coffins just standing on the street. I visited the hospitals where the injured children were being treated. Do you know how I was greeted by a boy whose legs had been crushed – the school had collapsed in the middle of a lesson! 'Auntie Raya, Auntie Raya! I shall never go to school again!' he shouted from his bed almost before I entered the ward. What could I say to him? How could I console him? Whatever happens to our children – even if it is an act of blind fate – we adults look into children's eyes at such times not only with sympathy but also with a feeling of guilt as well.

    — *All the same – what did you tell him?*

    — I begged him to be strong. 'You are a man,' I said. 'And your mother is beside you.' I said we would build new schools in his town, beautiful and strong, in which there would be no need to be frightened. I held him by the hand, and he gradually calmed down. Nowadays no one is surprised at someone's performing acts of charity, and certainly not an American reader. And I would not wish to give an account of my 'good deeds'. I only want to say that concern for children and charity work in that field is today in our society not a matter of passing fancy or of fashion but the most pressing necessity. I did not hesitate in making my choice about where to direct my efforts. I had no difficulty in deciding upon the field of children's welfare. I am a patron of the Central Republican hospital for children in Moscow which treats children from practically all our republics. Mikhail Sergeyevich hands over the fees and other awards he receives, including his Nobel Prize, mainly for the needs of the health service. He often entrusts me with the task of handing over the money or medical equipment. In this field he has done a great deal for the medical institutions in various parts of the country – in Byelorussia, Ukraine, Uzbekistan, Kazakhstan – and including the hospital in the Red Guard district of Stavropol where he was born.

The hospital of which I am a patron has also received through my husband a good deal of modern foreign equipment and help with hard currency. The doctors, mainly quite young people, and fanatics for their work, have had the possibility of working in the best clinics in the United States and Germany. The Soviet Union is now receiving substantial humanitarian assistance from various countries. I want to especially thank future American readers. A considerable part of that assistance, some of it addressed to me, comes from the United States. The readiness of the American people to respond to our needs evokes a warm feeling of gratitude in Soviet people and in me personally. I visited Chernobyl along with my husband. I came across many children whose lives were shaken by that disaster. I visited the offices of the association 'Haematologists of the World – For the Children', the aim of which is to treat children suffering from leukaemia, and I also visited the headquarters of the fund set up by the Japanese businessman Sasakavi called 'Aid for the Children of Chernobyl'. Quite recently I paid one of my regular visits to the radiological department of the hospital, where I met and chatted with the patients, with those under observation by the hospital, and even with their families.

There is something with which I can never reconcile myself – and that is the feeling that people are doomed. I have already told you about the Republican children's hospital. The children who are the most seriously ill are sent there from the whole of Russia, actually from the whole of the USSR. Alas, there are among them some who are incurable. I went along with a crowd of children to see their common playroom. It was also full of children. There prevailed a sort of suppressed, rather tentative noise. You know how children play when they are very sick. And in among that crowd of children – and there were children in the hospital from practically all our nationalities – there was a young woman sitting on a low chair, clutching to herself a three-year-old boy while she stared motionless ahead. When she suddenly caught sight of me, she said in a muffled, tired voice without any hysteria, at the extreme limit of human strength of which only a woman's, a mother's heart is capable: 'Raisa Maksimovna, help us! Do something! We came to Moscow seven times and only at the seventh time did we succeed in getting a place in this hospital, in the haematological department. But they simply examined us and said: "Go back home, there is no hope for the boy." Help us!' I felt unsteady on my legs. I took the little boy from his mother, stroked his head, and exchanged glances with the mother, after which words have no meaning. Later, in the chief doctor's office, the doctors tried to convince me that it made more sense to send the boy home: he was practically doomed. If he were to have an operation, which he was unlikely to survive, there was only one chance in a hundred that he would live. 'But there is that one chance, and who knows, he...' I begged them to do everything possible and even more. 'I beg you,' I said. The boy's name was Dima. I learned yesterday that there had been no miracle. He had died.

When I departed that evening, I took a bundle of letters with me in my briefcase. Later, at home, I spent a long time studying them. The letters already bore evidence of having been sorted: they had little pieces of paper pinned to their corners with handwritten notes on them, saying who they were from and when they were received. Some of them were distinguished by having cardboard folders with official abbreviations on them. I looked at the envelopes and then understood how the selection had been made – the letters with a cardboard cover were the ones that had been addressed to 'Mrs Gorbacheva, The Kremlin, Moscow'. Those with an even shorter address – 'Gorbacheva, R.M., Moscow' – they had no folder, but just a scrap of paper indicating from whom the letter came and when. A real office at home.

More than in any other country it is the custom in Russia to address letters to the top people. This epistolary link between the people and the centre of power is completely in accord with our national tradition. The same is true of the habit of assuming that the big bosses are accommodated exclusively in the Kremlin although there has not been a single apartment there for ages, with the exception of Lenin's, and that is no longer lived in. The wives of our biggest leaders have not, I believe, been written to for several decades, though I may be wrong. There are so many letters that she now needs an office to process them. But she apparently does not have one yet: the scraps of paper were signed in the very same familiar writing. There was no indication of the assistant who should have handled the documents. There was just a gap. What are these letters about? They are asking for some request to be carried out. In Russia that kind of letter must of course contain requests, more requests and still more requests, dictated most often not by a passing fancy but by the imperfections in our society and by hopes placed in the 'top' people. That's what the letter writers expect from the people they write to.

These letters turned out to be all connected in some way with children. The boys and girls of the Kemerovo musical school express their thanks for being received in Moscow during their concert tour in the capital. Thanks again for two 'Yasnaya Polyana' accordions made specially for the 'New Names' programme of the Soviet cultural fund by the Tula 'Melodiya' association and handed over to the school as a gift. A long, rambling letter in a very elevated tone from the actor and director Rolan Bykov about the needs of the children's film centre in Moscow. A little blue, patterned and even, it seemed, scented envelope slipped out of the bulky bundle reminding one of the Smolny Institute with its genteel archaic manner. Natalia Sats: 'I hope to see you in the middle of May and to tell you about my project for organising an association called 'Art for the Children''. The sheet of paper the letter was written on was also very fancy, blue, and crisp like starched material.

There were some letters written in a firm, strong hand on thick sheets of paper, at the top of which was printed in Russian and English: 'Bekhtereva, Natalia Petrovna, Member of the Academy of Science of the USSR, Director of the Institute for Experimental Medicine, Head of the Department of the Neurophysiology of Man, etc.' In short, one of the most 'titled' women in the USSR. 'At last, quite recently, we managed, after overcoming an endless series of obstacles, to conclude a contract with a Swedish firm for the supply of a positron-emitting tomograph which for me will always be associated with you – thank you for your help. We are doing everything to realise the possibilities that are opening up and to produce our own analogues as quickly as possible...' And further: 'From what I know of the mechanisms of the brain our society is now passing through a phase which alone will enable it to achieve a new level socio-politically and economically...' In every one of her letters there is at least a line about the long-expected tomograph – how it 'feels' and how it is working for the benefit of the Soviet health service. Then, at the end: 'I think about you, but now for some reason, when you look so well on the screen and you are received so warmly everywhere, I worry about you...' The language is clear and Russian, and the handwriting also looks as if it were printed. When my hostess handed these letters over to me for a time she said in a sad tone: 'Natalia Petrovna has suffered a tragedy. Her son and her husband died almost simultaneously.'

Concerning the hospitalisation in West Germany of the boy Valeri Uvarov. Because of the impossibility of providing in the USSR the treatment for the disease of the blood diagnosed in the boy, his parents sent a letter to Mikhail and Raisa Gorbachev asking for help in organising treatment in the German Federal Republic, where the necessary methods of treatment and medicines are available. Reacting to this letter, Mikhail Gorbachev approached Helmut Kohl with a request to help the boy. The request was well received. Today V. V. Tyutyunov, councillor at the Soviet Embassy in West

Germany, reported that Valeri Uvarov has been admitted to the children's clinic in Hanover. Treatment is being directed by professor Hubert Polivoda. The treatment is being administered by professor Hans–Jurg Rum. The cost of the boy's and his mother's stay is being borne by the charitable organisation 'Care Deutschland'. V. Aleksandrov, assistant to the secretary of the Central Committee of the Communist Party of the Soviet Union. Since our last meeting at the Republican hospital a lot of things have changed for the better. Professor E. B. Vladimirsky and I have organised a new institute based at the hospital, as well as two departments in the city to cope with Muscovites suffering from diseases of the blood. We are carrying out repairs in two departments on the floor where you inspected the blood bank. With help from German colleagues and the firm Stig we have started to organise in one of the departments the first children's department for transplanting bone marrow.

Yours – Professor A. G. Rumyantsev.

It seemed to me there was some connection between those two letters. A young boy, Ilyusha Malyshev, sends thanks for the guitar he was presented with and for the help given to his mother, his little brother and himself to obtain a long-awaited apartment. 'Raisa Maksimovna! In the summer I gave paid concerts in offices and factories. Along with your wonderful guitar we earned 340 roubles which we donated to the charitable project Samantha... They listen to "my" wartime songs and they go so well that people even say 'Oh, I know that boy'. Both the boy and his mother. I was present when R. M. Gorbacheva met them at the Culture Fund. As I understood it, the letter was written a long time ago, because the boy is now studying at the music school attached to the Conservatory. At the meeting he was giving a kind of 'report' about his creative work in the last two years. But I was moved not only by the boy, so slim and romantic, with an impressive head of hair and delicate, nervous fingers. I was touched by the simplicity and dignity with which the two women conducted themselves – Raisa Gorbacheva and Ilyusha's mother, Nina Davydovna. There was no hint of the 'benefactress' and the 'petitioner'. The two women chatted together calmly and sensibly, and not only about the gifted lad and his immediate future. To a much greater extent they talked about the life which was seething outside the house on the Gogol Boulevard where the Soviet Culture Fund was located.

Dear Raisa!
[*Signora Fanfani begins her letter, written in Italian*],

I am very sorry not to have been able to see you, at least to shake your hand and wish you happiness in the New Year. On behalf of Amintore I send the president the warmest and most sincere wishes for success in his work for the good of the Russian people. Baron von Thyssen, whom I met in Rome, sends you greetings and good wishes. I am sending you a list of the help which we have produced for your hospitals from October to the present day. I am happy to have been able, without help from the Government or the ministries, to carry out this voluntary mission and to have collected, prepared, and dispatched it all with my own hands. We have done it all with the best of will and in the hope that the Soviet Union will not need help in the near future. Then we shall visit Moscow only to become acquainted with its culture. In any case I would like you to know that you have a friend in Italy, a real friend who loves the Russian people and loves the Gorbachev family.

Dear Raisa Maksimovna!

From now on I have the right to address you in that way, because there is nothing dearer to me than your name. I shall always, to the very end of my days, be grateful to you and Mikhail Sergeyevich. Despite being so busy you found the time to help my son to overcome a most serious illness. I have already visited him twice in the clinic (the Burdenko hospital) and I am able to tell you that the danger of death has passed. Although his condition is still very serious and requires long and major treatment, the worst is behind us. According to what the doctors have told me, this is the first case in the world to date where a person with such an illness has survived. How grateful I am to you for your goodness and kindness! My son had a purulent abscess in the brain with the discharge of pus into the ventricles of the brain. The skilful hands of the doctors and your kind response to me in my grief performed a miracle. Four years ago, my wife died while undergoing an operation. She was my best friend, my comrade, and a person very dear to me. Now I have trouble with my son. My great grief prompted me to write to you with a request for help, and you and your husband helped me. I don't intend to write to the newspapers or make big speeches. I will tell you only one thing. Remember that there is in this country a man ready to give his all for you, even his life. I am a former airman and now a reserve officer. I have two sons, both of them officers, and one of them suffered a great misfortune. What you did for me, and my son cannot be expressed in everyday language. To the end of my days, I shall remember your goodness and kindness. Perhaps my letter will seem to you rather disjointed. But believe me when I say that these words come from the very depths of a father's heart. Again and again, I thank you and your husband for your kindness and sympathy. Not every person would be capable of carrying such a burden on his shoulders like the one you and your husband bear, and still find time to share the misfortune that has struck another person. But that's what you did. Greetings and unlimited gratitude! I am already 66 and have been around a lot, but such human compassion I have never met before. I wish you and Mikhail Sergeyevich the very best of health, joy and happiness and everything of the best. Once again – a huge fatherly and human thank you. With sincere respect and gratitude,

Sudakov Vladimir Dmitrievich.

I decided to quote this letter in its entirety. It was night-time when I read it, and beyond the dark I could see the man, the father, who had written it. There is plenty of grief in our country, but few, too few, instances of its being overcome. In this sense the letter struck me as being a rare human document. Let it fly away and scatter a glimmer of hope to all of us sufferers – in Russia, in America, wherever you like. Among the letters was a sheet of paper bearing a translation of a letter from Yoko Ono, widow of the legendary John Lennon. She wrote about the good impressions she had at a meeting of the international forum in Moscow and suggested they should write a 'women's' book together. And then another envelope, without any scraps of paper attached, fell out of the bundle. It had also been opened and I automatically took the letter out of it... 'Dear Rayechka, greetings...' It was something rather unusual. More even than Signora Fanfani's manner. I read the first line again, and no, I had not made a mistake. 'Dear Rayechka, greetings...' I then realised that the letter must have got stuck to others and had landed in my bundle by chance. I folded it up and put it back into the envelope. On the back of the envelope was the name: Alferova, L. Her sister? A relation? A friend? In a school photograph that I was shown that evening they are sitting there, the children of the forties, bunched around their teacher. They squeeze up to each other with a look of curiosity and something more... They cling to each other because like that it is warmer and safer in that insecure world. It is probably the same in this world today. It is a difficult business – in all ages – to be at the very centre, the focus of other people's hopes. To be the last resort for someone's desperate entreaties and sacred and so very just demands. Not a single man in the world (perhaps with the exception of the one and only, and he doesn't yet live in the Kremlin) is in a position to carry out everything that is expected of him. In that photo I recognised Raisa Gorbacheva by one single feature. By the same one that brought her to the very top of the very risky gymnastic pyramids at school in the 1940s. Look in the photo for the slimmest and smallest girl. That is Raisa.

University Years

I am on my way again to the President's suburban residence. It appears that winter has returned at last to Moscow, having been driven away by some natural or manmade disaster. It is a good sign. The surrounding forests are submerged in it. Even along the Rublyov highway, which Muscovites still call in the old way a 'government' highway, the snowdrifts mount up to the very windows of the car. The highway is fairly well maintained and regularly repaired, but frankly speaking, it is becoming less 'governmental' every year. The road is being democratised before our very eyes. I drove along it for the first time in 1984. Then it still existed in a state of mysterious, aristocratic estrangement from the other ordinary roads and footpaths in the Moscow region. A person driving under the arch made by the overhanging fir trees had a feeling of pride: he was driving along the road of official success. I recall how, as a casual passer-by, I was struck by the strict enforcement and the hierarchical perfection of the prevailing regulations: our Volga was forced several times not just to move to one side, but to dig its nose right into the snow and freeze, as small insects freeze at the sight of danger, and so free the road for the benefit of the grim-looking bullet-proof ZILs – the earthly means of transport of the Soviet gods – overtaking us or rushing towards us. It was in the direction of Rublyov that, for God knows how long, the country houses of the Soviet elite were situated. The regime operating on the Rublyov highway was an exact parallel of the regime of the rulers of the day.

Sometime in 1986 I began travelling by that road more or less regularly. I would not say that it happened immediately, but it was very noticeable that practically in front of my eyes the well-manned traffic police posts disappeared: several of their little sentry boxes are now simply empty, leading me to think of the demilitarisation of the very regime. Certain sacred rights vanished – the road became a road again and not an exclusive 'highway'. The average citizen with a little cottage in the country loads down his little Zaporozhets with long sought-after building material and scurries along, like a fish in shallow water, along the road which at one time he didn't dare to put a foot on. Then cars with foreign registration plates appeared on the road – too many, perhaps – because, as they say, all kinds of foreign enterprises began eagerly to buy up plots of land and buildings in that very Russian countryside for out-of-town offices. What is more, the number of ZIL limousines dropped sharply, as in Moscow as a whole: in the period of Perestroika not only was Soviet officialdom reduced in numbers, it also switched from the huge, period automobiles to more modest and economic ones which were also less noticeable in the life of the capital. It is sufficient to say that even the Politburo switched to using Volgas. One could not have imagined such a thing happening in 1984. No longer do drivers get pushed into the ditch by the all-powerful striped police baton (no face to be seen, just a baton sticking out from the window of the follow-up car as the very embodiment of authority). I saw the President's car several times on that road. What is more I could even distinguish his features – he was sitting on the front seat for some reason and reading a paper. It seems that even the ZILs have become more transparent in the time of Glasnost. I cannot say that there has been greater order on the 'Rublyovka' in recent years, but there has certainly been an improvement in the way people are treated. The road is very winding. They say that those frequent bends were introduced in the 1930s so that potential evildoers should not be able to take aim. The car went smoothly after the heavy snowfalls, giving the impression of moving rather like a sleigh, not a machine, not something mechanical. All the same the journey took ten or fifteen minutes longer than on the previous day.

But, you know, there is nowhere better for thinking than on a journey. Especially on a road that reminds you so well of the sleigh tracks of old, a road that goes through the snow-covered plains of central Russia that prompt unhurried thoughts. I was thinking that, after all, the nature of a regime changes under the influence of the character, and not just the character, but simply the appearance of a woman whose book you Western readers are now holding in your hands. Why? The fact of her appearing just once alongside the powers that be in 1985 made those powers more attractive, more accessible, and even happier. And younger looking too, which is also not unimportant if you bear in mind the fact that in recent years the personification of power took the form of feeble old age alienated from reality. Krasnoyarsk, Norilsk, Donetsk... A kindergarten, a nursery school, a children's home... The appearance, among the usual collection of male official faces, of a woman's face, is attractive because it is sharper and more sympathetic: both joy and sorrow are more noticeable. That retentive memory and those observant brown eyes, developed probably in childhood, when her very way of life – practically a life on wheels – the kaleidoscope of faces, places, railway stations and country halts – forced her from her earliest years to look closely at the world coming towards her. This time I arrived at the residence with a new toy – a Grundig tape recorder. I had brought a recorder with me last time, but it was a small Japanese one, half the size of my hand. It was convenient for my conversations with Raisa Maksimovna, but it was not very convenient for Ira, the typist I had asked to transcribe the tapes. So, this time I turned up with the Grundig. It was well made in the German manner, not just a Japanese toy, and, most surprising, it needed no batteries. It was plugged into the mains. No matter how I tried, my jacket thrown off, the Grundig plug would not go into the socket above the sofa. Then I drew attention to the fact that there was one free socket next to the President's desk, one side of which was simply covered with wires.

But the gap between the desk and the window was so narrow that I began to doubt whether I could get through. Eighty-five kilos live weight ... And it wouldn't be right to move the desk: it was after all the President's desk. Raisa Maksimovna caught the look of doubt on my face.

— You can't make it? Let me – I can get through. Diet.

— *But it seems to me to be your natural shape.*

— Oh no [she said, smiling], I'm very strict with myself.

— *But thank God, I also got through. The reel on the Grundig began to turn noiselessly.*

— Georgi Vladimirovich, I understood that we were going to talk today about the years of my youth. But even in this section I

66

shall find it difficult always to be saying 'my'. I shall probably more often be saying 'we' – Mikhail Sergeyevich and me. But nevertheless, at the outset it will be 'me'. About the years of childhood and youth and the dearest memories of that time. Youth is, after all, just a moment, but it is the moment, the spark that you always carry in your heart. For me youth was above all my university years. Without them, I tell you, there wouldn't have been any youth. That's what I think. And I believe that without those years we would never have become what we have become.

— *We would have. Only we would have been different.*

— I agree. I define youth as a time of poetry, of self-assertion, of seeking for the truth and for answers to the age-old human problems. But what was my youth distinguished by? What was it associated with? The first half of the 1950s. The country's post-war years. A special period in our nation's history. Those years contained so much: both tragic and heroic. I still find myself unable to explain how people could do, could achieve what they did in those unforgettable years. From where did they derive the strength? Factories, electric power stations, towns and villages were rebuilt, and the land, devastated by war, was restored to life. Lord! What joy we took in everything, how proud we were. Although we continued to have an unbelievably difficult life. In the collective farms the pay for a day's work was so little and so useless that they used to say: 'We work for nothing'. The most essential goods were missing from the shops and daily life. There were tremendous problems with housing ... Yes, a lot of things happened in those

67

years. Testing of the atomic and later the hydrogen bomb. The end of the United States' monopoly of nuclear weapons. The Warsaw Pact. Fresh alarms for the fate of the peace that had cost us so dear. These were not abstract things, you know. It is all very important for an understanding of us and our youth. But that's not all. There was the 'Leningrad Affair' concerning Party officials, 'The Moscow Doctors' Affair'. Those last convulsions of Stalinism were especially humiliating for a people who had been victorious and had over-come disaster at the cost of unbelievable sacrifices and suffering, and for the moral and social experience that the people had gained through the war. Stalin died on the 5th of March 1953. We were in Moscow at the time.

What was I thinking about just now? A person's life is com-posed of certain external circumstances and events and his own actions and behaviour. And also, of the life within himself. It is easier, of course, to reproduce the former, the external side. More difficult to reproduce the internal side. But you will agree that the sense and essence of life lies in their unity and mutual interdepend-ence. A person's internal state, his peace, the range of the feelings possessing his spirit – it is precisely these that are often decisive in a person's taking certain decisions or performing certain acts. But identifying them is more complicated. And so, it is 1949. I am on my way to Moscow. I am going to study.

— *By train?*

— Of course. And what a train! The carriages were overcrowd-ed. All the seats taken, whatever ticket you had, and the luggage racks were occupied too. Nowadays people put their luggage up there. But in those days people occupied the racks. What seats? People travelled standing, in the corridors and on the outside platforms. The trains crept along slowly, with long and frequent stops. Not just ours; all the trains in the country were the same. There were no sheets for the beds, and no one thought of asking for any. Instead of a buffet on the train there was only the tank of boiled water at the stations and the station markets to which everybody dashed during the stops.

— *And no one was afraid of missing the train.*

— In my view it was impossible to miss a train in those days. Even if you missed it you could catch up with it all the same. The peasants brought things to the train to sell: boiled potatoes, milk, eggs, loaves of bread, home-distilled spirits, vodka, apples, and water from the well – for five kopeks a jug. Pickled cucumbers and berries. True, it was all very expensive. For the journey you had to rely mainly on what your mother had provided. I was sad to be setting out for the first time on my own on such a long journey. The sadness of parting from my family. Parting from my school friends. Those who came to the station to see me off stood there before me. Parting from the world in which I was at home and understood. Sadness and anxiety. The beginning of the unknown, of an independent career. But at times the feeling of uncertainty and sadness would be replaced suddenly by a sense of happiness, joy and pride – the awareness that I was going to study in Moscow! Moscow is Red Square, monuments, museums, theatres, and libraries, and these would all be mine. I was going to study at the Moscow State University, where many pillars of the country's science and culture had also studied. I was travelling in a train, but at times it seemed as if I were flying on wings.

The university is my alma mater. Mine and Mikhail Sergeyevich's. Do you know what it means literally when translated from the Latin? 'Bounteous mother.' True, with material food the universities always went short, but with spiritual food... Our university did indeed become for us an intellectual 'bounteous mother'. To a considerable extent it determined the development of personality and the future course of our lives. We were part of the second post-war recruitment of students. My generation, the generation of the seventeen-year-olds, came to the university straight from school. But among those in the first recruitment were many much older people, thirty and even thirty-five-year–olds. The 'Old Men', as we used to call them. They were those who in the war years had for various reasons interrupted their education: they had been in occupied territory, been employed somewhere, fought with the partisans, had been evacuated, or had simply not been able to obtain an education earlier. But the majority of the 'Old Men' were men who had fought at the front and been demobilised who didn't even change their military greatcoats and uniform throughout their student years. They just didn't change their clothes. Both because they really had nothing special to change into and because they were in no hurry to part with their front-line youth and their front-line comradeship. This has, in my view, been depicted very well in Yuri Bondarev's *Silence* and Yuri Trifonov's *Students* and in other novels and stories of that time. Some of my age group, when they come to recall the 'Old Men', now point out first of all that they drank vodka – the front-line fighters. They did drink, of course. But those people introduced into our environment something more important. They brought a special diligence, a devotion to their work, a sense of responsibility and a realistic view of life and human relationships. They were a sort of university within the university.

The university gathered us together from the most differing corners of the country. Russians, Uzbeks, Ukrainians, Byelorussians, Kazakhs, Azerbaijanis, Jews, Armenians, Latvians, Kirgiz, Georgians, Turkmen and more. A cross-section of the country as a whole. There were also foreigners studying with us. Albanians, Bulgarians, Yugoslavs, Czechs... And they lived in the same rooms along with us. Germans, Spaniards, Koreans, Chinese, Vietnamese... We were all close to each other. We studied together in the same libraries and in the same lecture rooms. We sat our examinations, wrote our degree theses, and ate in the same canteens. We made friends and we got married. The spirit of youth and comradeship – that was the prevailing atmosphere in the university. In addition, all of us in those years were united by our optimism. Youth, the sense and awareness of our youth, comradeship, and optimism. God knows where we took it from, but that's how it was. Optimism united us all. But perhaps it was simply that I perceived life like that? No, even if it is the way I perceived it, it was all the same real optimism. How many years have flown past! And I am proud when I see, observe, or hear by some echoes reaching me, that the years that have passed and sped away have not destroyed that youthful sense of fellowship and humanity in those who were then with us. They have not destroyed it.

— *She pauses and then repeats:*

— In the majority of cases, it was not destroyed. At any rate in the case of those with whom I have been in contact. For example, there was Merab Mamardashvili who died recently. He studied on the same course as mine. A Georgian who became a major authority in the world of philosophy. He married a girl from my room, with whom I had lived for some years. Therefore, we were especially close. Merab was one of the regular visitors to our girls' quarters. There were several of them. We became accustomed to the regular visitors to our room. Merab married one of my friends and the sociologist Yuri Levada another. Even at that time we respected Merab for his intellect. I remember how he used to help us girls to digest Das Kapital. I knew Merab very well. True, life later led us apart. He had a complicated career. Do you realise that, to his very last days, he tried to calm down the nationalist passions that were flaring up between the peoples? He had the courage to oppose extreme nationalism. I am proud of Merab.

— *Perhaps that courageous opposition to any kind of raving extremism wherever it came from, is the clearest indication of a genuine philosopher?*

— Perhaps. But I want to say that that was what made up our years. It was what united us. And it was what remained, in spite of any differences we may have had. Zdenek Mlynar was on the same course as Mikhail Sergeyevich. He was also a friend of ours. As you know, he is a Czech. In 1955, to mark his graduation from the university, he presented my husband with his photograph and a copy of his thesis entitled 'The general supervision as part of the Prosecutor's work and ways of putting it into practice.' On the gift is written: 'To Mishka, a good friend, to remind him that we are lawyers with a broad profile.'

— *The profile did indeed turn out to be broad! He was the future ideologist of 'socialism with a human face' and, figuratively speaking, its strategist and practitioner.*

— We met Zdenek again in 1967. He came to Stavropol.

— *Mlynar was in Stavropol in 1967?*

— Yes, he came to visit us.

— *In 1967?*

— Yes. On the eve of all the events. And we had a meeting with him. We met Zdenek and his wife again later, in 1990.

— *And there were no meetings in between?*

— Mikhail Sergeyevich had some meetings recently, but they were official ones. There were no private meetings. We had a meeting in 1990. And recently Zdenek sent a letter in connection with the award of the Nobel Peace Prize to Mikhail Sergeyevich. I will read it to you: 'Dear Misha! On this occasion we shall probably not manage to meet. That is why I have decided to write you a brief note. You know that I don't like formality, but all the same I want, in my own name and Irina's, to express our most sincere good wishes in connection with your receiving the Nobel Peace

Prize. You have earned it and by so doing you have done more for our common cause than could have been expected from a single human being. Yours sincerely – Zdenek. P.S. If you need anything from me, I am always ready... I am worried about a lot of things at the moment, but I know that it can't be otherwise, and I am on the side you are on.' Our student days remained with us. We lived, of course, modestly. Very modestly. In poverty, as it might appear to someone today. The old, ancient buildings of Moscow University, in the lecture halls of which my husband and I studied, are situated, as you know, in the centre of the city, on the corner of Herzen Street and the Mokhovaya. The student hostel was then located in the Sokolniki region, on the Stromynka on the Yauza river. It was a huge, four-storey, rather forbidding rectangular building with a large courtyard inside. The three top floors were occupied by students and postgraduates, distributed according to their faculties – philologists, historians, philosophers, physicists, lawyers, biologists and so forth. On the ground floor was the library, the reading room, the student club, a hospital, a tailor's shop, the canteen, and a buffet. In the corner building opposite the hostel there was a food shop. It is still there today. On the other bank of the Yauza, in the Preobrazhensky district, or, as we then called it, the 'Preobrazhenka', was a street market.

— *Could you make the transition to that free market?*

— A transition? We just crossed the bridge [she smiled]. It was a market for food, not for clothes. Our Stromynka, Preobrazhenskaya Square and the Preobrazhenskaya Embankment are all, according to tradition, part of the Preobrazhenskaya *sloboda* or special district which has gone down in the history of Moscow. It was built by Peter the First. It was said that the building housing our student hostel had once served as barracks for the Petrovsky Preobrazhensky regiment. Later, in the Soviet years, two floors were built on. The nearest Metro station to the hostel is Sokolniki. It is just three stops by tram. Yes, if my memory serves me right, three. And the nearest cinema is the Rusakov club. The building, if you have ever noticed it, is of a very unusual shape, in the constructivist style. In our first years each room in the student hostel provided accommodation for from eight to fourteen persons. It was only the students in the senior classes and postgraduates who were able to arrange themselves with four to six to a room. The furnishings were of the simplest, practically monastic; beds, a table, chairs, bedside tables, bookshelves, and a wardrobe. Each floor had a communal kitchen and toilets with washbasins. Our 'wardrobe' at that time was also very modest, if the clothes that we wore year in, year out could be dignified by the title of 'wardrobe'. There is much, very much that one might say about it.

— *Never mind – it's interesting.*

— Well, one fact at least. In the minus thirty-degree Moscow frosts – and the winters were more severe then and I remember it being even forty degrees below – we, with very few exceptions, had no warm winter footwear, warm underwear, stockings, or winter headgear. And many of us did not have even a winter overcoat. We economised on everything. On food, I remember how my friend

Nina Lyakisheva's aunt tried so touchingly and in such a motherly way to feed us. (Nina was left an orphan during the war and was brought up in a children's home in Tashkent.) Nina and I went down to see her in Balashikha, a town in the Moscow region, and her aunt probably had more than eloquent grounds for believing that we visited her mainly for one purpose – to fortify ourselves with a little food. We also saved money on transport. How? We simply tried to travel without paying. Both on the trams and on the Metro.

— *And on the Metro?*

— Yes, we had a great many tricks for doing it. But I am not going to talk about that now. My own secrets! But, no matter how we economised, ten days before our scholarships arrived, we had no money left. As the poet Nikolai Rubtsov says: 'I pat my pocket and it doesn't sound; I try the other – nothing there; If I shall be famous one day, I'll take a holiday in Yalta.' How many amazing adventures befell us for that reason! But we always found a way out of trouble. I tell Mikhail Sergeyevich now that, whatever law they may pass, there will always be someone who will think up a way of getting round it. We ourselves travelled free on the trams and the Metro.

— *Mikhail Sergeyevich too?*

— Georgi Vladimirovich, you are asking provocative questions. As for the Metro, I can let you into one revealing detail: in those days there were no automatic machines. There were tickets. The conductors on the Sokolniki trams reluctantly accepted our silent requests. And when of a morning the thousand-strong (I don't know exactly – there were five or six thousand of us living at the Stromynka) crowd of students filled up the tram and were jammed into it nobody asked for any tickets. Only a few conscientious conductors growled at us, but the others, the majority, paid no attention to us: they resigned themselves to the situation. We bought the cheapest possible tickets for the theatre. They were tickets that had stamped on them: 'Top gallery, uncomfortable'. The gallery, the gallery! Whenever I enter a theatre I still look up to that gallery, because it was from there for the first time in my life that I heard an opera performed in the Bolshoi Theatre – Bizet's *Carmen* and for the first time heard a performance of Tchaikovsky's First and Sixth Symphonies. It was from the 'gods' that I saw my first ballet – Minkus's *Don Quixote*. And Chekhov's *Three Sisters* at the Moscow Arts Theatre.

— *And did you ever glance up at the government box, the 'Tsar's' box?*

— I don't think so. It didn't really interest me. As for the government box, I can tell you about another episode concerning the present day. Do you recall that that amazing tenor Luciano Pavarotti came to Moscow recently?

— *Yes.*

— Mikhail Sergeyevich and I heard him sing in the Bolshoi Theatre. One aria after another. A storm of delighted applause. I leaned across to Mikhail Sergeyevich and said: 'Surely he's not going to leave out Ave Maria?' 'Just wait', he said, 'be patient, he will

surely sing it.' But he went on singing other things, but not Ave...
Again, I leaned across: 'Surely? ... 'Listen,' he said with a smile, 'if
for some reason he doesn't sing it, so be it – I will sing Ave Maria
for you right here." And he added: 'True, I fear it will be my last
public performance... Can you imagine Ave Maria being sung in
the government box...

— *I can't imagine it... Well, and did he sing it?*
— Who?
— *If the president were to sing not only Moscow would have
known about it – the whole world would have known.*
— I have Schubert's Ave Maria sung by Pavarotti recorded on
a record – 'Pavarotti's Greatest Hits'.
— *I have never heard how well the president sings, but I – and
not just I – noticed long ago that he has a fine sense of humour.*
— Yes, he has no time for singing at the moment. And, as
for his sense of humour, you are right, it is a feature of his mind.
A fortunate feature. Often, in a moment, unexpectedly and in
a flash, it can remove internal tension, tiredness, or an awkward
situation. Two examples that have suddenly come to my mind. It
was during an official visit to West Germany in November last year.
We were flying at night in a helicopter on the way to the airport
at Frankfurt-am-Main. We were sitting in silence, weighed down
by the strain of the past day. The helicopter came in to land. The
people waiting for us on the ground tried to protect themselves
from the gusts of wind that always accompany a helicopter's landing or take-off. Mikhail Sergeyevich then said: 'So we've combed

the hair of the welcoming party. Now we can shake their hands.' And that wisecrack seemed to make everything easier, as though it had lifted from us the tiredness and burden of the whole day. Do you remember Barcelona and the famous museum, the House of Picasso? It has a collection of the early, student works of the great artist, his ceramics, a series of variations on the theme of *The Maids of Honour* by Velazquez, which impressed Mikhail Sergeyevich and me, and a whole row of rooms entitled 'Pablo and Jacqueline'. The rooms contained nothing but portraits, paintings, and sketches of his beautiful wife Jacqueline. A hundred Jacquelines look down from the walls. There were some at which Felipe, the young heir to the Spanish throne, who was accompanying us, was embarrassed to halt our large, formal procession. On one of these occasions Mikhail Sergeyevich said: 'If I were to draw Raisa Maksimovna like that she would never sleep again.' Everybody laughed.

Let us return, however, to the student years. We were 'working' students. We took jobs wherever we could. Unloading trucks of vegetables and coal at the Khimki river port and at Moscow railway stations was the sort of work our boys did. Of course, there were young people studying in our groups whose parents were 'Stalin' prize-winners, people of merit and those who were simply well provided for. Moscow society consists of many layers, like no other city in the country. Those young people did not live in the hostel. They enjoyed completely different conditions. They relaxed differently and they dressed differently. But I do not recall that I personally or those in my immediate circle felt ourselves to be reduced or deprived because of that. No. I will say more. We were happy. Happy in our youth and in our hopes for the future. Even just at being alive. That we were studying at university. That was what we valued. Our lecturers and teachers were leading scholars. Such was the tradition. I don't know what happens now, but I hope the tradition has been preserved. The most distinguished scholars in the country were invited to lecture to us. The authors of well-known textbooks, for example. Our logic lectures were given by Asmus, author of textbooks on logic and the history of philosophy. Rubinshtein, Leontyev and Lurye lectured on psychology. Courses in philosophy were given by Oizerman, Narski and others. We were deeply involved in the process of acquiring knowledge and we were carried away by it.

— *You were acquiring knowledge at first hand.*

— Yes, our teachers at the university were people whose names were the pride of Russian scholarship. And in our age group there were many brilliant and highly gifted young people. At times two-thirds of the student body consisted of boys and girls who had finished school with a gold or silver medal. In that post-war period the country was eager to get on with life and it was amazing then how much talent emerged from its depths, apparently drained dry by the war. I believe that it was not just by chance that there are quite a few academicians, doctors of science, professors and well-known statesmen, politicians, journalists, writers, economists and philologists today who were among those who graduated from the university in those days. A student scientific society was active in the faculties and contributed its intellectual migh to the university's intellectual atmosphere. We all belonged to scientific societies. Our programmes provided for the study of a very wide range of disciplines and subjects as well as specialised and classical literature. We spent hours in the library and reading room. As soon as we woke in the Stromynka in the morning we had first of all to occupy a place in the reading-room and then go about our daily chores. We would 'stake out' a place, do our chores, and then return to the library to work. For the whole day. It was impossible to study or work in our living quarters: there were so many of us. We did our serious study in the reading-rooms and our university library and later, as senior students, in the Lenin Library. But we spent a great deal of time in the library at Stromynka. The 'search for truth' continued at seminars, lectures and even at meetings. I remember with what exultation, at a meeting of the faculty's Komsomol organisation, we 'discovered' the law of the negation of the negation – Hegel's law of dialectics, 'not recognised' in Stalin's works. The student meetings of that period! – they were already forerunners of the 'Thaw'.

The shell of inertia, silence and total fear was beginning to show cracks – at any rate at student gatherings. René Descartes's aphorism – 'I think: therefore, I am' – was our slogan. We did not discuss in those days the question of student self-government. But questions of the distribution of places in the hostel, the maintenance of order and the organisation of our leisure time were decided with the very active participation of the students themselves. I remember how vigorously we defended the rights of the student family. At a conference of the university Young Communist organisation a satirical newspaper appeared with a drawing of the rector trampling with a big boot on a marriage registration certificate – no more and no less! There was no room for the young married people to squeeze themselves in, and some student or graduate families already had children. They needed their own corner. It was an age-old problem. And it still exists. But at that time, it was particularly acute. Later, years later, when I was busy with scientific and teaching work, delivering lectures on philosophy, the history of atheism and religion, and ethics, I realised that the system and methods applied in education both in the schools and in higher institutions were bound by too many dogmas and constraints. It was that in particular that deprived me at the university of a lot of knowledge relating to the history of Russian and world culture. We were obliged to learn off by heart, for example, Stalin's speech at the 19th Congress of the Party, but we spent very little time studying the history of Russian humanitarian thought. Solovyov, Karamzin, Berdyayev and Florensky – it is only now that we have obtained real access to these philosophers, historians, and writers. There was too much that was schematic and lifeless. And that, of course, deprived us of a great deal of knowledge. And again – it deprived us of the possibility of acquiring a real knowledge of a foreign language. At the university we learnt German and Latin. But later we did not have any opportunity to practice foreign languages. I think that was a great loss for the whole of my generation.

I remember that there were quite a lot of surprised reactions when it was discovered that it was possible to communicate in English with the wife of M. S. Gorbachev, member of the Politburo and Secretary of the Central Committee of the CPSU, when she accompanied her husband on what was practically his first – in his new role – trip abroad. It was unusual. High-ranking Soviet wives were usually incapable of speaking English or German or anything else and were even more tongue-tied than their husbands. I was also present and saw Raisa Gorbacheva start up a conversation in English with somebody abroad. True, it happened most frequently not with official persons or their 'other halves', but, as they say, with 'the man in the street'. With children, housewives or simply pedestrians who recognised her and surrounded her in a tight ring everywhere, on the streets and the squares and in the museums. There, in those surroundings, she is not ashamed to use her English. In the same way, incidentally, as the people around her, the public, are not ashamed of their Russian: 'Raisa, Raisa!' can be heard on all sides. If people are carrying placards or posters, she also reads them out in a loud voice. The people like it and so, I think, does she.

— I have never in my life felt envious because someone was wearing a dress or other adornment that was more beautiful than what I was wearing. But I really do envy people who speak foreign languages fluently. And I still do. I learnt English late in life... I have tried to make up for lost time.

— We were discussing the atmosphere at Moscow University in those days.

— Yes, despite all the obstacles there was also both radicalism and creative teaching in the MGU, and they created an unrepeatable university atmosphere. You know, I would even be more precise. With all the shortcomings in our system of education, nevertheless the teaching and the social activities in the MGU, unlike the other higher institutes, contained more radicalism, more excitement, and more creativity, and so compensated in some way for the failings of the teaching process. Thanks to the university and the atmosphere in it I acquired and have retained for ever a love of the student lecture hall and the company of young people. That's where I feel rather special. And, I have to confess, I always miss it. The very atmosphere of a young people's lecture hall, if you like – its very air, is liable at any moment to change into laughter, its special characteristic perhaps...

— *Whenever I go down into the Metro I immediately get submerged in the smell of my own youth. People who know say that it smells of warm rubber and dust, but it seems to me to smell of the 1960s, the smell of the Metro is linked with the smell of my own student youth – never in my life did I travel so frequently on the Metro as I did in those days.*

— It is possible that I have this attitude [to university life] also because I myself taught for many years. I don't know. But I believe it derives from that period, from my student years. Youth is an everlasting source of life: its worries, its fullness, and its variety. The atmosphere prevailing in an audience of young people was similar wherever I worked, wherever I studied and wherever

I visited, including places on the Soviet President's official trips. With young people all around you, you feel younger yourself. I experienced that feeling in lecture halls in Stavropol, in Moscow University, the Charles University in Prague, in the Humboldt University in Berlin and at Stanford. I carried that feeling away with me from Wellesley College in Boston. During the President's visit to the United States in June 1990 Mrs Barbara Bush and I travelled to Boston to the prestigious women's college, Wellesley. We attended the ceremonial presentation of degrees to graduates. I remember a young girl, Christine Bicknell, speaking on behalf of the graduates. I will read you an extract from her excellent speech printed in a magazine that also published the speeches that Barbara Bush and I made. 'Let us hope', said Christine, 'that in our years after Wellesley we can have the courage to look at who we are and to deal with the difficult issues that confront our lives. I believe that we are strong women, well educated women, women who have a commitment to bettering the world in which we live, and I believe we will meet the challenges that the world holds for us.' You see how our approaches coincide! It is obviously the spirit Common to youth.

— *It seemed to me that you and Mrs Barbara Bush faced the girl students with a difficult choice.*

— In what way?

— *You personified for them two different paths. One is the path of almost exclusive, self-sacrificing service to the family. The other is the path of professional self-assertion combined with the management of a family. In my view the young, intensely ambitious graduates were impressed by the reference the head of the college made to your doctoral thesis.*

— But I recall something else – the wave of applause evoked by Barbara's remark that she was sure that in that very auditorium was sitting somewhere, perhaps in the back row, the future spouse of a future president of the United States – or the future president herself.

— Indeed, you complemented each other very well not only on the platform but also away from it.

— I have the warmest feelings and great respect for Mrs Barbara Bush. I am impressed by her natural and direct manner with people. Young people approach life with the age-long confidence of being able to introduce something of their own, to achieve something and change things. That is why I love that eternally young student body, inspired with a bold sense of self-reliance. It was at the university that I met Mikhail Sergeyevich. That is where our family originated. I am often asked how we came to meet and how Mikhail Sergeyevich courted me. I suppose that is an important point in the reminiscences of every family. But for me there is something that is far more important and precious. Our relationship and our feelings were from the very beginning perceived by us... You know [and she put her piece of paper down] I have been thinking for a long time how to express it more precisely. And so – for me at any rate what is more precious is the following. Our relationship and our feelings were from the very outset perceived by us as a natural, inseparable part of our fate. We realised that our life would be unthinkable without each other. Our feelings were our very life itself. Do you remember the poetess, Natalia Krandieskaya? Wife of Aleksei Nikolayevich Tolstoy? She wrote these lines:

They call the sky blue,
They call the sun golden,
They say that time is irreversible,
They say the sea is boundless,
They say a woman is beloved,
They say death is inevitable,
They say that truths are sacred,
They say passions are fatal.
What then shall I call my love,
So as not to repeat the others?

Our first meeting was at a dance in the students' club in the Stromynka. Mikhail Sergeyevich came along with his friends Volodya Liberman and Yuri Topilin. In those days, Georgi Vladimirovich, we did not study our horoscopes. To tell the truth we didn't know horoscopes existed. They are now all the rage. But we really didn't know the meaning of Capricorn, one of the signs of the Zodiac, under which I was born, or of Pisces, under which Mikhail Sergeyevich was born. We didn't know if our relationship would be lasting according to the signs or not. Whether our marriage would be harmonious. We didn't even think about it. It didn't worry us. Financial considerations didn't concern us: legacies, family connections, somebody's position, protectionism. No. There were no legacies and no family connections. All we had was ourselves. All we had was with us. *Omnia mea mecum porto* – 'Everything I have I carry with me.'

— *But I thought that was an English saying.*

— No, it's Latin. Like that other maxim: Dum spiro, spero – 'So long as I breathe, I hope'.

— *In her speech, always correct, an occasional Latin word slips in, revealing maybe what once attracted her to study at the university.*

— We were friends for a long time before we got married. I shall never forget the long walks we took around Moscow – from the university and the Mokhovaya to Sokolniki and the Stromynka. Just imagine what walking that involved! Strolls along Gorky Street, the Petrovka and the Neglinnaya. I mention the routes we were fond of. From the Lenin Library to the Arbat, Kropotkinskaya and the Volkhonka. From the Preobrazhensky Square (which was also on our favourite route to Sokolniki) to the old building of the Mossoviet theatre. All that was our romantic lesson in Muscovite geography. Not to be forgotten are our joint excursions to visit exhibitions, the cinema, and the theatre. Then there were concerts by Lemeshev, Kozlovsky, Aleksandrovich, Zvezdina, Ognivtsev. Plays with the actors Mordvinov and Maretskaya. Performances by Nabatov. Also, not to be forgotten was our beloved Sokolniki park with its deer pond (I don't know if it is there now, but it was then), and its winter skating rink. Have you ever been on a Moscow rink? Which one?

— *Ten years ago, I took the children to Sokolniki.*

— You know, in our day they played just one and the same record at the skating rink. I am trying to remember what it was. For some reason I haven't come across it anywhere. 'White snowflakes are falling: Catch me up, catch me up.' Yes, they played it only at the rink.

— *I too remember the repeated 'Catch me up'.*

— I have never heard that tune again. I can't recall it. But it was certainly at the Sokolniki ice rink that it was played. I cannot forget either how we welcomed the New Year – 1954 – in the Hall of Columns. The fir tree and the music. Young faces all around, and we were there. I remember that people seemed to notice us.

— *You were a good-looking couple, no doubt.*

— They were sort of drawn towards us. And it gave rise to a reciprocal feeling of warmth and friendliness. Perhaps it was a general holiday – of youth, of the happiness of youth? The New Year celebration in the Hall of Columns in 1954. But perhaps it was also connected with the fact that it was the year 1954 – that the old life had been left somewhere behind us in 1953. We got married in the autumn of 1953. Our marriage took place in the Sokolniki registry office, on the other bank of the Yauza. But when we returned to Moscow later and went to look for it, we could no longer find the office. They had transferred it to the Wedding Palace. There is now some kind of municipal services agency. But in the past the registry office was immediately opposite our hostel.

— *All very logical – the student hostel and the marriage office opposite.*

— The building has been preserved. It's a large building. On the other bank, in the Preobrazhenka, there are very large buildings. The registry office was on the ground floor. We celebrated our wedding in the Stromynka. It was a student affair, very jolly, with singing, drinking and dancing. Mikhail Sergeyevich earned the money needed for the wedding, for a new suit for himself and a 'wedding dress' for me (not a proper wedding dress – we'll put the word in inverted commas – they didn't make special dresses to measure in those days. And there was no wedding ring. But the dress was new). To tell the truth, our parents knew nothing of our intentions. We let them know at the last moment. That shows how little young people care for their parents' opinion – both then and now. So, there you are – we're having a wedding, we don't need any money, we've got some. And that's the only announcement. Well, our parents didn't have much money either. But we lived with a constant feeling of responsibility to them. For example, I tried all my life not to overburden my mother and father in any way; not to ask for more than they could manage, and not to take much from them. After all, I was the eldest, and they had two other children and they didn't find life easy. Mikhail Sergeyevich earned money in the summer as a combine driver harvesting the wheat. True, we didn't have enough money to buy me a pair of shoes. I had to borrow shoes from a girlfriend in our group. But there was the dress – it was our first joint acquisition. The dress was made in a real Moscow tailor's shop that I remember very well, near the Kirovskaya Metro station. In the summer of 1953, before our wedding, Mikhail Sergeyevich and I parted for three months. His practical work in his training as a lawyer coincided with the holiday period. He did it in his own Red Guard district. In those days it was called the Molotov district. We spent those months waiting for letters from each other.

I had long since noticed that Raisa Maksimovna had those letters. By the time we had set up the tape recorder and taken up our positions for our conversation – she at the table and I in a chair opposite – I had long been eyeing those sheets of paper taken out of a lined exercise book, known for some reason as 'general'. I had realised long ago that they were letters. Whatever they are written on, letters always give off something that makes it possible for you immediately to determine: this is a letter. If everything that has spent some time in a person's hands bears in some way the imprint of humanity, then a letter is doubly so. Especially an old one, so thin you can see through it. I myself still have some of those faded letters. But I do not have and there never were any letters from my mother: she was still illiterate when she died. I had of course already guessed whom the letters lying on the table were from. I had already been eyeing them on the sly, but they had never come into my hands. My interlocutor had, of course, noticed my curiosity but she had not suggested that I might look at them or hold them even if not to read them. On the contrary, throughout our conversation her hand had, consciously or unconsciously, rested on the little bundle of letters with their edges stained by time. What does Vysotsky say? I don't like other people to read my letters, peering over my shoulder? In that case that man of character was singing the views of this woman of character.

— As I re-read these letters from Mikhail Sergeyevich today, these lines written on faded scraps of paper – how many years have passed! – written sometimes in ink, sometimes in pencil, sometimes in the steppe on a combine harvester, sometimes in the district prosecutor's office in the lunch break or late at night after work, I think again and again, not only about the feeling that brought us together in our youth. I also think that the choice we made about life and our path through it that began in those early years was not a matter of chance. I would like to quote some passages from two or three of Mikhail Sergeyevich's letters. Not the whole letters, because they contain pages intended only for me – and they will depart when I do. Yes, there are things that are intended for me alone, however many years pass. But I will read you something from them. Look – this one still has the mark on it – 'Prosecutor's Office, Molotov Region'.

— *And I thought it was you who had placed those marks on them.*

— Nothing of the sort. Nobody has touched these letters. I've just decided to re-read them. Look – 'Prosecutor's Office of the Molotov District'. Even the date – 20st of June 1953. He was working at the Prosecutor's Office and began to write a letter on the first piece of paper that came to hand. '... I am so depressed by the situation here. And I feel it especially keenly every time I receive a letter from you. It brings with it so much that is good, dear, close, and understandable. And one feels all the more keenly how disgusting my surroundings are here. Especially the manner of life of the local bosses. The acceptance of convention, subordination, with everything predetermined, the open impudence of officials and the arrogance. When you look at one of the local bosses you see nothing outstanding apart from his belly. But what aplomb, what self-assurance and the condescending, patronising tone! The contempt for science. Consequently, a disparaging attitude to young specialists. I read recently in a newspaper a note from a livestock expert, a man called Movsisyan, a graduate from the Stavropol agricultural institute. It is really shameful. You can see your own fate in what happened to him. The man arrived here with great plans and set about his work with great enthusiasm, but he very soon began to feel that everyone was absolutely indifferent to it all. They all laughed at him and mocked him. 'Such passivity and conservatism...'

— *She interrupts her reading and says:*

— Thirty-seven years have passed. Did I ever think then that I would read it out? Aloud...

— *She speaks in such a tone that I begin to fear that the reading will be brought to an end. But a minute later she resumes, quoting from another letter:*

— 'I have been chatting with a lot of young specialists. They are all very dissatisfied. As usual I have a great deal, a very great deal of work. I am normally at my desk till late. At night I write my "diary", consisting of short comments. Later they will be signed by the procurator. I have been nowhere else in this place. But, to tell the truth, there's nowhere to go: it's all so boring. If it weren't for the work...'

— *As you are reading, I seem to see a young man who has been sent out of Moscow after university with what you call his fierce radicalism, his 'ideas' and his enthusiasm, straight into the depths of the provinces, the 'Land of Nod'.*

— The Land of Nod? I'm not sure about that... But where were we? Yes – 'Please write to me. I always long for them to come, your letters. It is as if you yourself were coming to me. And I really need you here. Yours ever, Mikhail.' And this [she picks up some other sheets of paper from the table] is a letter from the fields. He was working on a combine harvester and apparently wrote it with interruptions on two or three occasions: 'Rayechka! We have just begun to gather in the harvest at full steam. It's very difficult in these conditions...

— *That was probably why he wrote in pencil, because he was working in the fields?*

— Probably. [She reads another letter]. 'The wheat crop is plentiful and good, but with a lot of weeds in it. This has really complicated work on the combine. The day's work on the combine is like this: We rise long before sunrise. We prepare the combine for work and give it a technical service. That takes about three or four hours, and then we start harvesting the grain... We carry on as long as it is possible, that is as long as the wheat is dry. For harvesting at night there is a special light... Every day we spend twenty hours on our feet. And we work in horrible dust and on scorching hot metal. The sun beats down unbearably. We've had so many very hot days – thirty-five or thirty-six degrees. It makes you want to rip everything off. There's nothing to breathe. I will end here... How I shall send this letter I don't know. I wrote it on the seventeenth. When I shall send it, I don't know for sure...' Well, there's no need to read on.

— *And have your letters to him been preserved?*

— Do you really think men preserve letters as we women do? I have kept them all, every single one... I will read you a passage from one more letter. The same exercise book, the same pencil. Apparently, he wrote a couple of days later: "You were asking about the building of the house... I can't honestly call it a house... It's just an ordinary peasant cottage. It has now been roofed with tiles and the windows have been put in. In general, it is suitable for living in. The trouble is that I still can't get hold of timber for the floors...'

— *Very topical!*

— Yes, unfortunately. Throughout our life we suffer from shortages. By the way, it was a friend of my father's working in the village Soviet who helped him to buy my first coat. But we have digressed. [She continues reading from Gorbachev's letter.] 'We have even been in Stalingrad, but to no purpose. The rendering of the walls has been finished and they will be whitewashed later. Meanwhile we are all still in the apartment and it's very inconvenient in several ways. Mama is particularly tired of it. 'I know, Rayechka,

I haven't written to you. Our work team consists almost entirely of Gorbachevs. Papa is the combine operator; I do the steering and Semyon Grigorievich Gorbachev is the tractor driver. There is a girl on the straw collector – Anna Mikhailovna Gorbacheva, and the grain is transported from the combine in a truck by Vasili Alekseyevich Gorbachev. Our team is known as "The Gorbachevs". Papa, Semyon and Vasili are cousins... I must finish now... Warmest greetings from the sphere of production to the sphere of the intellect.'

— *Did he send that to you at home? Were you on holiday?*

— No, I was at the University. He had gone off to do his practical training, and I still had some examinations to pass. In that same year, 1953, we moved into a student hostel on the Lenin Hills. It was a new part of the University, built in the 1950s and later which included lecture halls, administrative buildings and common rooms, libraries, clubs, canteens, a polyclinic and an up-to-date and, as it seemed to us, amazingly comfortable hostel for students and graduates. It was all very well done. Everyone had a separate, though tiny, furnished room. Two people shared a shower and a lavatory. Our transfer to the new university building coincided with our completing our studies at the MGU. This was a very different stage in our life as students. Mikhail Sergeyevich and I were now always together. We wrote our theses and prepared to take the state examinations. We read a great deal. We studied the German language. We even translated together some of the texts we used. I had the opportunity to observe at close quarters with what enthusiasm Gorbachev, student at the law faculty of the MGU, set about his studies, always trying to get to the essence, to the very heart of the matter. We gave serious thought to our future. In my last years as a student, I was often ill: a cold that I did nothing about complicated by rheumatism. The doctors insisted on a change of climate. After graduation I was recommended for postgraduate study. I passed the examination and began my studies. Mikhail Sergeyevich was offered a choice: to take a job in Moscow or to do postgraduate work. But we decided to drop everything and go to work in Stavropol, his birthplace.

— *Raisa Maksimovna fell silent, lost in thought.*

— Of course, there is a sort of secret. The secret of the feelings and the laws that unite two people. Especially people who become indispensable to each other. And it is beyond the powers of people, or of science, to penetrate that secret. And it is a good thing that there is something secret in the world. As I return to those years in my thoughts, I ask myself again: what was Mikhail Sergeyevich like then, in his youth, when he came into my life? What kind of person was he? An intelligent, reliable friend? Yes. A man who had his own opinion and was capable of defending it vigorously? Yes. In my youth I came up against the fact – and it was one of my very painful disappointments – that some people are not able to stand up for their own opinions, and do not even have such opinions. But he was a man who had an opinion of his own and was capable of defending it and standing up for it with dignity. But that's not all. Today, Georgi Vladimirovich, I am thinking about something different. In the fierce struggle now going on between good and evil, loyalty and treachery, hope and disillusion, generosity and venality, vengefulness, I think of his inborn love for his fellow men. His respect for people. And it really is inborn. It is not, after all, something that can be cultivated in a person, I am quite convinced of that. And it is not to be acquired along with a degree, any kind of degree. Respect for people and for their dignity as human beings... I think about his inability (my God, how many times have I thought about it!) to assert himself at the expense of others, their dignity, and rights. No, he is not capable of asserting himself by destroying another person. The person next to him. I can see his face and his eyes. We have been together for thirty-seven years. Everything in this life changes. But a constant hope lives in my heart: that he, my husband, should remain just as he was when he came into my life in our youth. Manly and steadfast, strong, and kind. And that he should be able in the end to sing his favourite songs again – and, let me tell you again, he can sing and loves it. And that he should be able to read his favourite poems and to laugh, openly and sincerely, as he always did.

The conversation was over. I quietly put the tapes away in envelopes and numbered them. Raisa Maksimovna remained for a time sitting there in silence, having pushed to one side the many pieces of paper, all covered with notes and scribbles. She stared thoughtfully ahead and raised her hand to her temple. Her face had become quite pale. Her last words were surprisingly like a prayer... In the intervals at that memorable Congress of People's Deputies in December I had observed how the deputies had appealed to her on more than one occasion: 'Raisa Maksimovna – why do you stay here listening to the debates? Just to make yourself suffer? You might as well be at home watching it on the television.' She did not go away, of course. It has been said more than once that she is practically always present when her husband speaks in public, both in the Soviet Union and abroad. At foreign press conferences she sits somewhere in the front row. In this country she doesn't sit in the front row in sight of the television cameras, but wherever he speaks he has no keener listener. But she listens not only to him, but also to the crowded hall behind her. It's not an easy fate, especially in Russia – to have all eyes focussed on you and people talking and expressing opinions about you. I believe he senses her presence in the hall even in the heat of an argument, and I don't think the Soviet political scene has known such a spirited orator since Lenin's days – when it seems as though he sees nobody apart from his immediate opponent.

'A secret not subject to the judgement of others...' As with any couple. But fate has decreed that these two have a much larger audience. And that means the judgement is more severe. When American journalists once asked Gorbachev which serious questions he discussed with his wife, he thought for a moment and replied: 'All of them.' Not everyone in his place would have permitted himself such manly directness, although, frankly speaking, are there any serious questions that we do not discuss with our wives? Of course not. Only some of us admit it while others prefer not to, reckoning that in that way they increase their masculinity and independence in the eyes of others. Gorbachev behaves

very chivalrously in his relations with his wife. I certainly would not be so stupid as to suggest that this is a result of Perestroika. I am not looking for any link here. I simply see a symbol. A sign. Although in Russia one's attitude to women, and especially to one's own wife, may also be an aspect of Perestroika and even demand a certain degree of courage from a man. At least in the Russia that I know best, because I was born and grew up in it, the old attitude towards women in my Russia is still very much alive. Raisa Maksimovna allows herself to express her own individuality in the form primarily of a sense of her own worth. Mikhail Sergeyevich treats this with invariable quiet respect. It seems as though much respect forms part of some code of honour that he observes with enviable self-control, even in situations where another person would have long ago burst into hysterics. If I were more daring, I would say that there is in the relations between these two people, who have both sprung from 'the people', a sort of aristocratism which I have come across frequently in good, traditional peasant families. In one of the letters addressed to Raisa Gorbacheva I read: 'Thank you! Thanks to you and your husband the image of the Soviet woman is changing in Russia and the world. She is regaining her dignity...' Gorbachev is paying his people the long-standing debts incurred by others, and this may be his most dramatic problem. He is also paying a debt called 'human dignity'. As I left, I said some nice things about her daughter, whom I had just met. Perhaps it was because I myself tend to judge people as good or bad by one single indicator – by their attitude toward my children.

— Thank you. Would you like me to tell you an amusing story? When our first granddaughter was born my husband and I went to see Irina in the maternity home. As we entered the vestibule I said to the nurse: 'Open the door wider – grandma has arrived!' The nurse opened the door, looked to see who was behind me and said: 'But where is the grandmother?' [And her brown eyes flashed with amusement].

— *You see? And you said it was diet.*

— That was a long time ago. [Smiling, she rose from the table.]

As for the last Congress that we were talking about, it ended up to the advantage of the president. After the first day the course of the gathering took a sharp turn and Raisa Gorbacheva remained to witness, not only some of the President's most difficult and dramatic minutes, but also the way the crisis was overcome. The chain of cause and effect here is unbelievably complicated, but it really seems to me that simple human courage, loyalty and patience also deserve to be rewarded. 'A prophet is not without honour save in his own country.' To bring the subject of this chapter to an end I will quote one other letter:

Allow me, Mr General Secretary, to thank you for the hospitality you have shown us and to wish good health to yourself and Mrs. Gorbachev, whose presence at your side created a new perception of your country – of charm and culture. It was especially agreeable for me and my wife to see her here… Francois Mitterrand

The Test of Real Life

— *Raisa Maksimovna, our last conversation ended at the point at which you decided not to do postgraduate work and chose to move to Stavropol.*

— Yes, I gave up the idea of doing postgraduate work, although I had already passed the examination for it and had joined the course. Mikhail Sergeyevich also turned down Moscow. We chose Stavropol, his birthplace. Stavropol – they say that every human being cherishes in his heart his own little homeland, the place where he was born and grew up. If that's so, can you imagine what sort of 'little' homeland I have? The whole Soviet Union – so many moves from one place to another that I went through in childhood. But Mikhail Sergeyevich's little homeland is, of course, the Stavropol region. What did I want to tell you about Stavropol? It's an amazing region! A region of an abundance of sunshine, wheat, and gardens. And of the sunflower that moves around to face the hot sun throughout the day. A region of wonderful mountains and steppes. The steppes are full of smells. What do the steppes of the Stavropol region smell of? You, Georgi Vladimirovich, ought to remember.

— *In my birthplace in the summer the steppes smell of the grasses.*

— That's right, and of thyme as well. Apart from that it's a region of health–giving, healing waters, sources of mineral waters, a very rare mixture produced by the sands of the desert and the mountain glaciers. If you have ever been in Kislovodsk you have probably seen Lermontov's words carved in the rock: 'I love the Caucasus like the sweet melody of my homeland.' It was in Stavropol, the centre of the region, that Mikhail Sergeyevich and I arrived after completing university, as young specialists, full of plans and hopes. It marked the beginning of our working lives, the start of a totally new life in a new environment. You asked me, Georgi Vladimirovich, what I thought of Stavropol after Moscow. Both Moscow and Stavropol are cities. But what a difference between them! They say that the first impression you have of a person is the most lasting. I don't know about persons, but it is certainly very true when it comes to cities. My first impression of Stavropol remains in my memory for ever. Stavropol struck me with its greenery. It is a flood of green. It seemed as though the city had been decked out in luxurious green clothes. Lombardy poplars and such a lot of chestnuts. And willows and oaks and elms. And lilac. And flowers everywhere. In the autumn this apparel gives the city a beautiful crimson-gold, touchingly gentle look. The appearance of the city at that time is the very image of autumn. I have never come across anywhere with a better autumn, and I believe that autumn is by far the best season of the year in the Stavropol region. In my childhood I loved the springtime – springtime in the Urals with its babbling brooks and floodwater. But in the Stavropol region I came to like the autumn. Spring is quickly over here, whereas the autumn is long, very colourful, and warm.

I was impressed by the city itself, the centre of the region, which had a certain restraint and tranquillity about it. The main square, the streets and the houses seemed to have preserved the spirit of our ancestors – Russians and Cossacks who came here two hundred years ago. Oh yes, when I spoke about the greenery, I forgot one detail. Struck as I was in my first days there by its beauty and plenty, it was only later that I learned that the beauty is the city's 'hobby' and a good and long-standing tradition among the people of Stavropol. Later I enjoyed playing my part in keeping the city green.

— *In the Stavropol region every little town is 'cultivated' like a garden.*

— I remember there was even a film made about Stavropol – *The Greenest Town in Russia*. The second thing that struck me was the measured pace of life and the patriarchal quiet in what was the centre of one of the country's biggest regions. The pace of life was dictated by the fact that people walked everywhere. There was no transport problem, no 'rush hour' in those days in Stavropol. Wherever you were going – to work, to the shops, to the baths, the hairdresser, the polyclinic, or the market – it was possible to get there on foot. Only the central square and a few streets were paved. Only a few administrative buildings and blocks of flats had central heating. Drinking water had to be carried from standpipes. And in the very centre of the town, opposite the teachers' college, there was an enormous sea of mud. All the year round it stayed there and there was no way, on foot or on wheels, that you could get through it. It was like Gogoli's 'Mirgorod'. Of course, Stavropol is a very different place today. More than three decades have passed. Modern industry has arrived, new scientific, educational, and cultural centres have been built, and the population has almost doubled. That fact alone, of course, has changed the content and the rhythm of life in the city and its appearance. But at that time, for the centre of a vast region in Russia, which in those years included two autonomous regions, Stavropol was excessively provincial. The cinema was called, of course, the Giant, as in every small town. There was the Lermontov theatre of drama, whose repertoire we knew backwards in the course of two or three months. In that theatre I knew by heart everything they performed. There was the regional library, an orchestra, a museum of local history and two more cinemas – the October and the Motherland – and a few clubs and film-showing rooms. That was all the cultural facilities there were.

— *You arrived in Stavropol with a university education obtained in the capital, in Moscow. In those days that was very rare. How did your workmates regard you? What were relations like where you were employed?*

— There weren't any.

— *I don't understand, Raisa Maksimovna.*

— There's nothing to understand – I had big problems trying to find a job. In the first few months in Stavropol, I simply couldn't find any work. Then for a year and a half I had a job I was not trained for. Then I had two years of work in my specialty but with no real rights. Either I was paid by the hour or on half-salary, with occasional dismissal when the staff was reduced. So, there's your 'person with a university education from Moscow' and 'a rarity in those days'. Yes – actually I did not have a permanent job for four years.

— *Why?*

— I think there were two reasons. I believe that in those years there were problems throughout the country with the employment of specialists with a higher education in the humanities. I knew, for example, that in Stavropol at that time about seventy per cent of the teachers were working part-time. But no less important in my view was the second reason. Yes, it's true – in Stavropol in those days there were practically no specialists with a university education, certainly not ones from a Moscow university. I don't know exactly, so I stress the word 'practically'. Well, perhaps there were two or three. In the faculties of the colleges where my professional training might have been used the appropriate disciplines were taught by people with teaching qualifications obtained very often by correspondence.

As a rule, they were graduates of their own Stavropol teachers' college. I do not wish to throw any doubt on their professional qualifications. When I came later to work among them I met people who were carrying out important scientific research, and were doing it very capably, delivered excellent lectures, enjoyed the well-deserved affection of the students, and gave themselves over entirely to their profession. But there were a good many who were simply not able, and who didn't want to engage in research of any kind. They didn't want to and weren't capable. Such people delivered lectures prepared by someone else at some other time, used other people's material, and had noticeable difficulty in pronouncing philosophical categories and concepts. Great difficulty. But the institute regarded them as 'its own' people – people they knew, who knew its ways and were easy to manage. It made them better off financially. In our country the rate of pay remains stable, depending on the position and the title, but not on the quantity and certainly not the quality of the work performed. I even came across people who were quite incapable of delivering lectures but who nevertheless received a lecturer's pay. They received the pay, but other people delivered their lectures. Competitions held to fill vacant places on the staff were conducted as a pure formality. The college did its best to hold on to its own people. Moreover, specialists invited to Stavropol from outside would need accommodation. Where would one find it? Every collective had more than enough people waiting for flats. Even if the students were not satisfied with the quality of the lectures and the seminars, there was nothing considered terrible in that. They were obliged to attend the course just the same, irrespective of whether the course suited them or not.

The quality of the teaching, the system employed and the way the teaching was organised affected the training of specialists throughout the country and not only in Stavropol. Everything in the colleges was strictly controlled. Everything that was and was not permitted – the relationship between the students and the teachers, the list of members of the staff, the teaching load, and the hours devoted to the various disciplines. The number of scientists and teachers employed by the college was always determined by the size of the student intake. It was more to their advantage to take in more school leavers and to release exactly as many as were admitted. Otherwise, the staff had to be cut down. This alone can explain certain episodes in my teaching practice, about one of which I want to tell you now. A correspondence student was having his third attempt to pass the examination. I had a talk with him, trying to extract an answer at least to the very simplest and elementary questions. I tried to get him to say what philosophy was. Alas, all my efforts were in vain. Then, suddenly, when I was already exhausted, he said with feeling: 'Raisa Maksimovna, I am so sorry for you.' 'You are sorry for me,' I asked in astonishment. 'Well, why do you get so upset? You are wasting time. This is the third time you try. But I do the same with everyone. I do all my subjects like that. True, they all give me a 'three', and I am through. And everyone's happy. What's the difference?' he asked me.

— *And how did you mark him?*

— I gave him a 'three' as well. I acted against my conscience – not for the first or only time. I am glad that we are giving serious thought today to the problems that have piled up in Russia in the field of education of every kind – general, vocational, and higher education. We are seeking ways to make it more democratic, to improve all its branches, to raise the quality of the teaching, and to raise the status of higher education in our country. So much has become a pure formality. We have been training specialists

without knowing what they are for. The number of degrees we
have created! Many a time I have asked in the college: why do
we award a degree to a person who is not really educated either
in the professional sense or in the general sense? When he turns
up to work with his degree, he will demand the same rights as a
properly educated person, a real specialist in great demand. You
see, it's a vicious circle – the production of the unwanted. There is
a great need for major changes in this field, and it is a good thing
that they have already begun. Take, for example, the President's
latest decisions about granting autonomy to institutions of higher
education. These are tentative moves towards improving a hitherto
stagnant system. Even in the past, experience was, of course, being
gained, traditions established, and progress made, but there was
also a good deal of stagnation.

— *Raisa Maksimovna, let us return to Stavropol.*

— Sorry, I didn't keep to the subject, I digressed. The subject
of higher education is a professional weakness with me... Stavropol.
Mikhail Sergeyevich arrived there from Moscow in the same year
as he finished at the university and a little sooner than I did. He
arrived with a lawyer's degree at the disposition of the regional
prosecutor's office. But he worked there for no more than ten days.
He wrote to me: 'No, working in the prosecutor's office is not for
me... I met some comrades with whom I used to work in the Komsomol.' And in another letter: 'In view of my experience of work
in the Komsomol, both in school and university, they have offered
me a job in the regional Komsomol organisation. You know what

my attitude is towards work in the Komsomol.' And again: 'I had a long and unpleasant conversation with the regional prosecutor.' And in another letter: 'After more talks with me and after berating me in every way, they have agreed to my leaving to join the regional Komsomol.' The next sentence was: 'I have been confirmed in the position of deputy head of the department of agitation and propaganda.' Incidentally, the regional prosecutor at the time was B. N. Petukhov, the man with whom Mikhail Sergeyevich had the 'long and unpleasant conversation'. Petukhov is an outstanding man. He has devoted almost fifty years to work as a prosecutor and investigator, and he has written a number of interesting accounts of his work. He presented inscribed copies of two of his books, published in 1970 and 1981, to Mikhail Sergeyevich. And he wrote a letter which I will also quote to you: 'I think today with tremendous satisfaction that I acted correctly when I did not stand in the way of your career.'

— *He was a far-sighted man!*

— Mikhail Sergeyevich's pay amounted to 1000 roubles a month in 'old' money, as we say.

— *That's supposed to be 100 roubles in 'new' money.*

— After paying various taxes and membership fees to all sorts of organisations we were left with 840 roubles. I remember it well, because, bearing in mind my lengthy 'unemployment', that money was for a long time our only income. Apart from some food parcels that Mikhail Sergeyevich's parents sent us occasionally from the country. They were not able to help us more than that. When he worked in the Komsomol Mikhail Sergeyevich frequently had to make trips round the region. On one such 'business trip' he wrote to me...

— *He wrote to you from such trips?*

— Yes – is there anything surprising in that?

— *Nowadays, as far as I know, men don't write to their wives even from trips abroad. And he wasn't far away – only travelling round the region.*

— It depends on what kind of husband. So, in one of his letters, he wrote the following: '... I don't know how many times I've been to Privolnoye hearing them talk of just twenty roubles – where were they going to find such a sum? Despite the fact that my father works day and night the whole year round. I am simply overwhelmed with shame. Honestly, I can't keep back my tears. At the same time, you can't help thinking that, after all, they still don't live too badly. But what about the others? There's a great deal yet to be done. Our parents and thousands like them really deserve a better life…

— *Those words seemed to me like something out of Ovechkin's Provincial Routine.*

— He was a very keen student of the life around him: it was as though he wanted to make up for the time spent studying in Moscow. His worries didn't give him any peace and he had a constant need to express himself, which was probably one of the things that prompted him to write so many letters to me when he was on his trips. They were really like studies in provincial routine. Life wasn't so very cheap in those days. Out of our eight hundred roubles we

paid two hundred for the flat, a little room in a private house that
we rented.

— *Whereabouts was it?*

— I will show you a photo of the house now, and you can
guess where it is, since you also call yourself a Stavropolian.

*Raisa Gorbacheva selected a little snapshot from a bundle of pho-
tos she had prepared. The snapshot was quite faded. In the foreground
there were trees – wherever you take a picture in Stavropol there will
always be trees in the foreground – through which you could see a typical Stavropol 'private' house built of the local limestone. I once rented
space in such a building. Even in my day at the end of the 1960s
three-quarters of Stavropol consisted of such houses, all overgrown with
hops and grape vines. So just try and guess where that one is – on the
Osetinka, the Tashla or near the Lower market?*

— *I suppose I must be a bad Stavropolian, Raisa Maksimovna,
or I left Stavropol too long ago – in 1973. I don't recognise the street.
Tell me what it is.*

— Do I need to? The house is still there. But I wonder whether we ought to attract attention to it and disturb the peace of the
people living there who are relations of our former landlord. No,
better that I should tell you in greater detail about the little room
that we rented there and which I can still see so vividly.

— *Well, if that's how you feel...*

— We had difficulty in finding room in it for our possessions
at the time. A bed, a table, two chairs and two huge boxes full

of books. In the centre of the room was a huge stove. We had to buy our own coal and wood. I used to cook on a paraffin stove in the narrow corridor. But our 'apartment' had its advantages. The little room was very light, with three windows all looking out onto the garden. It was a big and very beautiful garden. And the owners were good, and kind, and I count that as another good thing about the room. They were former teachers now living on a pension. The old man was very strict and not very talkative, unlike his wife and daughter. And it was only when he had had a drop too much to drink and was not quite sober that he would instruct me that I must 'look soberly at life'. It was in that room on the 6th of January 1957, on the eve of the Orthodox Christmas, that our daughter Irinka was born. At the maternity home they entered into her medical record: 'Weight at birth – 3 kilograms 300 grams. Height 50 centimetres. Weight on leaving maternity home – 3 kilograms 100 grams. A healthy child.' I remember that entry by heart: in those happy days the words were music to my ears. In the same year, thanks to efforts by Mikhail Sergeyevich's colleagues, we obtained a 'government apartment' in a building in which the two top storeys were intended as housing. The ground floor was to serve as offices. But because of the difficult housing situation the lower floor gradually came to be used as housing too. Our 'two-roomed' apartment, which had previously served as an office and reception room, was the last bastion to fall. More precisely – for someone or some department it was a defeat, but for our family it was a victory. Consequently, the whole floor became one huge unit of eight apartments with a common kitchen at the end of the corridor and a communal toilet.

— *That means you lived in a communal apartment?*

— Yes, our neighbours were a demobilised lieutenant-colonel, a mechanic from the garment factory, a welder, a hospital employee... They were all people with families. And there were four single women, two living together and two in separate rooms. And we – Mikhail Sergeyevich and I – for the first time in our lives had our own apartment. It was a little sovereign state with a great variety of sovereign subjects, to use modern terminology. It was a state with its own unwritten but universally understood laws. And in it people worked, loved, separated, drank like Russians, quarrelled like Russians, and made up again like Russians. In the evenings they played dominoes. We celebrated our birthdays together. To speak disparagingly of others or to display arrogance was completely out of the question. It was a sort of direct, natural, human world. Mikhail Sergeyevich used to make fun of me. Interestingly enough, he was then already using the sort of parliamentary jargon that we use today. In one letter – he wrote so often because we had no telephone, as in those days few people had telephones – he wrote: 'It is up to you to maintain diplomatic relations with the other sovereign units. I hope you will take pride in conducting our foreign policy. But don't forget the principle of mutual interest.'

— *Really a quite modern formulation!*

— In that house I got to know people with whom I maintained good relations throughout our years in Stavropol. One such person was Zoya Vasilievna Karetnikova, wife of the lieutenant-colonel, who had not had an easy life but was generously gifted. They had moved to Stavropol from Lvov on account of the state of health of the husband, Pyotr Fyodorovich. He is no longer with us – may he rest in peace. Because her husband was a military man Zoya Vasilievna had been unable to complete her studies as a geologist. She was from Moscow. She had golden fingers and a natural artistic taste. I have to tell you that there were no tailors or dress shops in Stavropol, and for twenty years Zoya Vasilievna made and remade everything I and my family wore. I was friendly with her for twenty years and her loyal and constant customer.

— *I believe you continued to have her make things for you even after you became the wife of the 'first man'.*

— Yes.

— *Stavropol is a relatively small town, and I have heard it said that the wife of the first secretary was always well turned out.*

— That only goes to confirm that Zoya Vasilievna really did have golden fingers.

— *And that was your special dressmaker?*

— You could say that. In Stavropol I also got to know Ksenia Mikhailovna Yefremova, an employee in the garment factory. Her fiancé was killed in the Finnish war, and she was left completely alone. I do not know, of course, whether my former neighbours and kind helpers will ever come to read this little book. But I want to thank each one of them. And special thanks to Ksenia Mikhailovna for the help she gave me at a very difficult time in my life when I was doing a job, writing a thesis, going on long trips and when my daughter was often very sick.

We all come from the people. In the early 1970s I heard an unexpected continuation of the quotation: how are we to return to them? The relationship between those who 'emerged' and the environment, the 'people', from whom they emerged, can be extremely complicated. Too often the dominant factor becomes the almost complete mutual alienation. Some of the big bosses or wives of the big bosses don't want to be reminded where they have come from. Others detect that reluctance. For some reason it is not the bosses themselves but their wives who most frequently do not wish to be reminded. In this case the situation is quite different. I long ago noticed Raisa Maksimovna's ability, without special effort and without trying to ingratiate herself, to understand and accept the world into which she was born. The natural relationship she had with that world and a certain feeling of obligation towards it has long been characteristic of the Russian intelligentsia. I don't expect you to be affected by this; I just ask you to note in your memory for the future the 'communal flat dwellers' of 1957. How often, as we move 'forward and upwards', we cast off our old friends like old clothes.

— For me work was not just a means of earning money. It was also a cause without which I would have thought my life was a failure. Student lectures, seminars, academic conferences, meetings, and debates – can you imagine how much effort, time, intellectual tension, and even sleepless nights they demanded? But they gave me a great deal. They gave me the incomparable feeling of moral satisfaction. Then there were the arguments and discussions we had in our spare time – in the student hostel, on the collective farm, where we were all, teachers, and students alike, sent to gather in the corn, the grapes, and the potatoes. They went on too in my flat, where my students also came. We discussed everything – new plays in the theatre, new films, events in the life of the college, the region, and the country. We argued till we were hoarse, of course, about the meaning of life – there would be no student debate without the 'key' question. In short, we discussed everything, starting with the eternal human problems. The flowers that I have been sent and the letters I have received from students who have long since become independent, with families and are no longer young – these are the most precious presents I have received. In exactly the same way I value their strict but just opinions of me and of my work. I remember very well the first lecture I ever delivered in a large auditorium. It was when I was still a student in Moscow. The society called Znaniye (Knowledge) arranged for me to deliver a lecture in a factory club. After the lecture there was to be a dance – that was the tradition. Quite a large number of people gathered, mainly young people who, I suppose, had their minds on the dance. I went up to the platform and to the microphone holding my lecture notes.

— *Were they written on scraps of paper like you are holding now?*
— Of course not. It was all very proper and thoroughly done. I looked at the audience and there in the first row I saw an old man

with an enormous grey beard. I can still see him sitting there! And I took fright. The subject of my lecture was 'Sleep and Dreaming in the Teaching of I. P. Pavlov'. I had prepared my lecture properly and done a lot of research in the Lenin Library. But I was apparently conscious of the weaknesses in my knowledge of the subject and the theoretical concepts I set forth. I felt even more vulnerable on account of my age compared with that of the learned old gentleman who was, I thought, quite capable of delivering a lecture on the subject of dreams himself. I read my lecture page by page without looking up and then waited, terrified, for the reaction. Not from the audience but from the old gentleman, the 'magician'. But, you know, there was complete silence – not a sound, not a single comment. And there wasn't a single question either during the lecture or after it. The old gentleman also remained silent. Apparently, everything was absolutely clear to him and to all the others present. Or was he also just waiting impatiently for the dance? But most likely [she smiled] the audience sensed what the young lecturer was going through and took pity on her. I would like to explain to my foreign readers what the Znaniye society is. Its purpose is to spread scientific and political knowledge. And, although I did not make a very good job of the first thing I did for the society, the contact I had with it, lasting many long years, was both useful and very interesting.

— *Why do you say you did not do well? That there were no questions means you explained everything clearly...*

— I said that I attributed it to the dance. Anyway, when I was in Stavropol, I was a member not only of the society's panel of lecturers but also of the presidium of the regional organisation. That enabled me to get to know many different representatives of the world of scholarship and art in Stavropol – scholars and poets, writers, actors, doctors, composers, artists, and teachers. I knew many of them very well and had frequent meetings with them. I remember also my first lecture as a teacher at the college. It was in Stavropol at the medical institute, and it was on the history of philosophy. It so happened that on that very day an important commission arrived unexpectedly at the college, officially to 'exchange experience with teachers of social science', but actually to check up on the faculty because of some petty quarrels that had taken place there. The commission included the heads of all the faculties in the town and the best-known social scientists in Stavropol at the time.

— *And that coincided with your first lecture?*

— Yes. In fact, they had not come to see me but to inspect the college and the faculty. It was quite an important faculty. But the head of the faculty for some reason thought that the best solution was to send the whole commission to visit my class. Although I had only just begun to work at the institute. I was terribly worried! On the whole I have a good memory. I practically never read my lectures. Only occasionally in the course of explaining the subject I would check my notes for particular quotations, facts and figures. As you know, a lecturer has to work twice – first at his desk, preparing the lecture, which allowed me later to feel completely at ease at the second stage, before the audience. There I could see the faces, hear my students, observe their reaction, if necessary, elaborate something, add, or repeat something, or reorganise the argument. But then, when I delivered my first teaching lecture to the students I had absolutely no experience. I had no idea of how much time a given amount of material would take to deliver, how much was needed for a two- or three-hour lecture. I hadn't worked out the ideal rate at which to speak. I had no 'spare' subjects for speaking to the audience if the lecture ended before it was due. That all came later. I forgot to say I had a good attendance – about 200 people. But I finished my first lecture thirty minutes before the bell went. I just didn't know what to do with that half an hour, or what to do with myself, to get away from the students and from the commission! When the lecture was over there was a discussion about it. The commission considered the usual questions. Had the purpose of the lecture been achieved, had the key issues been correctly identified, had the lecture succeeded in establishing the link between philosophy and natural science, and so on.

Suddenly the head of a faculty at the agricultural college asked a question: 'Excuse me, but how long have you been delivering lectures?' I replied, neither alive nor dead: 'This was my first lecture.' So that you should have a better idea of the situation I will describe to you what I looked like in the face of those venerable professors and the awesome committee. I weighed just fifty kilograms and wore a green dress with a little scarf. You know, during my first years at work I tried always to put on more clothes, so as to look more adult and substantial. Even as a child I used to get into trouble with my mother for it. I would put on every piece of clothing I had, and Mama would scold me: 'Now then, what on earth is that? Come on, unpack yourself!' I did the same at college, wearing jackets and sweaters, again in order to look more important, I suppose. It was the fashion at that time for girls to look like women in Deineka's paintings. "You say it was your first lecture?' The head of the faculty rose. 'Shame on you, colleagues,' he said and left. The next year he took me on to the staff of his college. He switched to part-time himself and suggested that another of the teachers should do the same, and he appointed me to the place he had made. He frequently repeated Khrushchev's remark, very fashionable at the time: 'We are coming back from the fair, comrades.' And he would add: 'And we must help the young specialist.' And he would point jokingly at me. In that way I became a sort of symbolic figure in the faculty – the young specialist – and naturally I tried not to let the head of the faculty down. But he died soon after, unexpectedly.

— *Do you remember his name?*

— Of course I do – Nikolai Ivanovich Khvorostukhin. He died of cancer, and I soon lost my place in the faculty because of a reduction of staff.

— *That was a real upset.*

— A very typical situation, alas. How often something good depends on a single good person! Throughout my long professional career, frankly speaking, I have never become accustomed to lecturing, in the sense that it never became for me a routine everyday obligation. Every lecture was an examination for me. I was always nervous when I began a lecture, especially before a new audience. Calm and self-confidence came only when I felt that I had made contact, that I had aroused the listeners' interest and held their attention. Because of the specific nature of the subject I taught – philosophy – and the nature of my research work, which was connected with sociology, the subjects of my lectures were very varied. I can say without boasting that sometimes women I talk to are surprised at how much knowledge in a variety of fields I have, often in spheres of knowledge very far apart. It is simply because my profession covers such a wide field. The dialectics, for example, presupposes an acquaintance with the natural sciences, physics, chemistry, and the general laws of their development. And historical materialism? My work on practical sociology was exceptionally useful for me. Moreover, I was not responsible only for student courses. I delivered lectures to graduates and to evening classes attended by mature students with the wisdom of years of experience and with high qualifications and who would not be fobbed off with elementary truisms. As I said, the subjects of my lectures were very varied: from the history of philosophy, Hegel's *Science of Logic*, Kant on the antinomy of pure reason, Lenin's theory of reflection and of the methods and forms of scientific perception, the problems of consciousness – to the role of the individual in history, the structure, and forms of social consciousness, contemporary sociological concepts, philosophical trends in foreign countries, and so forth.

Of course, we were affected by the conditions in the provinces, the shortage of specialists in the colleges. Efforts to achieve a narrower specialisation in the teaching of philosophy and in the programmes of public lectures were not successful, mainly because of the shortage of specialists. You had to be a jack of all trades. A scholar working in one of the big centres, like Moscow or Leningrad, usually lectures on only a few subjects – those he is himself working on. But in a provincial college you are always being asked to deliver lectures on widely different subjects, especially if you are young. It is often impossible to persuade the older lecturers to do that, and so they exploit the younger people. I was one of those they used in this way: apart from my basic disciplines I taught ethics, the history of atheism and religion. Not for long, it's true, but I did it. But there was a bright side to it... In the 1960s the Bible, the Gospels and the Koran appeared in my library, or more precisely in my life... With what difficulty I obtained them! By what strange routes! But I had them then and it was then that I read them. And it was then that for the first time I thought seriously about faith, tolerance, believers, and the Church. An exceptionally important part in my professional career was played by my interest in sociology. In our country sociology practically ceased to exist as a science somewhere in the 1930s. It turned out – and here too I want to be precise, because it is important – to be 'unwanted' and perhaps even 'dangerous' in conditions where a bureaucratic command system was being formed. Sociology is the embodiment of what we call 'feedback', and for that reason alone a system of command is organically alien to it. Just as it is alien to the system.

The revival of sociology began at the very end of the 1950s and essentially at the beginning of the 1960s. It began slowly, with difficulty and in contradictory ways. Sociology, a science dealing with the nature of society, the various forms it takes, what they have in common and how they interact, came up against some very real obstacles in the 1960s and 1970s, against the blind dogmatism of theoretical social thought. Nevertheless, many people, including myself, saw sociology as a phenomenon absolutely essential to social thought as a means of overcoming the gap between theory and practice. Work in sociology opened up for me a whole world of new ideas about society and the names of many talented scholars, philosophers, economists, and sociologists both Russian and foreign. It brought me into contact with some remarkable people, the country's leading sociologists, great enthusiasts for their cause, devoted to it and believing in it. They did not have an easy time. It required strength and courage to withstand the resistance to everything new and even its suppression in the 1970s and the early 1980s, in the period later known as the time of stagnation.

— *Too often sociology tells us rather unpleasant things that don't fit in with the official doctrine.*

— Yes [she said thoughtfully], I consider it very important that I chose the peasantry as the subject of my sociological studies. The Russian village is where we all have our roots and the source of all our strength and perhaps our weakness too. It was important for my development as a young scholar and for my personality and, finally, for the formation of my attitude to life. By no means unimportant also was the fact that my study of the peasantry and its real role was taking place on the basis of material gathered in Stavropol, the region that had been regarded traditionally as an important source of Russia's agricultural production. At that time we made use of every available means of research to study life in the villages – statistics, all sorts of documents, archives, questionnaires, and interviews. You know, I personally collected about 3000 questionnaires in those years. Moreover, I felt that, to a certain extent, I was myself 'inside' the processes and the events taking place in the countryside. I didn't feel like an outsider. On the collective farms I visited the farmworkers' homes, the working brigades, the farms, schools, libraries, shops, medical centres, pre-school nurseries and old people's homes. It was then the first homes for the elderly appeared in our region. In Grigoripolisskoye, for example.

— *I remember Grigoripolisskoye. It had a children's home. My youngest brother was educated there for a time. I used to visit him. That was also in the 1960s.*

— You see, it's a small world. I also visited homes for the elderly and have a very good idea of their actual state at the time. I not only visited them: I tried to help them where I could. I delivered lectures and ran discussion evenings. And I had a lot of meetings with the village intelligentsia, most of whom are such selfless people, especially if you bear in mind the conditions they live in and their limited resources. I also spoke at regional meetings, scientific conferences, and seminars, analysing the situation and making recommendations and proposals for the reform or improvement of some aspect of life in the countryside. The immediate subject of my personal research which provided the material about which I later wrote my thesis was the peasant family, its material condition, daily life, cultural demands, and the nature of relationships in the family. Bur, along with other researchers from Stavropol and Moscow, I carried out elaborate research into the region's collective farms – their economics, labour resources, system of wage payments, conditions of life, leisure facilities, and the structure and functioning of the administration. Not everything went as we wanted it, of course. Nevertheless, I can say without exaggeration that our work acted as a stimulus to the region for other scientists and also for the efforts being made by agricultural specialists, collective and state farm managers. The institute began to receive from various enterprises requests to draw up plans for the social development of working collectives. Our faculty did a great deal in this field, and I know it continued to do this work even after my departure to Moscow. The sociological research in which I took part for many years brought me into such close and revealing contact with people and life as I shall never forget. Hundreds of people whom I have questioned on a whole variety of subjects, their recollections, stories, and opinions of current events, remain in my memory and are part of my life. I know what their daily life is like and what their problems are. I have travelled hundreds of kilometres along country roads, in a passing car, on a motorcycle or a cart, and sometimes on foot in rubber boots.

A collective farm chairman I know says that a good agronomist always goes around on foot. It doesn't have to be barefoot; he says – times have changed. But he still has to go around on foot. The same is probably true of sociology. It is precisely for the reason that my host did her surveys on foot that her thesis, despite its rather optimistic title – 'The Development of New Features in the Life of the Peasantry in the Collective Farms' – does not stray too far from reality. As someone once said, in Russia truth still moves in the old way, on foot. Thank God it's not barefoot.

— My 'practical sociology is sociology with a human face, with the faces and the lives that have become part of my life. It has deepened very sharply my conception of 'real life' and my understanding of life and people. And it was in the course of such meetings with real people, and not from books or newspapers, not from plays or films, that I came to understand many of our misfortunes and the questionable nature of many undisputed assertions and established concepts. It was in the depths of the country that I experienced again the living pain of war, the sad aura of which still enshrouded the nation's life, although it was already twenty years since the war ended. As I conducted comprehensive social surveys of family life, I discovered that every fourth or fifth homestead in the villages of the Stavropol region consisted of a single woman.

Can you imagine it? A woman who has lost everything, whose life was literally destroyed by war. Of course, I quoted the factual material in lectures and articles, but I hadn't given them enough serious thought, I suppose. More precisely, I didn't perceive the situation as vividly, as visibly or as painfully. But when I came to carry out polls in the villages and every fourth or fifth house turned out to belong to a single woman, then I saw with my own eyes both the homes and the women. Women who had never known the happiness of love or the joy of motherhood. Women living out their lives alone in old, tumbledown houses that were also at the end of their days. If you think about it, we are talking about people whom nature intended to be the givers of life and to be at its centre. And it was amazing to find that the majority of those women had not become bitter, did not hate the whole world and had not withdrawn into themselves, but had preserved the selflessness and the sympathy for the misfortunes and sorrows of others that have always animated the Russian woman's heart. It is really amazing!

— *Do you think that fate possibly chose you to act on behalf of those women?* '

— *I don't know,' she replied, with a quick glance at me. But I could tell by her look and her reply that that was a subject she did not wish to pursue. But now that I am alone, sorting out the notes of our conversation, I keep returning to my question. And once again I see in my mind the face of my own mother, who was also left alone by the war, a single mother. How many such women are there whose intended husbands were taken by the world war and by that other war that a poet called 'war with your own people'? There was simply nothing left for them to do but to have children by 'illegal' husbands so as to fulfil their main destiny in the long-suffering Russian land. Illegitimate husbands produce illegitimate children. In my birth certificate, where it asks for the name of my father, there is a blank, while a friend of mine has a sad and eloquent word written – 'illegitimate'. I would like to believe that the woman I have these conversations with not only was well aware of the fate of such people as my mother but that she will often look with their attentive eyes at the world that is opening up before her. There is not a scrap of envy in my attitude towards her. Perhaps it is because I now know a little better than others how she feels being at such a dangerous height, the summit of Power. Power and height are the same thing, and to be next to the Power is even more dangerous, because next to the height there is always the neighbouring precipice. Or maybe it is because I am a man and it is, after all, women who are inclined to be more envious of her. I think they will be the main and most 'penetrating' readers of this book. Or perhaps fate has chosen her in the name of all those unknown women who have tragically missed so much that is good and enjoyable in life.*

— There is something else. I suppose a person who has suffered more feels more sympathy for others? I remember one woman at whose house I turned up late in the evening with my questionnaire, with so many questions to answer. After we had talked and she had answered my probing personal questions she sighed and asked me:

— 'How is it, daughter, that you're so painfully thin?'
I said, — 'Oh no, just my usual weight.'
Still, she went on: — 'I suppose you haven't got a husband?'
I said, — "Yes I have.'
She sighed. — 'I suppose he drinks?'
— 'No. '
— 'He beats you up?'
— 'Certainly not.'
To which she said, — 'Come on, daughter, why try to deceive me? I've lived a long time and I know people don't go round from door to door unless they're driven to it.'

Twice, I noticed, Raisa Gorbacheva's voice trembled in the course of that long evening: once when she recalled the peasant woman who, after answering the learned questions asked by the young sociologist, began to ask questions herself – very precise and even more down to earth than you find in any questionnaire; and the second time, when she spoke about her daughter. Then I realised that the woman really follows her around the world. She has not faded away.

— When I think of my past, I often think also of that woman who embodies a great deal for me: the fate of our country, the fate of our village toilers and – and this is also important for me – a sort of national assessment of our sociological activity, which at that time was essentially selfless. 'People don't go round from door to door...' – she said then, as though in confirmation of my observations. Yes, it was, after all, a selfless activity which, despite the shortcomings and problems, tried in those years to establish knowledge and truth about life, however unpleasant it might be. As for my thesis, it was partly based on those thousand questionnaires. Nowadays, in the time of Perestroika, democratisation, and Glasnost, as I observe the development of sociology and the work of sociological services, I wonder if sociology is making full use today of all the possibilities available to it. Is it assisting scientific prognosis and the management of social processes? Or has it again been brought under the control of someone else's subjective will (and it makes no difference whether it is the will of the Government, the Party, or the interests of some group) and becoming ever more politicised, departing from objectivity and from the great purpose of all scientific knowledge: to help people and to illuminate and not to obscure the road ahead.

— *You mean that it is again serving some people, rather than the whole of society?*

— Yes, that is important. There's a need for truth here too. I followed the work of the sociologists' congress: its proceedings were very difficult. But let's return to talking about our everyday life at that time. Our daughter was growing up. She went to the town nursery and then attended the state school for her general education, the normal local school in our district. She studied music and spent her holidays with her grandparents in the country. We always lived on our own, without the older generation. Our daughter shared with us the joys and sorrows of those years. She helped to keep the house clean, to cook, to do the shopping, and she learned how to make a card-index of our library and even how to arrange my numerous sociological questionnaires and other documents. I must say that my daughter learnt very early in her life to compile a library index. That's a big job in our family because we always had lots of books. But Irina was only a child, and I constantly had and still have the feeling that at some point in her childhood I did not give her enough attention. I didn't give her as much as I could or, more precisely, as much as she needed. She was born at a time when the law provided for only two months' maternity leave. Our material conditions and our difficulties with employment did not permit me even for a short time to live on my husband's salary. I shall never forget how, early in the morning, I would rush her, only half awake and dressed in a hurry, to the nursery school, almost at a run. And she would keep saying: 'How far away we live! How far away we live!' I shall not forget her little eyes, full of tears and despair, her nose flattened against the glass of the door to the nursery as, when I had been kept late at work, I would again rush into the nursery to collect her. She would cry and keep saying: 'You didn't forget me? You won't leave me?' That's how it was.

— *Here her voice trembled for the second time.*
— She was often ill, and quite seriously. We took her to doctors and specialists and obtained various diagnoses and recommendations, often mutually exclusive. That all has an effect on a mother's heart. I tried not to get a doctor's certificate too often,

because there was no one at work to replace me. When Irina was older, she stayed at home alone. But when she was smaller, I have to admit, I often took her with me to the college. She would sit there playing patiently in the teachers' room and waiting for the end of the working day. People who noticed her as they passed by would ask her questions and she would surprise them with her answers. 'Who do you look like, little one?' 'Like Daddy – the palms of our hands are identical.' 'And what is your name?' 'Zakharenysh.' 'Really? And your mother?' 'Zakharik.'

— *That was a curious reply.*

— When I was an eighteen-year-old student I appeared in a photograph and it reminded Mikhail Sergeyevich of Zakharka, a figure in a painting by Venetsianov, a Russian nineteenth century artist. And he began to use that as a pet name for me, and so it came to be accepted in our family. Now it has come into use again, with the next generation. Nastenka, our youngest, four-year-old granddaughter, said recently in the presence of some very impressive guests, when Mikhail Sergeyevich asked, 'Where is Raisa Maksimovna?' – 'Your Zakharka has gone upstairs.' The guests exchanged surprised glances and laughed. There was nothing for it but to explain who 'Zakharka' was and why the name was used. In the second class Irina wrote an essay about 'Why I love my Mama'. It turned out to be because I had 'a lot of books' and because 'all the students like Mama because they "say hello to her"' and also, most importantly, because "Mama is not afraid of wolves." I still have the essay.

— *I see, you are really an ideal archivist.*

— Perhaps it's a sign of my profession as a sociologist and a lecturer. A sociologist without an archive is like a person without a memory. Irina was awarded a gold medal upon finishing school. In the course of ten years at school she had, as I recall, only one mark less than the highest, and that was for drawing. She finished medical school in the same way, without a single '4'. And I am very proud of that, you know. In her adolescence and youth my daughter read a great deal, and she admits to me now that she very often used to read into the night 'on the sly'. She says now: 'I appreciated the fact that no one ever told me what I could or could not read, or said I was too young to read something. All the books at home were completely at my disposal.' She still likes to read fiction. And some of the things by Tolstoy and Gogol, the short stories of Somerset Maugham, the plays of J. B. Priestley and Margaret Mitchell's novel Gone with the Wind were read over and over again. I believe she actually knew Gone with the Wind by heart.

— *It's the same with my girls. They talk to each other in the dialogues of Scarlett O'Hara and Rhett Butler.*

— You know, it's very understandable. Those books contain some strong characters and many fine people. There are wonderful female characters, and male ones as well. And directness and nobility attract the female nature.

— *I'll take you at your word.*

— When she was sixteen my daughter and her close friends

acquired their musical idols – Alla Pugacheva, the Beatles, Joe Dassin, Demis Roussos, and the musical *Jesus Christ Superstar.*

But Irina tells me now that she prefers the tangos of the 1920s and 1930s. And, like Mikhail Sergeyevich and me, she likes the music of Tchaikovsky, his symphonies and ballet music. She loves Schubert's Ave Maria, Leoncavallo's Pagliacci, Bellini's Norma. The tastes of the generations are getting closer. In 1974 she began her studies in the Stavropol medical school. In an interview she gave recently to a correspondent from *Medical News* Irina said that when she finished school she stayed in Stavropol because she did not want to leave her parents. What parent would not be touched by such an admission? In her first year at the school, she got to know her future husband Anatoli. They studied in the same group. Anatoli's mother is a doctor, a neuropathologist. Her father was tall and handsome, devoted to his work as a land surveyor. But he died young of cancer: he was only 56. He suffered a great deal before his death: it is very painful to recall it now. He was operated on twice here in Moscow where we were then living. Irina and Anatoli were married in 1978, and Anatoli became a member of our family. When I am asked how many children we have, I reply 'four' – Irina, Anatoli, Ksenia and Anastasia. But I have brought up one daughter; we had a one-child family. Nowadays they say that a working woman with two children already has enough on her hands. It is not easy to combine professional and public obligations with family duties, with the role of mother and wife. The right to equal pay for equal work, to material and social independence and to fulfil oneself as an individual – all this represents a tremendous achievement by the women of our day. I have conducted opinion polls among women, asking them whether they would give up their work if their husband was able to provide adequately for the family. Even so, the majority of women replied "No."

On the other hand, the family, that social and moral blood relationship, has always been and remains the most important human institution, the source of people's wellbeing and happiness or misfortune. Take for example the actual business of bringing up children. In my opinion our experience demonstrates very convincingly that, with all the tremendous possibilities of social education, and given the evident necessity for it, it is essential that it be combined with a proper upbringing in the family. It is essential! Nothing can replace the emotional, loving relationship between the child and its parents. Not nursery schools or kindergartens or boarding schools or children's homes.

— My personal experience of boarding school certainly confirms what you say. Children who have been deprived of parental love, especially those who have been handed over to state institutions, later often, as adults, try to take their revenge on the rest of society for the way they were treated as children.

— I believe that, so long as Man himself is fated to exist, the natural feelings of paternal and maternal love will also continue to be experienced. Those same opinion surveys showed that the proportion of women who did not wish to have any children at all was extremely small. How can we reconcile a woman's desire to work and have a profession with her desire to have a family? I suppose that it is today a universal, worldwide problem and a very difficult one to solve. The conditions affecting women's work and its payment, and the state's support of the family, in the Soviet Union, to put it mildly, leave much to be desired. And if you also take into consideration social conditions in our country, the public services, the health service, and the housing situation. And, on top of that, the everlasting shortage of goods. The country now has great difficulties with the supply of foodstuffs and manufactured goods. But as far as I can remember there never were enough of them. For example, for as long as we lived in Stavropol all our main purchases – I am not speaking of foodstuffs – were made somewhere else – in Moscow or Leningrad or on trips abroad. In a word, where we happened to find things. As soon as a business trip to Moscow or some similar occasion arose, we would start drawing up a list of our own and our friends' needs. The list would include everything – books, overcoats, blinds, underwear, shoes, tights, saucepans, detergents, medicaments... You know how Moscow 'loves' to have all those people descend on it.

— And even people abroad now know all about our 'lists'. No sooner do you arrive than they ask you – well, where's your list?

— I can show you a dozen letters from Mikhail Sergeyevich written, say, from Sochi or from Moscow, saying he has managed to buy some shoes. The never-ending search for things! Taken together, all these real difficulties result in a situation where every woman resolves in her own way this problem of reconciling her professional and family obligations. She sets out her personal priorities and preferences, moves something to the foreground and pushes something else to the side. The result, in my view, is that the scale of values is often upset. I am sure that the problematic and complicated balancing of a job and family obligations in our life is one of the reasons for the lower level of women's professional qualifications and the slowness of their advance in employment. After all, the percentage of women with secondary education is not less than the percentage of men. And there are just as many, even more, women among students at university as men. But then, as they advance in years, the women begin to fall behind. Take the field of science, which I know best. There are, of course, fewer postgraduates among women scientists than there are among the men. Even fewer have doctorates. And among the living, 'full' academicians today, how many are women? You can count them on your fingers.

The situation is exactly the same when it comes to advancing up the ladder of power. At the very top the percentage of women is shamefully small! Despite the fact that there are quite a lot of women among lower-level officials. But as you climb up the hierarchical ladder the percentage of women drops. And it is in no way the laws of nature that are to blame for this but the same imperfections in our society. I have no doubt that they also are partly responsible for the fall in the birth rate and for the adoption of the idea of the 'one-child family' in our society. I believe it is not so much the women who are responsible for the tragedy of the voluntary refusal to have any children – and I do regard it as a tragedy. At least it is not only the women who are to blame. Lysistrata, the heroine of Aristophanes' play of that name, who brought a war to an end, is needed in every home. And in every family as a means of preserving it. Because devastating wars can break out in families. But Lysistrata is herself in need of protection and help. The widespread and, on the whole, very attractive image of the woman as the custodian of the home appears to me today to be something less than ideal. The times demand that women should play a more active part. Contemporary woman probably has as many roles as she has strength and imagination to fulfil them. Georgi Vladimirovich, have you seen the statue of Garibaldi in Rome?

— *I don't recall it.*

— But I do. There is a statue of Garibaldi in Rome. And do you know who is standing next to Giuseppe Garibaldi in the frieze around the statue? It is Anita Garibaldi, his wife. It is a statue to Garibaldi and, in fact, to Anita Garibaldi, his wife, who accompanied him through all the liberation campaigns and died during one of them. She shared with him equally the ups and downs of his career. She was, after all, a 'custodian of the domestic hearth'. But let us return to Stavropol. Mikhail Sergeyevich worked in the Komsomol until 1962, when he switched to Party work. As Party organiser he was responsible for the administration of agricultural production on collective and state farms in one of the Stavropol region's districts. Later he became first secretary of the Stavropol city committee of the Party, and then second and finally first secretary of the Stavropol regional committee of the CPSU. That covered a huge period of time that was very complex and very unusual for the country and the Party. It was a time of hope, but also disappointment. It was the time of the 'thaw', the break-up of many accepted ideas and stereotypes, the development of new ideas and new approaches, and at the same time it was a period when it was impossible to realise fully those ideas and approaches. It was a time for encouraging democratic processes and initiatives and a time that saw the failure of the principal undertakings and reforms and later their complete abandonment. In April 1958 Mikhail Sergeyevich wrote to me from the 13th Congress of the Komsomol, at which Nikita Sergeyevich [Khrushchev] spoke: 'The congress left a very powerful impression... conclusions that one does not always arrive at inside their home... vindication for all my worries, strivings, and stress...' Then something personal: 'I am trying to carry out your requests... I'm not going to tell you what I've bought. I'm only sorry I have no more money... I have taken out subscriptions for you for a World History – ten volumes – the *Smaller Soviet Encyclopaedia* and Plekhanov's philosophical works... I will be back soon, maybe before this letter because there is a possibility I may catch a plane.

Let us recall in chronological order at least some of the main events that took place from the middle of the 1950s to the middle of the 1970s. February 1956 – 20th Congress of the Party, Khrushchev's speech, the resolution concerning the 'cult of personality' and ways of overcoming it. October 1956 – the events in Hungary. June 1957 – the Plenum of the Central Committee and the resolution concerning the anti-Party group of Malenkov, Kaganovich and Molotov. October 1957 – the launching of the first 'Sputnik'. April 1961 – the Soviet spaceship Vostok with Yuri Gagarin aboard completed a flight around the Earth. God, how we celebrated then! October 1964 – the Central Committee of the Party dismissed Nikita Khrushchev as first secretary and elected Leonid Brezhnev in his place. I have preserved a cutting from the newspaper Pravda for the 17th of October 1964. It said in a leading article: 'The Party is the enemy of subjectivism and drift in the construction of Communism... The building of Communism is a vital, creative cause. It does not tolerate office-based methods, one-man decisions, or a failure to take account of the practical experience of the masses.' What a difference between words and deeds! March and September 1965 – Central Committee meetings to deal with the situation in agriculture and industry. August 1968 – the events in Czechoslovakia, the introduction of Soviet and allied military units into its territory. 1972 – the signing of the first Strategic Arms Limitation Treaty; the world recognises Soviet nuclear parity with the USA. It was a period that required the rethinking of many fundamental things. Such rethinking does not, of course, come easily. That is why philosophers call the process of acquiring knowledge the 'tortures of Tantalus'. In the 1960s Mikhail Sergeyevich took a degree in the external faculty of the Stavropol agricultural institute, in the belief that he needed to extend his knowledge of economics to do his work properly. His studies were quite a good addition to his university education as a lawyer, and to his civic and professional experience.

— *As I understand it, you were teaching in the same institute in those years. Were you ever the examiner when Mikhail Sergeyevich took a test?*

— No. I avoided such situations. Along with his education, something that in my view was very important for his development as a statesman was his entry into the country's ruling circles – the Central Committee of the Party and the Supreme Soviet of the USSR. This opened up for him all sorts of possibilities, including personal contacts with the leaders of the Party and the State.

— *Raisa Maksimovna, I heard a story that, when Khrushchev visited Stavropol and travelled round the region, Mikhail Sergeyevich was among those who accompanied him, and that Nikita Sergeyevich apparently paid him some attention. And gave him his blessing. Is it true?*

— *This is* the first time I hear of it. I think it's just a story, except that Khrushchev really did visit the Stavropol region. What was important was the variety of contacts: not only with leaders of the Party and state but also with his colleagues at the time. Here you had an exchange of useful experience and also of something that was beginning to evoke concern, numerous questions and thoughts and sheer bewilderment. That thought process that went on within himself – believe me – never stopped for a minute. He is not one of those who is ever satisfied with himself or those around him. In April 1970 Mikhail Sergeyevich was elected first secretary of the regional committee of the CPSU. He was then, as they used to say, the 'first man in the Stavropol region', a territory comparable with any state in the USA. Mikhail Sergeyevich's father, Sergei Andreyevich, a peasant who had lived a very tough life, sent a letter on this occasion: 'We congratulate you on your new job. There is no limit to your mother's and father's joy and pride. May that joy never fade. We wish you good health and great strength for your work for the country's wellbeing.' That very simple letter can still bring tears to my eyes.

I very much regret that Mikhail's father did not live to see his son become secretary of the Central Committee. It seems to me that his pride in his son would have increased his strength and desire to live. You made the remark that Mikhail Sergeyevich resembles his mother. I would like to correct you – it is not an entirely accurate observation, although you may not agree with me. His facial features are certainly his father's. And his eyes are the eyes of his grandmother Vasyutka. She was his grandmother on his mother's side, the wife of grandfather Pantelei. She was grandma Vasilisa. They all called her Vasyutka, and she had beautiful, bewitching black eyes. Grandma Vasyutka's eyes were handed down to Mikhail Sergeyevich. Mikhail Sergeyevich and his father were very close to each other and good friends. Sergei Andreyevich did not have a systematic education. He attended classes for the illiterate and went to a school for mechanics. But he had a sort of inborn culture and sense of dignity, and a certain breadth of interest. He was always interested in what Mikhail Sergeyevich was doing and what was going on in the country and the world. When the two of them met he would shower his son with a stream of pointed and vital questions. And his son not only had to answer the questions but also to give account to his father, the peasant and mechanizer. Sergei Andreyevich would listen eagerly and long to what his son said. He died when he was sixty-six, in 1976, just before the 25th Congress of the Party. Mikhail Sergeyevich was already in Moscow but flew back home when he heard his father was very ill. We spent two whole days at the bedside of Sergei Andreyevich, but he did not regain consciousness and we buried him on the 23rd of February 1976.

At this point I will permit myself yet another digression. The portrait of his father that faces Gorbachev when he is working in his out-of-town residence near Moscow can also be seen in another place, very far from Moscow, in the Stavropol region, in the village of Privolnoye in the local village graveyard. On his father's grave is the same image, enlarged from an amateur snapshot and mounted on the tombstone. So much for Gorbachev's father. As for his mother, you may find the following episode of some interest. I heard of it from my younger brother. My brother lives in a district not far from Privolnoye and works in the telephone exchange. When the president phones his mother, who still lives in Privolnoye, the call passes through his exchange. One day my brother was instructed by his chief to go down to Privolnoye to see what was wrong with Maria Panteleyevna's telephone, because her son couldn't get through to her. An hour and a half later my brother arrived at the house, found Maria Panteleyevna, and asked her why her telephone was not working. She said that she thought it was working. So why couldn't they get through from Moscow? Then she realised: she hadn't been in the house – she had spent the whole morning working in her garden. The weather was too good to miss! It was beautiful weather: the end of March, the sun shining, gathering strength awhile, the earth was warming up and a mist was rising from it. The task had been carried out faultlessly and my brother returned to his duties. The President's mother lives in her village house and cultivates her kitchen garden... She lives by her biological, moral, or simply peasant time, the natural progress of which is not subject even to the magnetic influence of her son's career. Now say that Russia is a country whose foundations have collapsed. No, we are not just dust in the wind. Maria Panteleyevna has two sons in Moscow: Mikhail Sergeyevich and Aleksandr Sergeyevich. Aleksandr Sergeyevich was born in 1947, after the war, and is sixteen years younger than his elder brother and an officer in the Soviet Army.

— Mikhail Sergeyevich's election to become First Secretary of the Stavropol regional committee was an unusual move for those days. In the first place, he was a local man. As far as I can remember, the first secretaries before him were all people from outside the region. They were all 'outsiders'. Incidentally, among the hundreds of congratulations we then received was a letter from the poet Volodya Gneushev. Did you know him?

— *Of course. He helped me when I was young.*

— The letter is dated the 14th of April 1970. It also hinted at the fact that Gorbachev was a 'local boy'. The letter read: 'Dear Mikhail! It was only today that a newspaper arrived in Zagedan from which I learnt of your election as First Secretary. I am sincerely glad, not only for you – your election is fully deserved and right – but also for the region which has acquired in you a boss and a friend. That's very good.'

— *Acquired a boss! The vocabulary of the time.*

— Perhaps. After all, we are all people of our time. Why deny it? Maria Sergeyevna Larionova, head of the school that Mikhail Sergeyevich attended, also sent congratulations: 'If it were possible, as it was then in the school, when it was announced that the school-boy Mikhail had been decorated with a medal, to call a meeting, I would like to say to people: "May our region be prosperous. It is now headed by a 'homegrown' secretary of the region who even as a little boy in Privolnoye made the work of a farmer famous throughout the land".'

— *It would appear that the word 'homegrown' can have a totally positive meaning!*

— As you see... Secondly, Mikhail Sergeyevich was young, just thirty–nine. In those days that was reckoned to be too young for such a position.

— *Why 'in those days'? Even now there are practically no thirty-nine–year–olds, not only among party secretaries, but generally among leaders.*

— That may be. But I would like to read you another message of congratulations from another Stavropol writer, Yevgeni Karpov. He writes: 'Dear Mikhail Sergeyevich! The saying "The egg can't teach the hen" was thought up by stupid, evil, and power-hungry people. After all, life itself teaches us that youth means daring, renewal and a fresh wind. Youth is the sunrise, and however wise and beautiful sunsets may be, people still long for the sunrise. It is, of course, far from being just your youth that delights me and my comrades about your election. I send you my heartfelt congratulations and I wish you good, following winds, strong and even stormy ones! Yours…' Although the process was agonisingly slow, nevertheless the pressing need for a renewal of government and Party officials and a change of generations forced its way through. You see, the same people had been in charge everywhere for decades and not only on the district and regional levels but even in the central ruling bodies. In 1978, when the forty-seven–year-old Mikhail Sergeyevich was transferred to work in Moscow, the average age of the members of the Politburo was sixty-seven, and for government ministers it was sixty–four. The natural process of renewing officials of Party and state, essential for the normal functioning of any society, had been interrupted. In the few years that Mikhail Sergeyevich worked in the Stavropol region practically all the secretaries of the local committees were replaced. Along with the appointment of new and younger officials, there was an improvement in the moral atmosphere, there was a new and more dynamic spirit infused into work that embraced not only the Party but all other branches of activity. There was a new spirit and style, characteristic of Mikhail Sergeyevich – frankness, close contact with the people, the ability to listen to and respect other people's opinion, and not to keep down the person working next to you but rather to encourage and support him.

— *I get the impression that in the course of the last year there has been some change in his manner of communicating with people. Take those 'walkabouts' in the street. He used to do more speaking himself, heatedly and with enthusiasm. Now he tends more to listen. At such meetings he does not have the look of an orator as he did in the early, romantic days of Perestroika, but rather that of a listener. I see him more frequently in that role, which he probably does not find so easy, given his political temperament. One gets the feeling that, as you put it, there is a great deal going on within him. These changes impress me personally, as does the way he listens patiently to his own people even when the people are clearly 'wrong'. History knows such situations.*

— Are you saying that some people have the right to speak, while Presidents should mainly listen?
— *Probably.*
— He always knew how to listen. He is not only receptive, he is simply 'hygroscopic' in the way he absorbs other people's views. But he acts mostly in the way he thinks necessary.

— *Is that another privilege of Presidents?*

— Up to a point. You know, even today we are still receiving letters from comrades who worked with Mikhail Sergeyevich at some time. In recalling those years, they remember especially and value the fact that, while Mikhail Sergeyevich demanded a lot from them, at the same time he gave them freedom of action – a great deal of freedom. He once said jokingly in the family circle: 'For me, Perestroika began in 1970 in the Stavropol region.' His position as first secretary of the regional committee of the Party gave him the opportunity to achieve something substantial for the region and to put into practice quite a few ideas that had matured after long and painful debates. It was in those years that the Stavropol region carried out the intensive development of new branches of the economy – electronics, power generation and the gas, oil and chemical industries. Tremendous work was carried out on land improvement in the region because Stavropol is, you know, a risky zone for agriculture. Nearly half the territory of the region consists of steppe lands subject to drought or semi-desert. Agricultural production was reorganised. New ways of organising the workforce and providing the people with greater incentives were experimented with. A system of self–financing and piece work was introduced. It was in those years that the foundations were laid for truly record harvests in the Stavropol area in the 1980s. Programmes for the extension of social and cultural facilities and the reorganisation of the region's health resorts were worked out and to a large extent put into practice. A polytechnical institute was opened in Stavropol, as well as a cultural institute and many secondary technical schools.

— Raisa Maksimovna, I would like to ask you this: It is no secret that in those years the position of First Secretary of the region was a very powerful one. The temptation to exercise power was there, not only for the rulers themselves, but for their wives as well. How did you feel then in Stavropol in that role?

— The 'temptation' meant for me primarily fresh and never-ending alarms and worries connected with my husband's work in addition to my regular professional and family cares. First came our joint concern, of course, for the affairs of the region. But our new situation changed our lives to a certain extent from another point of view: it improved the family's financial state, provided better opportunities for medical treatment, and it extended our circle of contacts and acquaintances. Mikhail Sergeyevich always took his holiday in the autumn or winter, when all the agricultural work in the region was over. We took our holidays as a rule 'at home' – in Kislovodsk, Pyatigorsk or Zheleznovodsk. But when it was possible, we sometimes used our holidays for travelling. We visited Moscow and Leningrad. One year we went to Uzbekistan and saw Tashkent, Samarkand, Bukhara and the Kyzyl-Kum desert. Twice in the course of the nine years we went with a group of Soviet tourists on foreign trips – to Italy and France. By the time Mikhail Sergeyevich was elected First Secretary in Stavropol we already had our own separate, comfortable apartment. But we had to leave it and move into an official house traditionally occupied by the Secretary of the regional committee. The question of our move and of whether we ought or ought not to give up our apartment was not discussed. It was taken for granted, because the official house had everything necessary for the needs of the region's leader. This was the beginning of our life in official accommodation.

The next few years turned out to be extremely stressful, although those preceding it had not been easy, I tell you frankly: we were both working, continuing our studies, and bringing up a child. And still the nearly nine years that Mikhail Sergeyevich worked as First Secretary were especially tense for us. Only very rarely were we able to take a holiday or to have Sunday to ourselves. But when we did get a day off, we liked to spend it outside the town walking through the forests and steppes. In Stavropol we had no country cottage – neither private nor state-owned. We would put on tracksuits and cover fifteen or twenty kilometres on foot. Usually just the two of us, sometimes with Irina or friends. But the others did not as a rule want a long walk, preferring a short stroll or a game of volleyball. We had so many adventures on our walks, getting lost in the forest and caught in a blizzard in the steppes. The situation once took on a dangerous turn, but we were saved by an electric power line that led us back to the town. Friends had already raised the alarm, fearing we were lost.

— *And that was when he was already First Secretary?*

— Yes. You know, it was so pleasant to be on our own. What a pleasure it is! We would travel out of the town and then go on foot. The forests and the steppes belonged to us. We often got into dangerous situations in the mountains and, I tell you, the most frightening thing is to find yourself in the mountains in a thunderstorm. Then there was an occasion in the forest when some hooligans fired on us. We had reached the depths of the forest when suddenly we heard shots. We had to take cover. There are certainly things to remember.

— How did you celebrate the public holidays? There were probably some 'family gatherings' of the region's leaders, at least of the regional secretaries. Stavropolians are a lively lot who enjoy drinking and eating and singing...

— Of course, we used to get together – for the New Year and the November anniversary of the Revolution. We collected money for it in advance – that was Mikhail Sergeyevich's idea. We had a great many friends both in Stavropol and in Moscow, and we still have them, both from among colleagues at work and among other folk with whom a single meeting developed into a sincere friendship lasting many years. Among our closest friends are Aleksandr Dmitriyevich and Lidia Aleksandrovna Budyka. Lidia is a children's doctor with a degree in medicine. As a doctor she helped me to bring up Irina. Her husband Aleksandr is an engineer also with a degree, who has risen all the way from being director of a regional tractor station to being a minister in the Soviet government. They are both good and intelligent people who are devoted to each other. They have also been together since their student days. We have been friends with them for thirty years. They have two sons. Mikhail Sergeyevich likes to poke fun at Aleksandr Dmitriyevich:

'Sasha, you're all right but for one fault – you're too much of a liberal.' Budyka always smiles back at him.

— Doesn't he call Mikhail Sergeyevich a liberal in return?
— No, for some reason he doesn't. Lidia's great weakness is children. A children's doctor by profession, she will go anywhere at any time of the day or night if she can help or save someone. From childhood she has also been very fond of dogs. They always keep one and are always trying to present us with puppies. For thirty years now we have been friends. Their family has also not been without its sorrows. Lidia's father died young, having suffered the tragedy of false accusations and repressions. Her mother died in great pain. Aleksandr Dmitriyevich's mother is very ill and being looked after by Lidia. Moreover, Sasha himself is a sick man and no longer works. But Lidia, my Lidia, remains the same patient, kindly person she always was. She is such a good and sincere person. I will tell you in simple language: the mere fact that her invalid mother-in-law, who has a daughter of her own, has been living with her for years – that alone tells you something about my friend's character.

In my view, a detail that says everything. The following is an extract from a letter written by Lidia Budyka to the Soviet magazine Peasant Woman *and published in December 1990. 'There are so many things that come to life in my memory. The lovely, happy years in Stavropol, the walks together, the arguments we had, the games we played, the joyful experiences we went through. But for some reason it is the sadder events that tend to come to mind. That is probably because at the really difficult moments in life a person reveals more true character, exposes things deeply hidden, and so becomes closer and more understandable. That is how it was on that summer's day when Raisa Maksimovna and I flew from Moscow to Krasnodar for the funeral of her father Maksim Andreyevich Titarenko. The previous evening the telephone had rung in our apartment, and after a brief silence, Raisa Maksimovna said, in a controlled and quiet voice: "Lidia, you know, Papa has died." 'I believe that the thousands of pieces of gossip that are spread around about Raisa Maksimovna are motivated partly by envy and sometimes by hatred but also by the simple, naive desire people have to believe in the possibility of the existence somewhere or other of an utterly fabulous, carefree, happy life where there are no problems, no bitter disappointments, no illness, and no deaths of close friends. But why talk of others when I myself was often deceived when I saw on the television screen her kindly smile and her calm, welcoming manner...'*

The years passed and changes came about in the life we lived and the people we knew. We also changed. We managed to achieve something, but the problems remained. In the last years we spent in Stavropol I heard Mikhail Sergeyevich speak ever more frequently not only about the difficulties involved in the social development of the villages and towns in the region, the provision of materials and technology, the lack of balance in the terms of exchange of agricultural and industrial output, and the shortcomings in the system of payment for work done. He also talked about the need for profound changes in the country as a whole, in its administrative structure, that were holding up the development of whole regions and particular branches of the economy. He spoke about the difficulties involved in providing the population of the region with foodstuffs and manufactured goods. You see, the region that produced the famous Stavropol wheat, meat and milk and delivered thousands of tons of wool suffered constantly from a shortage of the basic food products and other goods. In 1978 a full meeting of the Central Committee of the CPSU elected Mikhail Sergeyevich to be a Secretary of the Committee. For both of us it was totally unexpected. Mikhail Sergeyevich was in Moscow, and I came home from work late in the evening, about 10pm. The telephone rang – it was Mikhail Sergeyevich: "You know, there is an unexpected proposal. There's a Plenum tomorrow. Wait for it. I shall not fail to call you.' On the 27th of November 1978 he became a Secretary of the Central Committee of the CPSU.

You ask me what sort of feelings I had on leaving Stavropol. Was there regret or was there joy at having at last escaped from the provinces. You know, it's not so simple. Our children really took the move to Moscow as the very height of happiness. Such happiness, as Irina told me later, they did not find in all the years in Moscow. For me the return to Moscow meant the completion of a huge diversion in our lives. It had not been a simple period, nor an easy one, but it is a time I remember fondly. It was there in the Stavropol region that we spent the years of our youth, and it was there that our daughter was born and grew up. It was there that we had close friends and family. And it was there, in Stavropol, that we were given the opportunity to realise ourselves. I was worried once again by that feeling of facing the unknown. I felt rather anxious. Immediately on our arrival in Moscow we were provided with a country house outside the city. Later we were given an apartment. We obtained accommodation from what was held 'in reserve' and according to what was prescribed in those days for someone with the rank of a Secretary of the Central Committee. Actually, it was only later that I understood the rigid system operating in this matter: everything is decided by the unwritten – and, surprisingly, it really is unwritten – Table of Ranks. You will receive only what is laid down according to your position on the hierarchical ladder, and not according to your real contribution to the country's wellbeing. Alas, the same system operates not only in Moscow but everywhere. Everything depends on the position you occupy and not on the actual contributions you make to the common cause. Just remember my own faculty or any other place of work – you get paid according to your position, and that's that. Position stood for everything and still does. Initiative, creativity, and independence, not only in big things but in the smallest everyday matters, were not encouraged, or not encouraged very much.

In accordance with the accepted rules, high officials in ministries and government departments and also those in the headquarters of the Central Committee of the Party were provided with country houses in special areas belonging to those organisations. The top political leadership – Members and Candidate Members of the Politburo and Secretaries of the Central Committee – lived in protected government dachas situated in the suburbs. Their houses were provided with servants and equipped both for relaxation and for work, and they were provided free of charge so long as the occupant kept his position. Similar houses in Moscow and other places were used for entertaining important foreign guests and other representational purposes. And there was accommodation in the country's health resorts set aside for Soviet leaders and leaders of foreign states. There is one other detail I would like to mention. Among the Party and government officials with whom I had come into contact in previous years the building of one's own private dacha was considered to be quite impermissible. Responsible officials in the Stavropol region had neither state-owned nor private dachas. They could have a plot of land for a garden if they wished, but they could not build on it. When we found ourselves in Moscow in 1978 one of my many discoveries was that, it appeared, some members of the country's leadership, including Party leaders, who already had dachas provided by the State, were also building their own private dachas, for their children, grandchildren and so forth. I was struck by such economic enterprise and daring. We were put first of all in an old wooden cottage which had been occupied in its day by Sergo Ordzhonikidze and was in need of a major overhaul. After two years we were given a different one, a new, brick-built house put up in the 1970s. Before us it was occupied by F. D. Kulakov.

In 1985, after Mikhail Sergeyevich's election as General Secretary of the Party, we moved to a new house that had all the conditions, facilities and means of communication necessary for him to carry out the functions he was entrusted with. That is where we are now, in Mikhail Sergeyevich's study. The one we left was taken over by Boris Yeltsin, who was then Secretary of the Moscow city Party and had just become a Candidate Member of the Politburo. As far as I know, he continued to occupy it until he gave up Party work. In our last years in Stavropol our monthly family income consisted of the 800 roubles Mikhail Sergeyevich was paid as Secretary of the regional committee plus the 320 roubles I was paid as a lecturer. It was on the whole a good income for those days. As a Secretary of the Central Committee Mikhail Sergeyevich was paid 800 roubles a month. If I am not mistaken, all the Secretaries, Candidate Members and Members of the Politburo and the General Secretary received the same. Apart from that there were additional monthly payments 'for food' – 200 roubles a month for Secretaries and Candidate Members and 400 roubles for full Members of the Politburo. We were permitted to acquire essential books free of charge. Not only the head of the family but his wife too was provided with free transport in the form of a car and chauffeur. The apartment was rent-free, and a sum of money was allotted to pay for holidays. In recent years, all these privileges, including the use of state-owned country houses, have been withdrawn. In accordance with decisions taken by the Congress of People's Deputies of the USSR, the Supreme Soviet passed a Resolution 'Concerning the remuneration, servicing and protection of the President of the USSR', and of the Chairman of the Supreme Soviet, the Vice-President, and the Prime Minister. The President of the USSR was allotted a salary of 4000 roubles a month. Taking into account the current level of taxes and other payments that means a 'take-home' pay of 2500 roubles.

He is provided with residences in the Moscow area and in the Crimea, an official apartment in Moscow, the necessary transport facilities and a specially equipped plane and helicopter. On his retirement the President of the USSR receives a pension for life amounting to 1500 roubles a month, is provided with a state-owned dacha with the necessary staff, bodyguard and transport. So much for the material aspects. When I come to recall 1978, I remember that the move to Moscow meant for me new professional opportunities, visits to my favourite theatres, concert halls and exhibitions, and meeting actors and musicians whom we met previously only occasionally when we were in Moscow. Irina and Anatoli transferred to the Second Medical Institute. Both of them passed with distinction and in 1985 Irina presented her thesis on problems of medicine and demography. She worked initially as an assistant in the faculty of social hygiene and organisation of the health service at the Second Moscow Medical Institute. Later she took up scientific research and joined the laboratory for medical, demographic and sociological research. Anatoli also took a degree in medicine as a surgeon. He has been working for more than ten years in the Moscow city clinical hospital. A year after our arrival in

Moscow our first real Muscovite – our granddaughter Ksenia – was born. We decided on her name before her birth. I chose it – they trusted me. The second real Muscovite, granddaughter Anastasia, was born in 1987. Her name was chosen collectively by the whole family. Mikhail Sergeyevich's proposal won the day, so that in that respect we are on equal terms. Actually, they twice prepared a masculine name – in case it was a boy. Then it would have been Mikhail. But all that is about the joys of family life. There were other things too. To say that we found ourselves in Moscow in a new and unfamiliar environment and atmosphere is really to say very little or even nothing at all. I will not take it upon myself to judge the atmosphere and the kind of relations there were among the leaders, Mikhail Sergeyevich's colleagues.

I rely only on my own experience and my personal impressions, mostly of the members of the families of the Soviet leaders at the time. The first thing that struck was the way people were estranged from one another. Whether you exist or not, whether you existed in the past or not was not to be gathered from the faces surrounding you. You were seen and somehow not noticed. Even the usual greetings were not exchanged. There was surprise if you addressed someone by his or her first name and patronymic. What? You actually remember them? In company people often displayed pretensions to superiority, to being one of the chosen. Judgements were pronounced categorically and often without tact. What struck me about relations between members of a family was the mirror image they provided of the same respect for rank as existed among the leaders themselves. I remember how once I wondered aloud about the behaviour of a group of young people. The woman I was talking to was very upset and exclaimed: 'What are you saying – that's Brezhnev's grandchildren there!' We women used to meet mainly at official occasions and receptions, and only seldom privately. But even when we met in a small circle of friends the same rules of the 'political game' operated. There would be endless toasts to the health of those higher up, nasty talk about those lower down, discussion of food and about their children's and grandchildren's 'unique' abilities. And card games. I was struck by the evidence of indifference and lack of concern. Could I call it 'consumerism'? For example, at one of the gatherings at a state dacha I warned the children: 'Be careful, you'll break the chandelier!' In reply I was told: 'Not to worry. It's government property, it can be written off.'

— *The children replied like that?*

— The grown-ups... I remember the reaction to a trip that Mikhail Sergeyevich made to England in 1984 at the head of a parliamentary delegation. With Konstantin Chernenko's permission I travelled with him. The delegation's trip turned out to be extremely interesting, substantive, and productive of good results. It was reported in our press but more fully in British and American publications. When I returned home, I heard people say: 'Why did they sing your praises so highly over there? Don't you realise what it all means? What have you done to attract the West? Now then, now then, let's look a bit closer at you...'

— *Turn round, young man?*

— More or less. Formalism and callousness penetrated even amongst the service staff. I always had warm but sad feelings when I recalled people who worked for us previously. Our chauffeur Anatoli Andreyevich Khamukha was demobilised from the army and worked for Mikhail Sergeyevich in Stavropol for twenty years. I knew his wife and his children, and we still exchange greetings on national holidays. Mikhail Sergeyevich's hopes that here, at 'the top', he would be able to solve some pressing problems were not realised in many respects. Our troubles were driven inwards and postponed for the future. Leonid Ilyich Brezhnev was a sick man and that had an effect on everything. In November 1982 he died. Then came the turn of Yuri Vladimirovich Andropov. But the hopes that were aroused proved not to be long lived. Andropov was seriously ill. It's an awful thing to recall, but at his funeral I saw some openly happy faces. Then came the time for Konstantin Ustinovich Chernenko. That period was even more complicated. The country was living in hope of changes, the need for which was felt everywhere. The number of people was increasing who openly supported and understood the necessity of ideas about reform and the practical steps needed to bring them about. But everything remained as it was in the life of the Party and of the country. Mikhail Sergeyevich and I would discuss things at length after he returned from work. We talked about a lot of things – about the same things as were being discussed in society with increasing concern and insistence. There's another matter that suddenly came to mind,

Georgi Vladimirovich. There are people, I know, who are interested in the external side of my life. They even envy me – for the clothes I wear and my 'apparel' on formal occasions... But I value something quite different – my participation in the tremendous undertakings that have fallen to the lot of someone close to me – my husband.

Never before had we talked at such length – six half-hour reels had been used up and a seventh was half used. A pile of prepared notes we had gone through lay on the desk next to Raisa Maksimovna. Since the pieces of paper were of all shapes and sizes the pile reminded one more of a Chinese pagoda with turned up edges... One can tell that she is tired, and who wouldn't be after several hours of such work?

— I had also prepared some photographs [she said, pointing to a fat, well-packed envelope at the end of the sofa]. But we probably won't look at them today, it's too late. Next time, yes?
  — *You know, I would quite like to look at them now, just to glance through them quickly. It's interesting. [I risked seeming impolite.]*
  — Very well. Have a look at them on your own. I'll be back shortly.

She handed me the envelope, or rather the packet, and went into the other room, the library. For some time I sat there alone, glancing through the photos in the packet. The Stavropol house I already knew. The students from the agriculture institute gathering corn. In sports clothes the young teacher is indistinguishable from the girl students.

Gathering mushrooms somewhere in the foothills of the Caucasus. Then Moscow. Meetings with lots of people, airports. Boris Yeltsin, who took over their dacha, handing Raisa Gorbachev a few carnations with a very elegant and polite bow. Strange but true! Somewhere, in Roy Medvedev's book, I think, I read a story that four leaders of the USSR once met on the platform of the railway station at Mineralnye Vody. One, Brezhnev, was still active as General Secretary – in so far as he could be called 'active' at that time. And there were three future general secretaries – Chernenko, Andropov and Gorbachev. Brezhnev and Chernenko were said to be travelling from the south and the sea. Andropov was holidaying in Kislovodsk. Gorbachev had naturally travelled from Stavropol for such an occasion. The platform is said to have been cleaned up and cordoned off, and the four men paced slowly up and down the empty platform on that late autumn evening beneath the dim, also rather autumnal, lamps. Like Russia, the long train waited for the signal to start moving. I know the station platforms at Mineralnye Vody too well to forget that story as I looked through the old photographs. But no such photograph did I find in the packet, and I would certainly have recognised that platform. All the same, there was a photograph of a platform. It was faded, just an amateur snapshot, but quite distinct. In the foreground was a young, laughing woman in velvet jeans, with dimples on her cheeks and a shock of dark, chestnut hair blowing in the wind.

— That was our first time in Paris as tourists. We had only just stepped off the train [she explained, glancing over my shoulder].

Her husband, I realise, was not to be seen: he was holding the camera. It was the only photograph taken of her in Paris at the time. Moscow was still ahead. Paris too, like Washington, Bonn and Madrid... When I proposed to devote one of the chapters of the future book to happiness and call it accordingly 'About Happiness', she thought a little and then turned the idea down:

— Do you really think, Georgi Vladimirovich, that I resemble a woman flitting from happiness to happiness?

No, she doesn't – I see that now more clearly. All the same, that woman on the empty platform had more than a laughing face – she seemed to me to be happy. But the state of happiness, they say, lasts only for minutes. All the rest is just life.

Things I Take to Heart

Everything was the same as before in the President's study with one exception: there was a pile of letters, telegrams and postcards lying on the leather divan. A few days previously the president had celebrated his sixtieth birthday.

— I am sorting them out [Raisa Maksimovna said]. We have already counted more than 3000 letters and telegrams. Would you like to see the present Russian Patriarch Aleksei II sent for the occasion?

— *Yes, I said.*

We went into the library, where I was shown an icon in a beautiful setting decorated in gold leaf. The Archangel Mikhail peered out sadly and severely from behind the glass of the icon case.

— *He looks rather sad, I said.*

— It would be strange if the guardian angel looked otherwise.

— *She then showed me a tiny ornament in the lacework.*

— Archistratig. The sign of the supreme leader of the heavenly host.

We stood there, admiring the thon. It was a dull day, but the icon seemed to gather together and focus all the light dispersed in the room and shone softly in the depths of the library. I then remembered that it would soon be Easter. I saw on a desk nearby two piles of books, both more than a foot high. What was on the top today? What are they reading now? An elegantly bound volume – Love Songs – poetry– frankly, something I had not expected – and on the other pile a volume of Pushkin. It was a blue, rather faded volume from the ten-volume edition issued in the 1950s. I opened it at the bookmark – Boris Godunov.

— That's what I am reading [she said from behind my back and took the open book from me].

> 'I feel there's nothing can reassure us
> Midst all our worldly cares
> Nothing, except maybe our conscience:
> If it is clear it will triumph
> Over malice and wicked slander.'

She read quietly, as though to herself, and then closed the book and placed it next to the icon. The Archangel Mikhail and the profile of Pushkin stamped on the book cover seemed to make quite natural neighbours. A minute later our final conversation was under way.

— Where shall we start? [she asked, without waiting for a question]. Konstantin Ustinovich Chernenko died on the evening of the 10th of March 1985. Nothing had been revealed concerning his condition and illness. On the 2nd of March came the results of the elections to the republican Supreme Soviets. They showed that

99.98 percent of the electors had turned out to vote, and that over 99 percent of them had voted for the nominated candidates.

— *What figures! How quickly we have changed our ways.*

T— hat we have done so is all for the better, I think. Chernenko was elected as a deputy to the Supreme Soviet of the Russian Federation. The press reported that the electoral commission had handed him the certificate confirming his election, and his address to his constituents and the Soviet people was published. But there was not a word about the fact that Konstantin Ustinovich was in hospital and very gravely ill. Moreover, on the 6th of March, in accordance with a longstanding practice in our country, his wife Anna Dmitrievna gave a reception on the occasion of International Women's Day.

It is given for the wives of the heads of foreign diplomatic missions accredited in Moscow. As was the custom, the reception included dances, songs and a concert. When Chernenko died Mikhail Sergeyevich was informed immediately, and he called an urgent meeting of the Members and Candidate Members of the Politburo and the Secretaries of the Central Committee. Decisions were taken regarding the funeral. An emergency meeting of the Central Committee was called for the next day, and at that meeting on the 11th of March Mikhail Sergeyevich was elected General Secretary of the Party Central Committee. A great deal has been written about those meetings of the Politburo and the Central Committee. All sorts of points of view, conjectures and opinions have been voiced. According to what Mikhail Sergeyevich told me,

neither in the Politburo nor in the Central Committee were any
other candidates put forward for the post of General Secretary. By
that time the majority of the members of the Central Committee
had probably arrived at a common point of view in their assessment of the situation that had arisen both in the leadership and in
the country as a whole. It was a very difficult, complex situation
of internal tension. Outwardly everything looked normal. Mikhail
Sergeyevich's election was unanimous. It was late when he returned
home. The whole family was there to meet him with flowers. Ksenia, who was then only five, said: 'Grandpa, I congratulate you.
I wish you happiness and that you will eat up your porridge.'
Mikhail Sergeyevich laughed and asked: 'And will you eat it along
with me?' 'No! My muscles are tired of chewing it.' 'But you must,'
said Mikhail Sergeyevich, laughing. 'I don't like it either, but, you
know, I eat it, I have to…' We grown-ups congratulated Mikhail
Sergeyevich and were happy and proud of him and had confidence
in him. But on that evening, of course, neither the children nor I
had any real idea of the burden that he had taken upon himself. We
couldn't imagine a hundredth part of what Mikhail Sergeyevich's
'new job' was going to mean in reality or what awaited him and all
our family in the future. You, Georgi Vladimirovich, will probably
want to ask: if I had known then that everything would be so complicated and so full of drama, would I not have tried to dissuade
Mikhail Sergeyevich?

— *That is a question.*

— Now I want to reply to it in complete sincerity. Despite
the burden of what we are going through today, I am not going to

say 'Yes' in haste. No, I cannot say it. We did not, of course, know that things would be as they are today. But tell me – do you not ask yourself today: what would it have meant for the country and the people if then, in 1985, someone much the same as his predecessors had come to power and, what is more, would remain there for another fifteen years or so? How would that have ended up? What kind of situation in the country would we be talking about today – if we were actually talking at all? Where would that have led the country? Six years ago, that was what we thought about in the first place. That was why Mikhail Sergeyevich made such a decision. A month later, in April, there was a full meeting of the Central Committee at which Mikhail Sergeyevich made a major speech. The Committee passed a resolution calling for the regular congress of the Party to be held in February 1986. That meeting, known as the April Plenum, is now regarded as the turning point. But we still had ahead of us the 27th Congress of the Party, the nineteenth nationwide Party conference and the First Congress of People's Deputies of the USSR. In 1985 Mikhail Sergeyevich made his first trips around the country – in May to Leningrad, in June to Kiev and Dnepropetrovsk, in July to Minsk, and in September to the Tyumen and Tselinograd districts. This later became a regular part of his work, and not only for him but for all the country's leaders. In that way new traditions came into being. But then it was something unusual and new. And those encounters with the people were not just for show: they were frank, and by no means always very pleasant, but always very sincere conversations about everything that was worrying people. They were heart-to-heart talks, sincere and concerned.

— *He acted similarly when he went abroad.*

— Yes, but that was later. The hour-long speech that Mikhail Sergeyevich delivered on the 17th of May in the Smolny Institute in Leningrad was also broadcast by television, which was regarded as something extremely unusual. In the first place Mikhail Sergeyevich did not read off a prepared speech, but spoke naturally, reasoning and explaining his personal understanding of the serious problems in the economy. He was consulting with the people. And, secondly, he was addressing the whole country, all the Soviet people, at once. Never before – with a rare exception – had speeches by leaders of the Party and the country at Party conferences, congresses and groups of activists been broadcast by television, and, what's more, transmitted 'live'. It must be said that the country reacted very quickly to these innovations. Remember those political jokes that went around?

— *You mean to say you heard them?*

— Of course – both those and some of the contemporary 'folklore'. For example, I recall one of the jokes going the rounds in 1985: a man living in the far north returns from Moscow and is asked: 'Well, how are things there at the centre, do they support Gorbachev?' 'No, they don't support him.' 'Really?' 'No, they don't support him. Can you believe it – he walks without any support.' And here's another wisecrack: 'This Gorbachev is quite illiterate.'

'How can you say that when they say he's got two degrees?' 'All the same, he's illiterate. All the ones before him read their speeches, but he just talks. In that same year, 1985, the General Secretary carried out official visits to France, Poland, Bulgaria and Czechoslovakia. In November he had his first meeting with the president of the United States of America, Ronald Reagan, in Geneva. Before he visited France, for the first time in our country's history, the leader of the Party and of the state talked with foreign, Western journalists on the television. That had previously been unthinkable. Also, in 1985 there was the first official visit to our country of the head of a foreign government since Mikhail Sergeyevich became General Secretary. It was the visit of Mr Rajiv Gandhi. In accordance with the protocol the ceremony of greeting the distinguished guest began at the airport and was due to end on one of the big squares within the Kremlin walls. But it rained that day. The very moment the cars drove into the Kremlin it simply came down in torrents. We who were there to welcome Gandhi had to take cover against the buildings... Rajiv and Sonia Gandhi had to shoot out of the car and dash across to us beneath an archway. They were young, handsome, and full of strength and optimism in the midst of a Russian downpour.

— *It meant good luck?*

— I hope so. Years later I was able to fully appreciate something else – their genuine civic courage[1].

Incidentally, changes were later made in our diplomatic protocol for greeting and seeing off the heads of foreign states and governments.

The ceremony for receiving guests by the Chairman of the Presidium of the Supreme Soviet of the USSR and later the president of the country no longer takes place on a square in the Kremlin but in the St George's Hall of the Great Kremlin Palace. Six years ago, Mikhail Sergeyevich and those who shared his views initiated some reforms which came to be known throughout the world as Perestroika. The reforms were aimed at finding new paths for the development of our country's domestic and international policy, in the conditions of a new period and a new existence for our common human home. The agenda included economic and political reforms, the replacement of the old and obsolete organisation of the administration and the bureaucracy, and the establishment of a state governed by the rule of law. The conception of new thinking in international relations meant, as I understand it, the recognition of the priority of political means over the use of force, non-interference in other countries' affairs, and the prevention of a nuclear or ecological catastrophe on a world scale. As I listed all that, Georgi Vladimirovich, I was thinking that nowadays for us and for many, many people in our country and beyond it such a programme sounds like something quite ordinary. We are used to that. But, you know, behind every statement, every sentence,

---

1 *This book was already in production when on the 21st of May 1991 came the terrible news of the murder of Rajiv Gandhi. It literally stunned Mikhail Sergeyevich and me, and we sent a telegram of condolence to Mrs Sonia Gandhi in which we said that Rajiv Gandhi was our great personal friend and that we fully shared her inconsolable grief. I would like to add to that personal message only one thing: that Rajiv Gandhi was not only our personal friend – he was a great friend of our whole people, and the news of his tragic death was received with sadness in every Soviet home.*

and every thought there is the agonising process of rethinking and reassessing the past. Truly agonising! It has been the most difficult search for answers to questions and problems that time has faced us with so urgently and imperatively. And what a struggle it has involved, internally, but not only internally. It is still going on. I was a witness of how, during the drafting of the report to the Party's 27th Congress and in the course of the most heated discussions between Mikhail Sergeyevich's closest collaborators, there emerged new ideas about the contemporary world, regarding it as a single civilization with all its contradictions and problems.

At that time Mikhail Sergeyevich said in the Central Committee's report to the Congress in February 1986: 'The course of history and social progress is demanding ever more insistently the establishment of constructive and creative cooperation between states and peoples on the scale of the whole planet... Such cooperation is necessary in order to avoid a nuclear catastrophe so that civilization may survive... That is the way, through a conflict of opposites, with great difficulty and to a certain extent just feeling our way, that a contradictory, mutually dependent and in many ways single world is evolving.' In 1986, such statements amounted to a revolution! The ideas behind Perestroika and the steps taken to bring them about turned out from the outset to be attractive to people and were eagerly seized upon by them. The solidarity and support in the feelings, the words and finally in the eyes of hundreds of thousands of people who came out to welcome Mikhail Sergeyevich on his trips around the country and abroad, became the emotional background of Perestroika. Support and unity were to be seen in the continuous stream of letters. In 1985 Mikhail Sergeyevich received up to 40,000 personal letters a month. Altogether in 1985 he received 402,500 letters! And those were, I repeat, only the personal ones and not the letters addressed generally to the Central Committee. In 1986 Mikhail Sergeyevich received over 60,000 letters a month, again personal ones. In 1990 he received up to 40,000 letters a month and in January and February 1991, 93,000. I am convinced that there is no more accurate, more revealing, or more honest document relating to the Perestroika period than those letters. The letters contain a history of Perestroika, an analysis of the ideas behind it, advice, suggestions, reflections, all the tension and drama of Perestroika. There is no point in concealing the fact that there were also letters full of malice, of hatred and of rage.

But the majority were letters of support, of hope and of determination to act. I would like, of course, to read a few of the letters, or at least some extracts. 'Perestroika is what the people long for. Do not stray from the path you have chosen, do not retreat – A. Lavrik, Svobodny, Amur region.' 'If there is a return to the past then better the hangman's noose' – that was in a letter from L. Sheveleva in Bratsk. 'We have faith and hope – A. Feklisov, Moscow.' 'Please take care of your health: the battle is just starting – E. Glushkov. Yuzhno-Sakhalinsk.' 'It is clear to everybody how much of your energy, time, intellectual strength, and health is being consumed by the colossal, inhuman burden you have brought down upon yourself. It is always difficult to build... Perhaps it will be a little easier for you if you know that the huge mass of ordinary people is entirely behind you, that they admire you and support you – K. Lasta. Leningrad.' 'God grant you great victories, you great and dear person. Mikhailina – Rovengan, Ukraine.' 'Dear Mikhail Sergeyevich. Dear man! I am not too shy to address you with that word because you are close to all honest people – Chermak family, Chernovtsy.' 'I am endlessly proud of you as I observe your efforts abroad. Mikhail Sergeyevich, the cause of peace is the most important thing for all of us. If necessary, all of us ordinary folk are ready to give up everything and to live on bread and water if only we can preserve the peace. I beg you to guard your health. You have totally conquered the love and gratitude of our people – Z. Potop. Kyshtym.' This letter I want to quote in its entirety: 'You know, it has become interesting to be alive... Previously I didn't pay much attention to what was being said on the television. And I must admit I wasn't very interested in reports of congresses and plenums. It seemed to be going on far away from me and hadn't much to do with me.

But now, whenever you speak on the television, I demand absolute quiet at home. I always watch the programmes with tremendous interest and read the reports of your meetings with workers and collective farmers. If there is something I don't understand I read it again. Now I even regret not becoming a member of the Communist Party. Just as, incidentally, I regret that we have only one girl. You know, there was constant fear for the future – what if war broke out tomorrow? Now I look to the future with hope and think: it is impossible that a man should make such an effort and so many peace proposals and not succeed in ridding us all of the madness of nuclear war... I have written you this letter so that you should know that we workers are with you heart and soul. There has been so much to understand and think about in the last year that I just couldn't fail to share with you my feelings and thoughts – L. Bardetskaya. Kirov region.' Here's another one. 'Hold on, right is on your side. My letter may be just a drop in an endless ocean, but I very much want to thank you, to support you and beg you never to retire.' The writer is, as you see, a maximalist – 'never'. He continues: 'You may sometimes lose heart on account of what is going on in the world. But don't give up, because right is on your side and your initiatives serve the interests of the whole world. Thank you for your courage. Thank you – M. J. Lelotte. Belgium.' Here are the very recent letters: One from S. Gersh in Yuzhno-Sakhalinsk: 'I want very much simply to voice my support in a friendly way for your efforts to bring about Perestroika, and to let you know that we have faith in you and your undertakings. In Sakhalin we have detected at least a glimmer of light, a little hope for a better future. So, I beg you to carry through to the end the cause you have started, however difficult it may be.' This one is from A. Aborvanov, a professional driver from the village of Donskoye in the Orenburg district. 'I and the people who elected me greet you warmly and support you.

To have supported the Church and at the same time to have awakened the people you have aroused a feeling of goodness and of mutual understanding in people which we so lacked in the period of stagnation. I advise you as a friend to keep to the course you have indicated, and which will lead our country into the future. Good health and strength and long life to you. May this letter give you more strength and confidence. I believe the support of the people is a good platform from which to perform good deeds.' Here is a letter dated the 6th of March 1990 from O. Turkina, who is an engineer in the Novolipetsk metallurgical complex. It is signed by her, her husband S. Turkin, and her sons Dima and Misha Turkin.

Greetings, dear Mikhail Sergeyevich!

I wanted to write this letter to you a year ago but had no hope that you would ever read it. Perhaps today you are in need of support and my letter will give you encouragement. A year ago, a second son was born to us, and we called him Mikhail Sergeyevich in your honour (my husband's name is Sergei). I am 34. I am not a member of the Party and I work as an engineer in the Central Heating Laboratory at the Novolipetsk metallurgical complex. From the first year of Perestroika, I have been your ardent supporter. Having called my son Misha (everybody knows it was in your honour) I have linked my fate closely with yours. I suffer badly when there are setbacks in this period, and I rejoice at the successes. It is painful to hear the avalanche of attacks on your good name. I have faith in you, in our country's future and in our people. I would be very glad to learn that you have read this letter...

The ideas of Perestroika captured the emotions and imagination of many members of the artistic intelligentsia. Their support and their inspired words were of tremendous significance in enabling society to understand the aims of Perestroika. Do you recall the poem Yevgeni Yevtushenko wrote in 1988, in which he used Mikhail Sergeyevich's remark that 'we can't go on like this' as a sort of refrain?

> When our country almost went off the rails.
> We kept it on by the skin of our teeth
> And realised as we held it back:
> 'We can't go on like this!'

In the last few years many authors have sent us signed copies of their books in which much of importance and significance has been said. We take great care of letters received from scholars, authors, cinema people and publicists. In reply to a note, I sent to Tatyana Ilyinichna Ivanovna about an article she wrote in *New Times*, she wrote me the following in 1990:

...Thank you for your kind words. Believe me, if I could and knew how to, I would do something very good for you. And, of course, for Mikhail Sergeyevich. But I can't think of anything. I would so like to give you some pleasure... In return for all the happiness that many (very many, you know) like me have experienced in the course of these last five years. My God, it is customary to say that youth is the happiest time of your life. But I am forty-seven and my happiest years began just five years ago. Moreover, it is a rather special kind of happiness – freedom and dignity are its main features. Gorbachev is a great man. Great and wonderful. Take his meeting with the young people – once again I admired the replies he gave. I am proud that I have such a President. I can very well imagine (as it seems to me) the impossible load on his shoulders and yours. I do the best I can. May you both be protected by fate, the heavens or God, if after all he exists. Keep well and young as long as you can. If people like me (and our number is legion) had risen from our seats along with the delegates to the Third Congress to greet Gorbachev on his election to the post of President, believe me – and let him know this – the world has never heard such ovations as he would have heard from us. I congratulate you, Raisa Maksimovna and Mikhail Sergeyevich, on the spring holidays. And on the best of them – the birth of Perestroika especially. Thank you once again...

N. A. Benois, the grandson of Nikolai Benois, and a remarkable Russian artist, representative of a famous artistic family that has done so much for Russian culture, wrote me from Italy on the 23rd of February 1988:

Dear Raisa Maksimovna!
I beg you to forgive me for permitting myself to address these lines to you although I do not have the pleasure or the honour of knowing you personally. But I have long had the intention of expressing to you and your brilliant husband the unlimited admiration we experience over the grandiose nature of Perestroika... in the field of the domestic and foreign policy of our vast and, in all

senses, great Soviet Union, thanks to which the whole structure of Soviet life will be radically renewed (and, I would say, rejuvenated) in accordance with Lenin's guidelines. So, the true paths for the achievement of genuine socialism will be established. So, permit me, dear Raisa Maksimovna, to express to you, since I have at last dared to write to you, my great admiration for the grandiose historical initiative upon which the ultimate fate of the great Soviet country will depend. And I wish from the bottom of my heart that you and our respected Mikhail Sergeyevich will be able successfully to perform further work for the good of humanity. But the purpose of this letter consists not only of my fervent desire to convey to you and your remarkable husband my feelings, but also to thank you from the bottom of my heart for the interest and attention which you have shown in the creation of the Benois family museum: in Petrodvorets on the outskirts of heroic Leningrad, birthplace of practically all the members of the 'creative part' of our vast artistic family...

Perestroika is all the time extending its front, digging in and embracing one new sphere after another. As a person, as a citizen, in view of my personal conviction, I could not, of course, remain aside from its development. But for me it meant primarily to be at Mikhail Sergeyevich's side, to help him and support him as far as my strength and abilities permitted.

— Raisa Maksimovna, I keep wanting to ask you: what about your own work? Did it occur to you, let us say, to complete your doctoral thesis?

— Yes, it did. But I had ceased to be engaged in my own professional work. I won't say that it was a simple or easy thing to do. On the contrary I agonised over it. For some time, I continued to gather material for the doctoral thesis and attended philosophical seminars and conferences that interested me. I continued to follow the philosophical and sociological literature that was published, and I maintained active contact with my colleagues. But the circumstances of my daily life faced me with a choice, and I made that choice. Other people can write doctoral theses…

— But you are contradicting yourself. Last time you were arguing in favour of women playing a more important role in science and for intellectual equality.

— Quite so. But everything in life is specific. Remember: 'the truth is always specific.' Today I do not regret the choice I made. It was what my family and I needed most. The position of lecturer in the faculty of philosophy remains the last position I held officially in my life. But to be completely honest, I must tell you that there was all the same a moment when they were going to make me head of the faculty. I only just managed to scrape out of that promotion. Tears were shed, and I had to ask my husband to intervene.

— He stepped in to prevent your promotion?
— Yes.
— That's the first time I have heard of that kind of protectionism. It usually serves the opposite purpose.

— All sorts of things happen in life. I linked my direct involvement in Perestroika as a citizen with public work, and in particular with social work in the Soviet Culture Fund.

— *Tell us more about that.*

— There already exist in the Soviet Union today hundreds of non-governmental public funds and organisations, of which the Culture Fund was one of the first to be set up. Its emergence was the result of a general public-spirited desire to become directly involved in the democratic reforms initiated by Perestroika, and with a desire for the spiritual renewal of life in our country. The fund began its life with the motto: preserve, develop, and augment. Its tasks were: to activate interest in and attention to spiritual values and talents, to extend the circle of enthusiasts and devotees of culture, and to develop a cultural dialogue between the peoples of the Soviet Union and cultural links with the peoples of other countries. Through culture to humanise relations between people. A special concern, in my view, was to care for the 'ecology of culture', the preservation and protection of what is known as the cultural layer in civilization which includes, as I understand it, on equal terms the works both of man and of nature. But before going any further I suggest you drink a cup of tea.

In the course of our work some little traditions had been born. One of them was to drink tea after two hours of talk, dictating and recording. While tea was being drunk the tape recorder was naturally switched off. But what Russians, and not just Russians, could drink tea in silence? Of course, we conversed and chatted, and these tea-time conversations were usually of an ordinary, everyday character. Sometimes she would talk to me about her grandchildren. I could sense that, like every grandmother, she could have said a great deal about them: I understood that she even writes down some of her half-joking, half-serious observations of their behaviour. But on each occasion, she restrained herself so as not to fall into the very common and, on the whole, completely forgivable sin of those who love children – talking too much about them. It is in general part of her nature to be attentive both to those around her and herself. She watches her behaviour and her appearance.

— They are very different from one another, the grandchildren. They are always together, but surprisingly different. Ksenia is very emotional, kind and a great joker. She never bears a grudge. For her everybody is very good. She likes small children, music, and dancing. For example, she may say something like this: 'Grandma, have you realised I am already ten – the years are flying by!' Or: 'Granny, has anything in your life made you really sad?' 'Yes,' I reply, and she says, 'I have a serious problem. I can't write the letter D properly.' They say that Ksenia looks like me, and like Irina who also, they say, resembles me. But there is one quality that she certainly gets from Mikhail Sergeyevich, and that is her sense of humour. Anastasia is small and quite different, well balanced, and placid. She has had a strong character from the day she was born. She always knows what she wants. If she wants to eat, she will eat and there's no need to press her. If she doesn't want to eat, then no persuading will make her. She talks about herself in the third person. She will, for example, sit down at the table and say in a reasoning voice: 'Grandma, she's fixed herself up well, hasn't she? Not bad, eh?' Or: 'Grandma, one mustn't live life too fast, isn't that right?' 'Of course,' I say. 'Anastasia, you are my little flower.' 'Grandma, I've got two legs and a flower has only one. So how can I be a little flower?' Again: 'Granny, give me a biscuit.' 'No, Anastasia, you'll get fat.' 'I'm fat as it is, so what's the difference?'

Sometimes talk about the grandchildren would be quite spontaneous – they would simply remind us of their existence themselves. Not in person – I never caught sight of either of them, though occasionally I would hear them running around and laughing. The last time I met with Raisa Maksimovna she was only just recovering from an attack of influenza. She was wearing a long, sleeveless jacket reaching down to her knees. Very nice, I said, taking my glass of tea. A present, she replied, realising at once what I was referring to. She didn't say who it was from, and I didn't ask. Something in her tone of voice hinted that it was from her husband. She reached down into the pocket of the jacket in search of her spectacles. How often in the course of those evenings had she lost her spectacles! Sometimes when she found them, she would put them down in front of her on the table where they could be seen. But never once did she put them on – I never saw her in glasses. She reached into her pocket and came across a piece of paper. She laughed, because it was a note from granddaughter Ksenia to her mother (from which I gathered that the jacket was worn not only by the mother but by the daughter too, something that always happens in my home: my daughters contrive to wear not only their mother's jackets but my sweaters as well, wrapping themselves up in them as if in a shawl. The girl's note read like this:

> *Dear Mama,*
> *I would like to find out from you whether we shall be going some-where else on my birthday apart from that stupid polyclinic? I have in mind a café or a circus. I am not likely to wait up for you; I shall probably go to bed, which is why I am writing you this note.*
> *The ending evoked a smile – I can remember it word for word: 'I await a reply, like your nightingale, and I'm waiting for the summer...'*
> *It struck me that all this – the sleeveless jacket worn by everyone, the note in the pocket and the way it was written – bore the stamp of the style accepted in the home and in that circle.*

— So let us continue our talk about the Fund. It is headed by Academician Dmitri Sergeyevich Likhachev, whom I had known previously as a specialist on ancient Russian literature and as author of *Notes on What is Russian*, reflections on Russian culture, the pe-culiarities of the Russian national character, Nature in Russia, and Russian landscape painting. Dmitri Sergeyevich told me: 'I very much want the Culture Fund to be a fund of really great culture. We must "reach for the heavens, for the very top." The Fund already has quite a few good things to its credit. It was the father of the rebirth of charitable work in Russia and it made its contribution to the abolition of 'blank spaces' in our literature and history of art and to the revival and development of various kinds of creative work. Under the auspices of the Fund some special programmes came into being: Local history and economy, Unique Historical Territories, The Restoration of Forgotten Names, The Great Silk Route, New Names, and The Preservation and Development of the Cultures of Numerically Small Peoples. A programme called Through Culture to Health and Charity has just been set up in our country.

Among organisations that have become active are the Pushkin Society and associations of collectors, bellringers, and restorers. A great deal of effort and enthusiasm was devoted to realising the idea of organising a museum for personal collections. A plan for a museum of modern art is now being put into effect. I am very pleased that the magazine of the fund, called *Our Heritage*, which is printed by the Maxwell Communications Corporation, is very popular. The Culture Fund strives to help specific useful causes in all corners of the country. In this connection I recall Mikhail Sergeyevich's visit to Sverdlovsk in April 1990. It gave me the opportunity to spend some time in places I knew as a child, in Alapayevsk, and with the backing of the Fund to support the efforts of the peoples of the Urals to develop the Alapayevsk Sinyachka cultural complex, including the setting up of an Alapayevsk children's School of Art. That gives me much joy. I had tremendous satisfaction from taking part in the organisation of a Rorich Fund. Nikolai Rorich was a great

Russian artist and thinker. As we know, he spent the last decade of his life in India, but he did not break off contact with his native land. I regard it as a great blessing that Mikhail Sergeyevich and I have made the acquaintance of Svyatoslav Nikolayevich Rorich, Nikolai Rorich's son and a well-known modern artist, and his wife, Devika Rani, an Indian cinema actress and niece of Rabindranath Tagore. I recall so well our meetings with them – our conversations that were so human and so profound: about wisdom, beauty, spirituality, goodness and 'Kanchenjunga', the sacred mountain of the 'five treasures'. And, of course, about fate. We discussed with the Rorichs the question of setting up a Rorich Fund in Moscow and opening a Rorich cultural centre and museum. We spoke a lot about Nehru, who was at one time close to the Rorich family. Svyatoslav Nikolayevich repeated more than once that he had great faith in Mikhail Sergeyevich and that everything of his would succeed. Rorich's speech is dotted with such old-fashioned and moving words – '*matushka moya*' and '*batyushka ty moi.*'

His inscription on the photograph he gave us says: 'Let us always strive towards the beautiful.' It is all symbolic, like an eternal summons... the call of human naturalness and wisdom. It is strange, but when I think of Rorich's work I keep recalling the fate of the Andrei Rublev Museum of ancient Russian art. I found myself in it for the first time some years ago and went through a whole range of emotions. It is impossible to underestimate the effect upon a person of the art of ancient times, whether it be articles of sculpture, of daily life, frescoes or, in the case of our Russian religious culture, icons. I realised that the Museum had more than enough difficulties, and I could not remain indifferent. I tried to play a part in the fate of the Museum. Unfortunately, it proved to be anything but a simple task to help it out of its troubles. But I am sure it is essential to do so. Such unique museums, centres for the study of the history of Russian culture must be a matter for our common patriotic concern. We don't have many of them. Russia is not Italy. When you travel in Italy you hear on all sides: tenth century, twelfth century, thirteenth century and so on, referring to buildings, museums, and whole cities. That is why I think all our historical monuments must be better appreciated by us. We must give them more attention and care. I think it is important that the work of such organisations as the Culture Fund should not only be based on the rebirth of morality and moral impulses coming from people but should be capable of evoking them itself. Priceless objects and works of art and of national crafts are being handed over by the Fund's many benefactors. It all goes to replenish the displays in our museums and mobile exhibitions. But no less important in my view is the fact that people are doing it selflessly, moved by the highest motives.

— *What about the return of our national artistic and cultural treasures from abroad?*

— I want to say something about that. People, and often people not connected by birth with Russia, hand these things over, not only out of a feeling of debt to our country and not only out of generosity, but also because they have faith that they are entrusting the things into honest and good hands: the image of our country has become more attractive and more human in the years of Perestroika. I am proud to have played some part in the return back home of our cultural treasures. It has been my good fortune to receive many such gifts, and I remember the warmth of people's hands, both old, even very old, and quite young ones, and it seems to me that that chain of warmth and concern is felt by all Soviet people at the present time, which is so difficult for us. I would like to express gratitude to the people in America, France, Britain, Italy, Japan, Spain, and other countries – to those who have emigrated from Russia, of whatever nationality they may be, as well as to those who have no formal relationship with Russia and were motivated in what they did by their own goodwill. From the earliest time I have loved books, the theatre and painting. I value very highly inspired creative writing, and I bow down before the original, gifted mind, human dignity, courage, and selflessness. I admire the beauty of the human face. As well as the beauty of the landscape, a flower, and a blade of grass. It is my belief that, by protecting beauty in any of its forms, man is in the end contributing to the salvation of his own soul.

— *But in recent times, Raisa Maksimovna, people in Russia are talking more about 'saving one's soul' in the direct sense. There has been more active interest in the Church, in religious literature and in religious teaching and ideas. One of the reasons is probably the lack of stability in our material existence and a certain emotional strain.*

— Yes, probably. But it cannot be denied that the changes that have been taking place in recent years in society have, on the one hand, permitted the Church to be bolder in coming out of the shadows and ending its alienation of so many years, and, on the other hand, have made it possible for people not to conceal or to be ashamed of their beliefs, or even just their interest, even when they do not coincide with the official view. For example, that same interest in the Church. It is not a question of 'maybe', Perestroika has definitely contributed to the rebirth of the Church and has removed certain constraints from its everyday life. Old churches and mosques are now being returned to believers. At the request of believers, I have myself had occasion to take part in such handovers, and I was glad to help a good cause. Today we hear again the ringing of church bells on feast days, and religious sermons are even broadcast on television. Theological ideas are circulating more freely. You remember, of course, that until 1985 even such books as the Bible and the Koran were considered to be bibliographic rarities. It was impossible to get hold of them or buy them. Today we are opening up for ourselves a rich multicoloured world inhabited by many forgotten and practically unknown thinkers, and zealots of the faith and spirit. In a word, a normal dialogue with the Church is beginning in society and the State. The 'iron curtain' that existed between them until recently is coming down. Do you remember the celebrations that marked the one thousandth anniversary of the arrival of Christianity in Russia? The Church today has joined actively in the peace making, charitable and patriotic work in society.

This is extremely important for us. Ours is a multi-ethnic country, with people in it of many different faiths, and social accord greatly depends on all the shepherds of our multi-million flock. I have had occasion to meet various dignitaries of the Church.

I met the late Patriarch of All Russia, His Holiness Pimen, and the present Patriarch, His Holiness Aleksei II, the Roman Catholic Pope, His Holiness John–Paul II, the Supreme Patriarch, Catholicos of all the Armenians, Vazgen I, and other spiritual leaders. And I have met ordinary believers, highly educated, and deeply thinking people. His Grace Pitirim, the Metropolitan of Volokolamsk and Yurev, is a member of the Presidium of the Culture Fund. And we are now discussing together all the problems of mutual concern. When I visit churches, I invariably talk not only with the clergy but also with the ordinary believers. You see, I understand that people come to church with their pain and their anxieties, and they come in a peculiar state, bringing their pain to God. That means that we people around them failed to notice their pain and did not react to it. Once when I visited the Svyato-Danilov monastery a woman, already old, asked me: 'Raisa Maksimovna, why did you not kneel before the icon?' What was I to reply? So, I asked her in turn: 'Do you believe in God?' 'Yes,' she replied. I said: 'Well now, that's fine. I believe a person cannot live without faith, that's what makes him a human being. But you will agree – faith can be of various kinds. Most important is: what sort of deeds does it express itself in? I know many worthy people who are atheists, I know people who do not believe in God, but believe in some kind of mysterious supreme force. Your faith does not prevent me from respecting you and your feelings and believing you. The most important thing is to be tolerant and to respect the other person's view. It is important that, in the name of some faith of our own, we don't start fighting each other or make each other suffer for it. That is my main article of faith, my ideal and my hope. So, tell me now (I continued) would it really be better if, simply to humour you, to please you, I were to kneel down here?' 'No,' the woman replied, 'you mustn't be a hypocrite. That would be worse.' Don't be a hypocrite! Those seem to me to be very important words and the key to understanding a great deal.

I am probably too interested a defender of Perestroika, and yet among its other contributions I would mention the fact that it has returned to people a sense of their own dignity. Even that natural interest in religion, which has so increased recently, is also in the last analysis founded on that – on the revival of a sense of one's own dignity. But don't be a hypocrite or act insincerely. To do that would be to diminish one's own dignity, would be to hurt other people's feelings, and to offend them. And not only to offend them. I am convinced that hypocrisy, the lie, is the true sister of evil, intolerance and cruelty. When I see with what ease yesterday's atheist and energetic propagandist for atheism today vows eternal loyalty to Christian dogmas, while some priest fights furiously at the barricades of political confrontation (and we have such people), I think to myself: is there in this even a single drop of faith – of any faith! – or is there only a soul-destroying lack of faith, lies and hypocrisy? Is there only that 'priceless legacy' of the past, ideological intolerance and confrontation, which it is so difficult for us to cast aside? Do you remember Evgeny Shvarts's play, *The Dragon*? The dragon, defeated by the knight Lancelot, says: my consolation is the fact that I am leaving you only ruined souls, worn-out souls, dead souls. They say there is nothing more precious than contact with human beings. It would be difficult, even impossible, to list the names of all the people whom Mikhail Sergeyevich and I have been fortunate enough to meet in the last few years. Statesmen, politicians, public figures, scholars, artists, doctors, housewives, collective farmers, industrial workers, and office workers...

People known the world over and those not known at all. Memory preserves the moment of meeting, words, images, situations, and atmosphere. They included so many talented, exceptional, brilliant, and unique people! I dream of bringing them all together one day in the pages of a book.

As I accompany Mikhail Sergeyevich on his trips around the country, I often visit schools, children's homes, nurseries, hospitals, markets, shops, cultural institutions, and people's homes. I do so, of course, not simply to satisfy my curiosity. My various encounters are unofficial and have a directness and degree of informality, and they provide an extra possibility for me to see and hear and understand things and if possible to help. A possibility for Mikhail Sergeyevich and me to see more. I recall a trip in 1987 to the Murmansk region and the towns of the Soviet Polar region. I remember the majestic, severe beauty of nature in the Far North. The very location of Murmansk was so striking – on three terraces like the three decks of an ocean liner. I remember visiting the gigantic Seve-ronikel non-ferrous metal complex. The heroic submarine K–21 is a memorial to the courage of our fighters in the Second World War. The museum of life in the region of the northern seas. I remember very well the children and the staff at the Murmansk pre-school children's home that I was able to visit. And, of course, I remember very well my meetings with women – in Monchegorsk, Murmansk and Severomorsk. We spoke of a lot of things: about the shortage of jobs, and the problem of finding employment for the wives of fishermen and of men serving in the armed forces. We spoke about pensions for northerners who do not want to move after they retire but want to continue living in the North. We spoke of the moral and material responsibility of parents who abandon newborn chil-dren and leave them to the mercy of fate and the care of children's homes. It is a problem in Murmansk and in other ports. We spoke of the quality of the food provided in the children's homes and the provision of the homes and boarding schools with transport.

We also spoke of everyday problems and about ecology in Monchegorsk. We spoke of the part that the women of Murmansk could play in the work of the Culture Fund and in the develop-ment of cultural links with people living in the neighbouring Scandinavian countries. And I am pleased that in dealing with certain 'women's' problems in the area I have taken a part and made a contribution, however small. Along with the Chairman of the Murmansk region council for women, Margarita Mikhailovna

Molodtsova, I prepared a note concerning the most pressing social problems and sent it to the Central Committee of the CPSU and the Council of Ministers of the USSR. Some of the proposals made by the women's councils in Murmansk and ideas put forward by the Party and government organisations in Murmansk – concerning problems of women, children and elderly people living in the North – were sent to the Presidium of the Supreme Soviet of the USSR, to the Soviet Women's Committee and to the Children's Fund. There were general resolutions summing up the results of Mikhail Sergeyevich's trip, touching on a whole series of problems, and our proposals were included in them. I am not, of course, in a position to help with everything I come across, or about which people write to me with requests. And although my heart aches and although, believe me, I would like to help everyone, one has to face the reality of life and recognise that no one is almighty. Most difficult of all are questions of housing, serious illness, the fate of invalids and of single elderly persons. In the last few years, I have heard quite a few kind words addressed to me. I have also acquired my own supporters, allies, and friends, both here at home and abroad – in the United States there is even a society of friends of Raisa Gorbacheva. I thank them all, my friends far and near, for their support, their good feelings and kind words. The pictures that have been presented to me, the books, poems, songs, and drawings – what could be more precious than such sincere gestures?

And the messages – simple, sincere, and trusting: 'With respect for you and gratitude for your courage and distinguished representation of the women of our country to the whole world. K. Tishchenko, Krivoi Rog.' I am going through quite recent mail: 'Dear Raisa Maksimovna! I congratulate you on the holiday of the 8th of March. I wish you Siberian health, Caucasian long life, the peace, and love of your family, and, of course, patience. I understand how difficult it is to be the wife of the President, but everything will be all right. I pray for you and await your call. There is a great deal that must be said. Respectfully, Raisa Alekseyevna Mukharamova. Ashkhabad.' Here's one from Ivano-Frankovsk, from the family of a man who fought in the Great Patriotic War. Congratulations on the 8th of March. 'On this beautiful day we present you with a million snowdrops...' This letter is from the USA – from Gloria Hatten Sapp, who lives in the state of Georgia.

Dear Mrs Gorbachev,

I sat in my home watching and listening to your first speech delivered to the students at Wellesley College and to the viewing public of the United States of America. I do not know how the citizens of the Soviet Union hold you in their opinions; I hope it is with the tremendous respect you deserve. Your words were inspiring, your poise was graceful, and your sentiments were shared by thousands. Your presence helped bridge the gap between our nations; a gap that is growing smaller and smaller at a quickening pace. I wish you, your husband, and your country triumph over the obstacles you face. I am thankful for all that you are and all that you are accomplishing for our world.

Most respectfully, Gloria Hatten Sapp.

Now here is another letter which I will read in its entirety.

Dear Raisa Maksimovna!

I don't know whether this letter will reach you or whether I ought to be writing it. But, believe me, I very much want to say some kind words to you. Frankly speaking, when Mikhail Sergeyevich began to make trips round our country and you joined in those trips, which were anything but tourist excursions but real working occasions, I was rather annoyed. But sometime later after your first trips I realised that they were actually work for you and not pleasure trips. And it was anything but easy work. It is a great social work and a moral obligation. Whatever your mood or state of health you have to smile at the journalists and the people around you. You have to understand what people are talking about and talk with people and reply to their questions, not with superficial answers, for the sake of answering, but much more seriously, knowing what their problems are and replying to all their questions. Then there is your ability to dress modestly but at the same time with taste and in accordance with the fashion. And you have the ability as a woman to dispose people towards you. In my view, to be the wife of the General Secretary is very difficult, when you are seen not just as a woman in general but as the wife of Mikhail Sergeyevich. It really is a very difficult job! I am writing this letter after watching the *Vremya* programme on the television, which showed you on your visit to Yugoslavia. And, my word of honour, I felt really proud of you, Mikhail Sergeyevich, Soviet people, and my country. Maybe my letter is rather confused and not all of it will be clear to you. I simply want you to understand my good will and best feelings towards you.

Larisa Gutsal. 28 years of age.'

Here is another letter, from Italy:

Raisa – that's the way they address you, without any titles or adjectives. We love you for the way you appear side by side with Signor President – modestly, quietly, and intelligently but at the same time lovingly. Confident, calm, and serene. You move, sowing the seeds of spring which are already producing shoots of the flowers of freedom and of joy. May your strength not betray you further on this path. Thank you.

Sister Anna Lonero. Naples.

— *Well, that's not prose but poetry.*
— I am deeply grateful to the five million readers of the British magazine *Woman's Own* who chose me as 'woman of the year' and awarded me in 1987 a prize for my international work. I am grateful to the international fund 'Together for Peace' and its chairman Signora Fanfani for awarding me the prize 'Women for Peace'. I was touched to the depths of my heart to learn that Mr Rivello in Italy, the Modzelewsky family in the USA, the Rejin family in Brazil and the Dimov family in Bulgaria had called their children by my name. A Polish firm, Vitroflora, and its owners,

husband and wife Anna and Karol Pavlak, have developed a beautiful and amazing new sort of flower and called it 'Raisa'. A firm in the Federal German Republic, Ogilvy and Meiser Fokas, has given my name to a new kind of rose they have developed. Believe me, I by no means seek such marks of attention. I do not thirst for such general adoration. But that's the way the human heart is made: it makes no mistake in detecting other people's goodwill and their attitude towards you. That is its best source of nourishment. It reacts to goodness with goodness immediately. I remember Sicily, Messina, the town of Linz in the outskirts of Bonn, Minneapolis... I shall preserve in my heart forever the gratitude I feel towards all those people who came forward in those memorable days to shake my hand and through me to express their confidence and gratitude to my country, my people, and my husband.

— *And yet it is not by chance that we Russians have a saying that 'you can't be nice to the whole world'. And it sometimes happens that the 'world' turns out to be kinder to you than 'home'.*

— It happens... In recent years I have, of course, heard other things said: that I have 'pretensions to play some special role', that I am 'meddling in things that don't concern me', that I am 'the Kremlin's secret weapon', that I am the Tsaritsa, Josephine, and so on. I believe, Georgi Vladimirovich, that it is not so much my individuality and not just the variety of human thought, attitudes and assessments that determine the contradictory nature of people's judgements. In my view, on the whole it is other circumstances that are important. Possibly it is primarily the fact of my appearing openly in public. The essence of the matter is that the concept of 'wife of the leader of the Party and the country' has become very abstract. It really said nothing. It is a matter here not only of the wife of the leader of the state. It seems to me to go deeper. It is a question of the attitude toward women as a whole, and especially to a woman as a wife and a woman as a mother, and of their position in our society. I have already discussed with you the fact that, having done quite a lot for women and children, the country was still not able to create the necessary conditions for realising Soviet woman's equality in practice and for the assertion of her human dignity with full rights. Moreover, there has been a re-evaluation downwards in the social awareness and in public opinion of the role of the family. At the same time there has been a depreciation of the role of the woman as mother and the woman as wife and – don't rush to conclusions – of the man as father. Oh yes, the reduction in the role of the woman inevitably reduced the importance of the man in the family.

The two are related. A typical detail: I remember that, when I was still a child, the family observed all holidays and celebrations, both public and family, together. Father and mother would always go out together, whether it was to visit friends or to the club for official celebrations and occasions. The following situation, for example, was not exceptional but quite natural. My father would have a formal meeting at his work. Among other leading workers he would be presented with an honorary certificate or a prize, while my mother would be there in the audience along with other wives of my father's colleagues. After the formalities were over, along with my classmates, I would appear on the wooden stage where my father had just been honoured. A concert would follow. We would sing and dance for the workers and construct a pyramid of gymnasts... And I knew that the most appreciative, the most intent and most 'suffering' of my audience were my father and mother sitting side by side somewhere in the front rows. The whole family would go for a picnic or a spring outing, and transport was even allotted for it so that entire families could take part in some event, always with the children. Nowadays, you know, colleagues at work celebrate people's birthdays without their wives or husbands. For national celebrations wives and husbands are not invited. Even a group visit to the theatre is organised on the basis of the collective at work. 'Tickets according to the number of members of the trade union!' – who has not heard those words? It has also become fashionable to go on leave or on holiday as a single person. It is a problem to obtain a holiday package for a whole family. Do we have many boarding houses or rest homes where families can stay? Practically none. We didn't think about it. We reckoned we were building something better than the family. Incidentally, it is only in our country and in a few countries that used to be close to us that official receptions and dinners take place without wives or spouses.

In my view there could be fewer such receptions, but it would be much better, more appropriate if wives were invited as is the practice in the rest of the world. And what happens when a highly placed official, speaking in the Supreme Soviet of the Russian Federation and watched by the 300 million television audience, insults his colleague, a woman? Somebody's wife and mother. When he was asked to apologise, he gave the impression of not knowing what he was to apologise for. In both the material and the moral sense, we have cheapened the value of the work that women do in the home and the family. It has now become not only bad form but practically 'improper' to be proud of a wife who is a housewife or to describe your partner in life in such a way. Here again and again I think of my mother. Yes, she was also a housewife. But, you know, she brought up three children, and what could be more to the benefit of the state than the work involved in that? She gave all her children, I repeat, an excellent education, all on our father's very modest income. In order to manage in such conditions there had to be devotion to work and even, forgive me, real talent. Her hands, on which so much depended, were not only hard-working, they were also talented. She sewed, altered, turned, cooked, washed, cleaned, cultivated the garden, looked after the cow and the chicken, treated the children when they were sick and watched every kopeck, and that's also a talent and a real one! It requires a lot of character and energy to run a house and a family. What a pity that we don't know how to appreciate it! Is it only the housewife who it is not fashionable to praise today? I believe that the situation of women and the family in the state is our common concern. Quite recently I read somewhere that, if the women are happy, the whole of society will be happy. Everybody cannot, of course, be happy at once, but it's a very interesting thought just the same.

I am interested in something else I have observed. Following the devaluation of the role of the father, mother, and wife, perhaps simultaneously, some irreversible processes have begun to take place in connection with the very concept of the home.

— What do you have in mind?

— I will explain. The attachment to the family home, which used to be so typical of everybody, began to decline and lose its strength. 'State-owned' housing came to be preferred to one's own home, lived in for generations. I am not speaking only of the parental homes around the country that have been abandoned and deserted. By continually moving ourselves from one apartment to another, from a communal apartment to a small separate apartment and then one day from the small one to a better one and obtaining each one by fighting for it and overcoming all the obstacles, we become willy-nilly enthusiastic practitioners of the 'exchange'. Of the process itself. We don't have time to become attached to anything or make a place comfortable and homely before it's time to 'spread out' or to move on. Perhaps that is why we do not take care of, or value especially, the state-owned apartments or houses and don't worry about them as we would worry about our own. We are always on the move, always lodgers. At the time of Mikhail Sergeyevich's meeting with George Bush in Malta I spent some time with a young Maltese family. They were newly married, charming and welcoming, and did not yet have children. But the flat already had a children's room and they were already equipping it quietly. The apartment was three-roomed, which they had purchased on a mortgage with their parents' help. They had immediately bought an apartment that allowed for the family to expand, and which would last them a long time, perhaps for more than one generation. That is how you lay the foundations of a family home. It is built as the swallows build their nests. Russia is not Malta, of course. The scale is different, including the extent of the shortages of accommodation.

We can't for the time being, even for money, provide every young family with the possibility of having an apartment like that: spacious, permanent and with provision for the future. But something could be done even now! If a person lives in the house in which his mother and father lived, he has a different attitude to its walls, and not just its walls. He has a more stable attitude to life and has deeper roots in it. After all, a house is not just its walls, it is something else that cannot be put into words, something mysterious. Once again, I remember my mother. I have already told you that we also had no permanent home: we trooped endlessly in the wake of my father the railway worker, endlessly changing our abode. But wherever we went, wherever we moved to, my mother stubbornly carted along with us an old sideboard, as if it were something very precious and living. Wherever we found ourselves that sideboard would be put in place, and we already had a home. There was already something of our own. Whatever you thought of it, it was our 'nest'. It brought warmth and security to us. And we never parted with that sideboard. It provided a link between Mother and all of us with those who in the past had composed our home.

— *It is difficult to believe what I am about to tell you, but it so fits in with your story. I had the good fortune to be with you on a visit to Turgenev's house in Bougival. And do you know what struck me most of all? I remember that my mother had a cupboard made, if I am not mistaken, of the dark wood of the plane tree. There was not a single nail in the whole cupboard or its shelves. It had been handed down to her by her mother, who had also received it from her mother. It was, as I now realise, the most valuable object in our home. It was, of course, already falling to pieces, but the wood was light, mature, and sweet smelling. I liked to stick my nose into the cupboard, not just in search of something tasty but simply to smell the air inside it – spicy, delicious, and mysterious. But my mother died, and I stupidly tried to make a sleigh out of the upper shelves. I tried sawing, but the wood would not saw; I knocked in some nails and the wood split. In short, I ruined the cupboard. Later the house was sold, we children were sent off to children's homes or boarding schools, and the things in the house were also sold or lost. The cupboard also vanished, like everything else. An old linen tablecloth remained and is with us still as a memento of my mother. And, with the passing of the years, I began more often and more painfully to recall that cupboard, perhaps because I felt guilty about it. For me it really was 'deeply respected' as in Chekhov's The Cherry Orchard. You can be nostalgic about things as well. So, thirty years later I visited Turgenev's house, now a museum, and what do you think was the first thing to catch my eye?*

— I can guess.
— *Yes, it was an antique cupboard in dark wood and, as it seemed to me, exactly the same as the one my late mother had in my parents' house. I was really shaken and spent practically the whole of the visit standing by it. I wanted to open the door, put my head into its spicy depths and sniff!*

— That's what you should have done. As I recall, the people in charge of the museum were hospitable and simple people. But in general, I understand you very well. The feeling of home is something one must not lose, that is dangerous. Every one of us must try to revive it. It is also the way to finding a sound foundation, putting down roots and gaining stability in every person's heart and in society. My house is not just my castle: it is also my world, my galaxy. That's what I think. Moreover, we must from childhood stop driving out of children the desire to work by giving them formal handicraft lessons 'work training', which most often teach them only how to wriggle out of any obligation to perform mandatory work, and give them the freedom to work themselves, wherever they want and where it is not harmful to their health. Best of all – in their own homes, orchard, or market garden.
— *Nowadays many of them simply dream of that – to have their own home and garden. Grown-ups as well as children, including my*

own. It seems that this is true on a global scale. In America the boom in private home building and gardening was associated with the fact that people born in the post-war years are now entering their active working life. It is the generation of the 'baby boom'. I think it also has direct relation to us. I personally believe and have great hopes in my generation – and I would like it not to be the generation of those who have 'nothing to lose', but of socialist property owners.

— I would do everything possible to encourage such a tendency. I would encourage everything that binds a person to his home, to his native soil, to a given order of things and gives him greater stability in society and the opportunity honestly to increase his wealth. It is time, already time, to stop shouting and howling and whipping up intolerance, hatred, and bad feeling and to start doing something positive – in the home. I also believe in hard-working and business-like – my mother would have said 'busy' – people, and I am impatient to see more of them on the path of Perestroika.

To finish with the subject of the home: this spring the President had planned to fly down for his mother's eightieth birthday. He wanted to go on his own – that I know for sure. But as it happened the miners wouldn't let him go. In his place went people who were to some extent able to replace him and give his mother pleasure comparable with the arrival of her son. Two personal representatives of the President flew down for the occasion: two little emissaries with bows in their hair – Ksenia and Anastasia. His mother was happy, though at the same time

sad – a state familiar to all our mothers, irrespective of whether they are waiting patiently on the family threshold for a President, a prime minister, or a general labourer. The fact that he is a son says everything.
— We started our conversation, Raisa Maksimovna, about the position in society of the wife of the country's leader.

— Actually, throughout the civilised world the position, rights, and duties of the wife of the head of state are more or less clearly laid down, either in some written regulations or according to certain traditions. For example, I was told that in the White House, to assist the President's wife to carry out her official functions at the proper level, there is the necessary staff. There is a person in charge of the office and the President's wife even has her own 'territory' and her own 'office' in a wing of the White House. Madame Mitterrand, wife of the President of France, who devotes a great deal of effort to the organisation France Liberté which she founded, acquainted me on one visit to France with the work of her own secretariat which, as a matter of tradition, helps the President's wife in her social and charitable work. Frau Kohl is very active and engaged in very varied social work and guardianship, and she also told me about the special office set up to give her the necessary assistance. It turned out, Georgi Vladimirovich, that I had at my disposal only one tradition, which took shape in Stalin's day – the absence of any right to a public, official existence. It even strikes me occasionally that a certain section of our society regarded my public appearance with excessive partiality, as if it were the 'big event' of Perestroika. Yes, my appearance in public alongside Mikhail Sergeyevich required of me as wife of the head of state that I should carry out certain official duties: taking part in meetings and certain government and social functions including some involving protocol. I did not, of course, have any special diplomatic knowledge and certainly no experience of 'high society'. I learnt as I went along, using my own everyday logic and intuition. I really acquired a great deal through intuition, and through a natural tendency to use my common sense. I learnt for the first time in detail that there are strict rules governing diplomatic ceremonies and protocol in international affairs.

There are general rules that are accepted in all international practice, and there are special, national rules and requirements of protocol connected with the different traditions of particular peoples and states. I learnt – no longer by hearsay but from 'primary sources' – that even such occasions as a 'lunch', 'tea' or 'fourchette' have their own 'individual' elements of diplomatic etiquette. For example, the 'dinner' is the most important kind of reception, which has to take place in the evening after seven o'clock or later, although it is called a dinner. It requires a strict and well-defined order of 'seating' at table and, as a rule, formal or evening attire. In some countries women are expected to appear in long evening dresses at official lunches. In our everyday life a long dress is something not very necessary, and in my opinion not necessary at all. Very elegant, of course, but it is a requirement that is rather wasteful to observe – do you often attend such 'dinners'? Again, it is a very small matter, but in 1985 a new rule was adopted in the diplomatic protocol of our country: at official receptions and dinners in our country now it is required only that the men should wear dark suits and the women elegant dresses of ordinary length.

— *We can reckon that our protocol is the most economical in the world!*

— Not the most economical, Georgi Vladimirovich, but the most democratic. Every form of representation requires attention to the peculiarities of everyday life; the traditions and customs of the people and the country. Attention to both big and small matters. I remember with gratitude, for example, the understanding with which Mrs Bush and the staff of Wellesley College treated my request that, when I attended the commencement, I should not have to put on the academic gown and headgear, because it was not the practice in our country. It would have embarrassed me, and I would have felt very awkward in it. As the place for Mikhail Sergeyevich to make his speech on our last visit to Britain the British government proposed the Guildhall, an extremely prestigious building in London which is the centre of the financial world, the City.

It is an honour only very rarely extended to foreign guests and a mark of special respect. But in accordance with ancient tradition a ceremony in the Guildhall presupposes certain obligatory forms of dress: a woman must wear a hat and gloves and a man tails, a morning coat or military uniform. An exception was made in our case. Mrs Thatcher respected our wishes and, contrary to tradition, decided that she, too, would not wear a hat or gloves. During the same visit Mikhail Sergeyevich and I went to Windsor and met the Queen. In England an audience with the Queen is the highest mark of diplomatic esteem. I had already learnt that Queen Elizabeth's favourite colour was blue – 'royal blue' – and usually appears somewhere in her attire. I also gathered that members of the royal family and guests of the Queen tried not to use that colour when they were in her presence. I also tried to maintain the tradition. In the course of official visits by heads of state it is the tradition for the hosts to propose a separate and additional programme for the visitor's wife, apart from the official visit itself. Such a programme is usually agreed beforehand through the foreign ministry. The hosts take account of the interests and wishes of the guests, but above all, of course, the guest also has to bear in mind the possibilities and the suggestions made by the hosts. I have sometimes heard people who were along with me, my own compatriots, say about programmes arranged for me: 'Raisa Maksimovna, do you really find that interesting? Can you really not think of something different?' You can think of something, but you certainly can't always carry it out. But quietly, discreetly, I also manage to slip away from a strictly arranged programme. In Finland in 1990 I got away 'incognito' to look at the 'church in the cliff' and to wander round the streets of Helsinki. In San Francisco, apart from the agreed programme, I undertook a sortie to the coastal district of the city, spent some time in Chinatown, in a family grocer's shop and on the platform of a sightseeing tram and talked to the conductor. She was so moved that she offered me the favour of making use of the services of her friend, a hairdresser who would, she said, give me a beautiful American hairdo.

— I particularly remember the grocer's shop. The right to choose which shop rested with the head of security on the American side. Your 'escape' was, of course, entirely his responsibility. He was not very talkative – mostly he just smiled into his moustache – but very imposing and greying at the temples. The spitting image of Faulkner in his prime. But when we entered the store with you, I was simply dazzled – bottles, bottles, and more bottles to suit any taste! Good old 'Faulkner' – he knew where to go!

— Yes, it certainly was a well-stocked wine department. The other sections were also very good. In France, in a little café called the Rosarie in Bougival, I drank coffee with some French women and had a purely women's conversation with them – not in the least diplomatic. Some misunderstandings as regards the rules of diplomatic procedure must have been, in my view, the basis for the rumours spread in the American press about 'friction' between Nancy Reagan and myself. I did not take, and I still don't take those statements seriously. Nancy Reagan and I were lucky because we were witnesses of, and in some respects participants in, the greatest and most important historic meetings between the leaders of our two countries. All our feelings, worries and anxieties were just a drop in the ocean of the hope born of these meetings and felt by people throughout the world: the hope of peace and a future for the whole of mankind. I remember the first meeting in Geneva in

November 1985. They got to know each other, studied each other, 'adjusted' to each other and had debates and discussions. The birth of understanding was difficult, as was the drafting of the official documents.

I remember the mansion, the Maison de Saussure, where Ronald and Nancy Reagan gave an official dinner in honour of Mikhail Sergeyevich and myself. We were still in the mansion at two o'clock in the morning. That morning we were due to fly out of Geneva, but they just couldn't arrive at a final draft of the joint statement. Every sentence, every word and every letter was fought over. All the same, Geneva gave birth to what was most important – a recognition that a nuclear war cannot be won and must not be fought. After Geneva a revival began to take place in scientific, cultural, and economic contacts between our countries that had previously been at a standstill or had not existed at all. Then came October 1986 and the meeting in Reykjavik, Iceland. How much has already been written about that Soviet – American summit meeting and its dramatic events! Yes, we all went through that, but we remember and understand its importance too – for without Reykjavik there would not have been Washington in 1987 or Moscow in 1988. There would not have taken place the meetings that turned out to be more constructive and more productive of results than the meeting in Geneva. There would have been no Treaty on the destruction of intermediate- and short-range missiles. And there would not have been that rare human mutual understanding and accord of the Soviet and American peoples that became apparent clearly and strikingly in December 1987 in Washington, in 1988 in New York, in Washington, Minnesota, and in San Francisco in 1990. There was accord in the name of peace and friendship. In Geneva Nancy Reagan and I took part in the laying of a stone for the building of a museum of the International Red Cross. Today the museum is already open. I would like it and all the work done by the International Red Cross and Red Crescent to symbolise for ever collaboration between all states and peoples in the cause of mutual understanding and trust and in the name of goodness and charity.

Out of the mass of impressions that remain in my mind after Mikhail Sergeyevich's trips to various countries, the most important is that of thousands of open, friendly human faces. I remember Delhi, New York, Minnesota, Prague, Krakow, Stettin, Berlin, Dortmund, Stuttgart, Shanghai, Madrid, Barcelona, Rome, Messina, Milan, Nagasaki... The crowded streets and squares of the cities. Sympathy and friendship on people's faces. Hope and faith in people's hearts and eyes: the belief that the world can survive without the use of force, that the world can be without war. Italy, the country of Dante and Petrarch. The source of European civilization. And the cathedral square in Milan with the amazingly beautiful, decorated marble facade of the cathedral itself. Monuments everywhere to a great culture. And the equally amazing and unforgettable outpouring of emotion by the many, many thousands of people gathered there as the people of Milan welcomed Mikhail Sergeyevich and the delegation. 'Gorby, Gorby, Gorby!' they were shouting in the square. Eduard Amvrosievich Shevardnadze and I were walking together. We had been left behind by Mikhail Sergeyevich and had to make our way through the dense crowd of people. I looked at him and saw that there were tears in his eyes, as there were in mine. He said to me then: 'For the sake of this too it was worthwhile to begin Perestroika.' I keep on repeating to myself, and not only to myself, one and the same question: ought Eduard Amvrosievich, a friend of Mikhail Sergeyevich and one who shares his views, to have brought it to an end in such a way? I have preserved the letter that Shevardnadze wrote on his sixtieth birthday, that was such a special day for him and for us, his friends.

Dear Mikhail Sergeyevich and Raisa Maksimovna,
This day in my life, a major award from my country, and the kind words you addressed to me on the occasion of my sixtieth birthday give me the moral right to express to you my heartfelt thanks. All the same, I would like in this written reaction to your congratulations and good wishes to go beyond the limits of what is for me an important day. It would be more correct, in my view, to speak of the importance of the whole period in the life of the Party and country of which my life and my work in the post I was appointed to is only a small particle. At a reception in the Soviet embassy in Madrid recently an elderly Spaniard, who was far from sharing our ideas but who had suffered agonisingly the tragedy of the 1930s and the long night of Franco's rule, said: 'At last people have appeared in world affairs with high ideals and pure

intentions, knights without fear or blame, like Don Quixote to
our Spanish way of thinking. At last, a great human ambition has
received a wonderful human embodiment.' It was you he had in
mind. You will remember what great personal anxiety and doubt
attended my new appointment. I am still not free of them. At every
step, every day, and every hour I experience a colossal 'resistance of
the material'. But, both just over two years ago and today, I found
and I find now the strength in myself to overcome that resistance.
The source of that strength is certainly not to be found in the fact
that I succeeded in fully mastering the complicated art of the new
type of diplomacy, the diplomacy of the period of new political
thinking: we have a long way to go for that. I see the sources of my
strength in something else. I see it in your support which I felt and
still feel in the hours and days of the most trying ordeals. I see it in
the policy that you have devised, of which the honesty, universal
appeal and scientific underpinning make it irresistible for millions
of people.

I see it in the positions taken up by the Party, society, and the
country – the positions that the world rightly identifies with you.
For a large part of my life, I too served the Party's cause as well
as I could. I have never concealed and do not conceal now that
I had my doubts, some uneasy thoughts, and occasionally inner
disagreement, but they were always kept down by my faith that the
decisive and critical hour would strike for our Motherland. Now
that it has struck, I feel for the first time that my life is in complete
accord with the life of the Party and the people. It is a great source

of happiness, and I am indebted to you for it. I know of no better award to myself. And I know no better response to it than to be always near you in the front ranks of Perestroika. That Spaniard was right about everything, except one: we are not dealing with windmills. But all the obstacles in our path can be brought down and we will revive the country for a life of happiness in a rejoicing humanity. I believed this and I still believe.

Yours ever, E. Shevardnadze

Even now I am very moved by what is said in that letter... People have often asked me and still ask me: is it an easy life to be wife of the President and General Secretary of the Party? I always reply that it is easier than actually being the President and General Secretary. I do not take any state or political decisions, do not take part in their preparation, and bear no responsibility for them. My work is purely social. Everything I do falls within that framework. So much for that. But the President and General Secretary is my husband. His life is also my life. His worries are also my worries. Can the anxiety for our country, which makes itself felt today in the heart of every thinking Soviet citizen, pass my heart by?

When I attend the Congress of People's Deputies of the USSR in the Kremlin Palace of Congresses, I sit among the people invited in the gallery and a lot of people come up to me – deputies, guests, and correspondents. They put questions to me, ask my opinion, and thank me for being present along with them in the hall. But some actually say: "Why do you do it? You just don't spare yourself, Raisa Maksimovna. Why do you upset your nerves and your mind, why?' Once when I was talking with our talented and popular singer Alla Borisovna Pugacheva I heard her say: 'I cannot sing to a theme, Raisa Maksimovna – it has to be from my heart.' I understand her. I can't live to a 'theme'. I can't live without putting my whole heart into everything I live by, into everything I do, in which I am involved and for which I am responsible. I remember another episode that took place, not in Moscow but in Paris. Mikhail Sergeyevich and I have visited the city several times and it so happened that on two occasions I had as my French guide and protector a very pretty girl called Isabel. On the last occasion, just before we were leaving, I had a curious conversation with her.

— 'Madame,' she said, 'in the course of my duties I see a lot of important people. I am worried about you. You are like me. It's going to be very difficult for you.'

— 'Why, Isabel?'

— 'You are too open; you worry about everything.'

— 'So, what can I do?' I asked.

The girl shrugged her shoulders.

— *But I remember another episode involving that girl.*

— Which was that?

— *You praised her for the elegance of her style of dress in the presence of other people, and she blushed with pleasure. Next day she appeared in even more stylish attire that in no way resembled a police uniform, even in Paris.*

— Well, that's all very true. A woman is always a woman. Our country is going through a difficult time, a very difficult time at present. The choice has been made. It remains firm and constant. Our society has set out on the path of renewal and of demolishing totalitarianism and the obsolete command system of administering the country. There is no way back. Only forwards, only along the path of democratisation, national revival, and the realisation of further political, legal, and economic reforms. But there are so many difficulties that have arisen and are still arising on that path! The endless 'black holes' that have been exposed in the economy, ecology, culture, medicine, social security, and the defence of people's rights in the Perestroika period were previously camouflaged and concealed. It turned out that we, society as a whole, did not know the real, factual state of affairs in all areas of our life. Perestroika has had to cope with Chernobyl, the earthquake in Armenia and the events in Nagorno-Karabakh, Sumgait, Osh, Southern Ossetia, Baku, and Lithuania... We have had thousands of refugees within our own country! The period of Perestroika is by no means easy or simple. All those dramatic events were a testing of the spirit, the mind, and the will. They involve incurable heartache and sleepless nights. The telephone rings out like a gunshot destroying the peace of the night. Nowadays telephones frighten me. They bring shouts of despair, entreaties, suffering and, sometimes, someone's death. I remember all those terrible nights – from the time of Chernobyl to the crisis in the Persian Gulf, when at two twenty in the morning Mikhail Sergeyevich was informed that the operation was due to start in an hour's time and Iraq was to be bombed. There was the night of the 19th to the 20th of January 1990 – the night of the events in Baku.

I recall that next day I could scarcely recognise Mikhail Sergeyevich – he had gone grey, and his face was grey too: he seemed to have suffered a nervous shock, to have gone through a mental crisis. And, you know, I was not alone in noticing the trauma that he went through. I have just come across an amazing letter, written on the 24th of January. It was delivered to the editorial office of the newspaper *Pravda*, but it was addressed to Mikhail Sergeyevich. It is from the town of Panevezhis and written by Y. I. Vasilyauskas.

Mikhail Sergeyevich! If there is a God or some other supreme force, may you be granted the best possible health and fortitude, especially now. I am simply afraid that you will give in and get away from all those: people who are now, openly, or covertly, hissing and gloating because of the fighting in the Caucasus. Why did I decide to write to you? Simply because for the first time I saw such sadness in your eyes when you spoke on the television about the events in Azerbaijan. I will not enter into any long discussion here, only to say: I understand perfectly well the feelings of a person who gives everything he can to people and tries to do his best and yet is often met with, it seems to me, only black ingratitude. I understand very well that in that case a man simply feels like saying: live as you please! That is a purely human reaction and it is to be understood. But, my dear Mikhail Sergeyevich, you often say in your speeches that without this or that Perestroika will fail... I am your most convinced supporter as a matter of principle, although like everyone I can have my own opinion. You know how to persuade people, that's a fact. But on one thing no one, even you, will persuade me that I am wrong: that if you now, because you are offended or for some other reason, decide to quit, that that would be an end to Perestroika. That is a thousand per cent right! You must not do it for any reason, not in any circumstances, you must not.

It must not be permitted. If you quit now, it will be the end of everything. Perestroika has already become a rather trite word, and therefore I say that your departure in the present conditions would signify the end of the hopes of all those who believe that after all there is light at the end of the tunnel... People are far from being angels, but what can one do? You have chosen your path, and however hard it may be you must carry on to the end. You must not quit! Not for anything! Therefore, even if you are put under pressure and accused of making mistakes, hold on, don't get depressed. I beg it of you. I simply do not understand how people, if they only exert a little thought, can fail to approve what you are doing and, in any case, do not understand one thing that seems to me to be elementary. It is something that ought to be clear even to an amoeba: that you are working exclusively for the benefit of people in our country and the world. That is your supreme objective, and it will not be seen only by a person who is blind or who does not wish to see. I don't take part in any demonstrations, neither for nor against, and I don't belong to any party. But I always support, without any qualifications, your policy, your aims and your ideas.

Without you there would be nothing. I am not a stupid sheep or bootlicker, and I don't need anything. I appreciate that you have the right to drop everything. But for God's sake, Mikhail Sergeyevich, not at this moment, whatever anybody says. God grant that I am mistaken and that my fears are unfounded, for God's sake. But one can draw such a conclusion from scraps of information and various rumours. Moreover, at the second Congress you said several times: let anyone who wishes take my place, I'm not hanging on to it. God grant that you said that in the heat of the moment.

Everything you have done so far, everything you have succeeded in doing, is not yet irreversible. Everything could still go into reverse if you quit. Don't do it, I entreat you! I am convinced that I am not alone in my opinion. There are millions of people who think as I do. And not in the West, but here throughout our country. Remember that all our hopes are centred on you. If my fears are unfounded, then thank the Lord for that! Forgive me for mentioning the name of the divinity so often – I am not a believer. But if I were I would pray to God that my letter should not have been written in vain. And forgive me for the confused nature of this letter. Perhaps in this case it will convince you of its sincerity. I remain your most convinced supporter. I wish you and those near to you all the very best. And again, I wish you to persevere and to persevere to the end. Forgive me for bothering you. It is a very emotional but also reasonable and sensible letter. I trust its author more than those people who keep saying, with obviously provocative intent in mind and with enviable persistence at this difficult time, that you can't carry out a revolution in white gloves. I have heard Mikhail Sergeyevich say more than once that the goals that we have set ourselves do not permit us to be indiscriminate in our choice of means to achieve them.

— *At a meeting of Secretaries of local Party organisations at the 28th Congress of the CPSU one of the women there, an Azerbaijanian, threw the charge at the General Secretary that amounted to accusing him of being the butcher of the people of Azerbaijan. He rose slowly from his seat and said, not immediately: 'You know, it is impossible to live with such an accusation.' There was an uproar in the hall, and the woman apologised...*

— Today, when the economic situation has become so difficult as well as the living conditions of the people as a whole, decisions have to be taken that are extremely hard. But they must be taken. It is obvious that they can no longer be put off. They have been put off too long...

But, you know, today it is not only problems of a material character that are putting pressure on us. Perestroika, democratisation, and Glasnost have made intellectual life in our society and life as a whole freer and more open. The social consciousness has been freed from many obsolete stereotypes and dogmas, the acceptance of the diversity of opinions has made it possible to take a new look at our history, the present day, and the world around us. It has become apparent that there is a great variety of views and interests in different sections of society. But here too we have come up against

Candle in the Wind...

Before wedding

Raisa Gorbacheva. Youth

Moscow, Stromyngrad.
Raisa Gorbacheva and Nina Lyakisheva

Student years. With friends

With husband and daughter Irina. Arkhyz

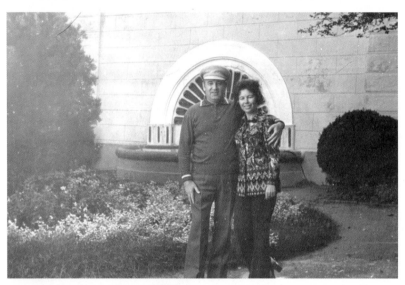

Stavropol region. On the walk

Mikhail and Raisa Gorbachev. Photographed by Yuri Andropov

Yuri Andropov often visited the Stavropol Territory and met with the Gorbachev couple

On vacation

Bashkiria, Kuyurgazinsky district, Ermolaevka

Under native sun

Summer!

Raisa & Irina Grbachev

Raisa Gorbacheva and Nancy Reagan

Moscow. Raisa Gorbacheva and Nancy Reagan

Raisa Gorbacheva and Nancy Reagan

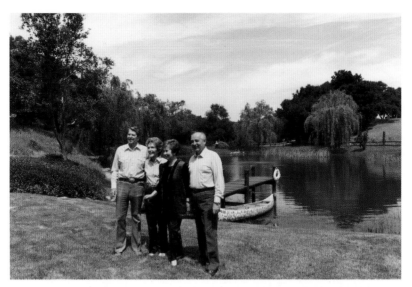

USA. Santa Barbara. Rancho del Ciego. With the Reagan couple

Great Britain. Checkers.
Mikhail and Raisa Gorbachev, Margaret and Denis Thatcher

Raisa Gorbacheva and Barbara Bush. In an aeroplane

Moscow. Raisa Gorbacheva and Barbara Bush at Novodevichy Monastery

Barbara Bush, wife of the President of the United States, Raisa Gorbachev, wife of the first President of the USSR, Marcela Temple Seminario, wife of UN Secretary-General Perez de Cuellar and Nancy Reagan, First Lady of the United States, the UN building

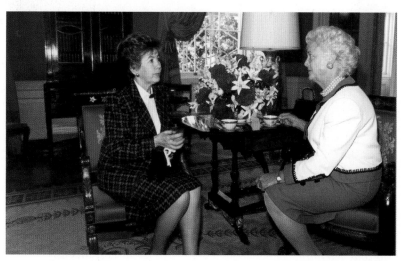

Tea Party with Barbara Bush

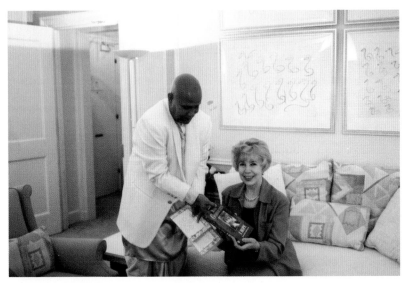

Sri Chin Moy and Raisa Gorbacheva

Moscow. Kremlin.
Mikhail and Raisa Gorbacheva, Svetoslav Roerich

Italy. The Vatican. With the Pope John Paul II

*Soviet Cultural Foundation. Dmitry Likhachev, Georg
Myasnikov and Raisa Gorbacheva at a board meeting*

Moscow. Raisa Gorbacheva and Dmitry Likhachev

Kazakhstan. With the presidential couple,
Nursultan Abishevich and Sara Alpysovna Nazarbaeva

With Barbara Bush. The flight went well

Germany. Willy Brandt, Alisa Freindlich, Raisa Gorbacheva,
Yuryevsky Pitirim, Metropolitan of Volokolamsk and
Dmitry Granin

France. Paris. Grand Trianon Palace. Spouses of the Heads
of State participating in the summit

Children's Republican Hospital

Raisa Gorbacheva at the Children's Republican Hospital

You are not alone!

Smiling can heal too

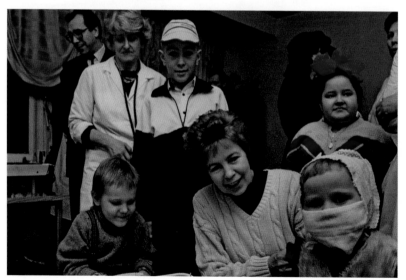

For god's sake, get well!

In the editorial office of the radio station "Echo of Moscow"

Raisa Gorbacheva at the conference on Sustainable Development

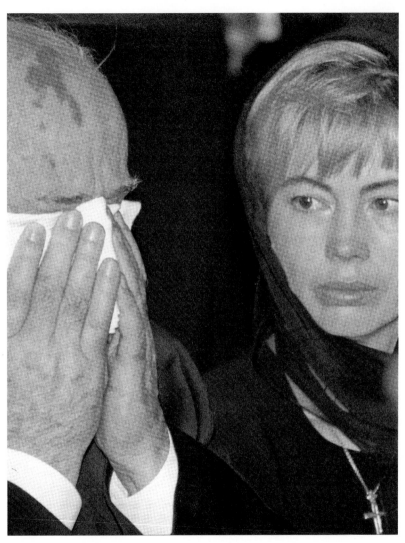

Farewell to a wife and mother

Moscow. Novodevichy Cemetery.
Monument to Raisa Gorbacheva

Raisa Gorbacheva: "I hope..."

very serious, and perhaps the most serious, problems. Nationalism and extremism have come to the surface. They are spreading today like a cancerous growth in the fabric of people's national self-awareness. It so happens that I have both Russian and Ukrainian roots. My father, as you know, came from the Chernigov area, while I was born in the Altai region, lived in Siberia, the Urals, Bashkiria, and the Caucasus with its very mixed national composition. For almost twenty years I have been living in Moscow. I have a good idea of what is meant by mutual relationships and links and mutual help between people of various nationalities. I am profoundly convinced that that is the invisible medium in which alone it is possible for each separate human life and our human civilization itself to survive. That is what made it possible for us to hold out, to endure or, as my mother would have said, to 'make it through' the bitterest years and days experienced by our Motherland. And I find it extremely alarming when I see holes appearing in that priceless medium for human morality. I was first struck by this with terrible force in Armenia, at the time of the tragic earthquake. If you recall, Mikhail Sergeyevich then broke off his official visit to the United States and, after a brief stopover in Moscow, arrived at the very centre of that frightful disaster.

We visited Leninakan, Spitak and Kirovokan. I shall never forget those days! Nor shall I forget the people's faces. There was so much sorrow in their piercing looks. I saw men driven frantic by the weight of their loss and I saw women sobbing over tiny graves and did what I could to console them. I saw crippled children in the hospitals. Like any adult person I looked into their eyes not only with fear but also with a feeling of guilt. Yes, it had been a natural disaster. Man had practically nothing to do with it. But I know that, whatever happened, whatever befell people, a person can never feel himself aloof from human suffering and tragedy. For that reason, moments of the greatest tragedy, such as happen in the course of human life, also become moments of uplift for the human spirit and human virtue. Incidentally, those days were full of that dramatic combination – of disaster and the heartfelt, nationwide, even worldwide reaction to it. The country remembered that it was one country, and that people were people, on whichever side and at whichever frontier they found themselves. And it is all the more frightful when, against a background of tears, sorrow, and the deaths of thousands of people and of groans and cries for help coming from the untouched ruins, I heard some people shouting slogans and demands for the 'liberation of Nagorno-Karabakh'. Then I learnt that at that tragic moment Azerbaijan's offer of help was rejected. Can such people really be entrusted with the fate of a nation? Truly, if a blind man leads a blind man both will fall into the abyss. I remember how, during an interval at the 4th Congress of People's Deputies of the USSR in December 1990, I was surrounded in the foyer of the Palace of Congresses. As usual there were questions and replies, arguments, and discussion.

Then suddenly a young, handsome man said at the very top of his voice: 'Raisa Maksimovna, everybody is putting down the Russians, can't you see? They are humiliating our nation, they have robbed us and brought us to our knees...' I had difficulty in interrupting him: 'What are you talking about? Stop and think about it for a moment. After all, it's from others that we hear that Russians like to be seen as the bosses, that they are lazy, not used to working and only exploit other people. Just think about what you are saying. One more step and we shall be looking for enemies. Who are they – these Georgians, Armenians, Estonians, Lithuanians, Jews, Kazakhs and Azerbaijanians – are they enemies? History has shown us more than once what that means. Or is other people's experience always just theory? The strength of the Russian people lies in the fact that we have never exploited anybody. We have never lived at the expense of other peoples. We have shared the joy of victory and the bitterness of tragedy with all the peoples of our country. And that is not a sign of weakness or of our humiliation but, I repeat, of our strength, our morality. 'Remember Dostoevsky: "I am only saying that the Russian heart is perhaps, among all the nations, the one best suited for universal, worldwide unity..."' These are anxious times, with much to be concerned about. About the future of the country, about the fate of the Union of peoples, and about everything that has been created in centuries of life together. Where did this all-destructive aggressiveness spring from? When fifty- and sixty-year–old men who have been for thirty years expounding the theoretical necessity for barrack-room socialism and its superiority and have been in charge of building that society – when they announce that they will 'gladly destroy it all and set about its destruction', I feel scared. Are we to have more Herostratoses in our country's history? Have we really not become wiser and not rid ourselves of the fatal virus of mutual destruction? Is every policy ineffective in the face of this evil?

And, generally, must one destroy in order to move forwards? It is contrary to common sense! I am convinced that people can be happy only by being constructive. What are the sources of this passion for besmirching the historical monuments of your own people and the tendency to present the whole seventy-year history of the Soviet period as a story of nothing but mistakes, crimes, and shame? And it's not just a matter of the writing of history. How many of them have emerged recently – people pretending to be supporters of Perestroika who are building a career, their personal wellbeing, and their prosperity by trampling on the dignity of their country, their own people, and their own history. What is happening at times with the traditions of our intelligentsia? Or have we hastened to dispose of those traditions like second-hand books? Some intellectuals have preferred hatred to them. They preferred the all-destructive passion of hatred, or they preferred to appease their conscience with such sayings as: revolutions are always started by intellectuals, carried out by fanatics and the fruits are harvested by rogues. So, I want to tell people to stop and think. Culture is both an intellectual phenomenon and a moral one. And, as I personally understand it, democracy exists so that, together and jointly, we can seek paths for the progress of society and the most effective ways to organise human life, and not so that we can fight and destroy each other. Democracy is, of course, valuable in itself, but it is still primarily an instrument for the creation of something more important. Or are we not able to live without enemies? An opposition has not yet taken shape in our country, but we already hear the cry: roll up your sleeves, draw up lists of reliable and unreliable people, appoint 'our' people and 'our' prosecutor and demolish the constitutional organs of power. How difficult the battle has turned out to be with the times in which we lived, and which formed us!

Intolerance towards other people's opinions, which penetrated society in the past, is spreading today into ever new forms of hatred, struggle, and confrontation. 'Raving democrats' on the one hand and 'raving conservatives' on the other. In practice the two extremes turn out to be one and the same. I remember some episodes at the 28th Party Congress, the Russian constituent Party conference, and the April joint meeting of the Central Committee and the Control Commission. The Party recognised and supported its leader in the belief that the country could not continue to live as it had in the past. But it appears that for some people – and quite a lot of them! – it would be nice to live and change, but without really changing, without accepting changes in the way of life, the new conditions and demands, and without reacting to them. And again, the same attacks, the same aggressiveness, and the same moral 'execution' of the initiators of Perestroika. During the 28th Party Congress a newspaper called *The 13th Microphone* was published. It interviewed Mikhail Sergeyevich and published what he said. I want to quote an extract.

'How much sleep have you had in the last few days?' 'I can't sleep: even in my sleep the conflicts continue.' 'What has pained you most at the Congress?' 'I have already spoken about that. I don't like flattery: I never have, since I was young. My friends from my student years know that. On top of that I can't bear brazen aggressiveness, which unfortunately was evident at the Congress. That was very hard to endure. There was a tendency to turn the Congress into a kangaroo court – that was terrible and upset me more than anything.' 'And what gave you most pleasure in these days?' 'However difficult it was, good sense is prevailing.'

I remember our trip last year to Spain: Madrid, Barcelona, the El Oriente palace, the palace of Zarzuela, the Olympic complex, the Complutens University and the Institute of Soviet Science and Culture. The Prado Museum – Spain's treasure house. Picasso's Guernica hangs there. A lot is said about the anti-fascist essence of that painting. But I took it to be not only a symbol of fascism but also a symbol of war in its most frightful form in history – a symbol of the horrors of civil war. Civil war! The painting is a summons to people to return to reason. Spain lived through a civil war, and the totalitarian Franco regime lasted nearly forty years. Many of us remember how, in the 1930s, we welcomed Spanish orphans snatched from the hell of a civil war. Thousands of them found shelter in our country. And they found a second mother among our Soviet women. Now the Spanish people have found in themselves the strength and the courage to leave dictatorship behind and to set out on the path of democratic development without resorting to war but achieving it through popular agreement. Our historical dramas are in many ways similar, perhaps that is why we found so much understanding and so many friends on our visit to Spain. They include King Juan Carlos I, Queen Sofia, and the socialist Prime Minister Gonzales, about whom my husband said after their meeting: 'Our talk together went on a long time: we had a most interesting discussion and came to some very important conclusions...' Another friend is Senor Villapalos, a professor of law, a leading scholar and rector at Complutens University. And there are the Spanish children whom we took in in 1937 and who have now returned home. So many of them came up to me, and they all asked what they could do practically to help our country. Perestroika is often described as a revolution. If it is one then it is practically unprecedented in Russia, a country of revolutions, because the main task Mikhail Sergeyevich has set himself is to carry it through democratically, without bloodshed or the use of force. Unfortunately, there have been some casualties in the years of Perestroika.

But, believe me, they would be incomparably greater in number if some forces succeed in making the President of the country to abandon the stand which he has taken up and defends quite consciously, resolutely, and courageously. In the words of Maksimilian Voloshin:

Both here and there in the ranks
Is heard the self-same cry:
Who's not with us is against us,
And justice is on our side.

But I stand alone among them
Amidst the roaring flames and smoke,
And with all the strength I have
I pray for one and all.

— *Very much to the point! And, unless I am mistaken, written in 1919.*

— In the vortex of political conflict today there is, in my view, yet another dangerous thing taking place: society has become excessively politicised, I believe that, in these conditions of total politicisation, adults have the obligation as never before to be attentive to the spiritual vitamins that our children are now being given. I am sure of this: after all, we are now harvesting the fruit of the childhood of generations who grew up on images and the condemnation of 'traitors' and 'enemies of the people'. That is why it is now so important to protect children from the influence of political passions and not to force them to be on one side or the other of the barricades. It is alarming and frightening to see columns of schoolchildren and adolescents at rallies calling 'down with' this or that. It is frightening to see our children's minds filled with those same images of 'enemies of the people' even if they are now 'modern' enemies. I have already told you once that I find it very sad and disturbing that, for example, the wife of a popular people's deputy informs us with pride in an interview published in *Ogonyok* magazine that her young daughter can tell intuitively by the look of someone appearing on television and by the way the person speaks whether he or she is one of 'ours' or is 'our' enemy. And I share the view of the author Anatoli Aleksin, President of the Soviet association *Peace for the World's Children*, which he outlined in the paper Soviet Culture: 'The seeds of enmity and hatred, of nationalism and chauvinism that are being scattered today in children's minds will never produce anything good and will never result in decent behaviour or internationalism. We are hurling the tragedy and confrontation, the burden and filth of the past, into the future, into our common tomorrow.'

— *Your husband's credo, which he has frequently stated, is a combination of politics and morality. What is your attitude to this supertask? Do you not regard it as idealistic?*

— Yes, Mikhail Sergeyevich likes to repeat that the interests of millions of people are the big issues in politics. Politics must be moral. Is that idealism? What if we try to see the larger picture? I remember a conversation I had in the course of Mrs. Thatcher's first official visit to Moscow. At dinner I asked the British Prime Minister, an outstanding politician: 'Mrs Thatcher, I would like to ask you as an ordinary person: is it moral to defend the idea that it is essential to preserve nuclear weapons on this Earth?' She replied: 'You are an idealist, Mrs Gorbachev.' I defended myself, saying: 'But there are many idealists like me and I'm sure there will be a lot more.' I recalled that conversation recently, following the tragedy of the war in the Persian Gulf. I attach extraordinary value to, and I respect the American people's feelings of patriotism. Nevertheless,

I dare to say that that war, like every other, was a tragedy. I recalled the conversation with Mrs. Thatcher after hearing a major political leader of a certain state say: very well, if force alone is effective then we shall manufacture our own nuclear weapon. So, what is that? What do you call that? No – no war, not even to punish an aggressor, is a good thing. Today people must learn to take into account each other's interests, if only for the sake of their own survival. I do not believe that, in this system of coordinates, the point where politics and simple human morality intersect is only idealism. No! No, it is here, at the point of intersection of politics and morality that we have the sources and the foundations of the finest and most productive results of contemporary politics.

— *Mikhail Sergeyevich is being accused of not making a decisive break and not cutting off his attachment and obligations to people, and especially to those comrades-in-arms with whom he set out on this path of reform.*

— Again, just think about it: is it really so bad? Is a purely pragmatic and opportunistic approach to circumstances and people so very moral? I do not deny it: there are sometimes, it is true, bitter lessons to be learned. For example, if fate had not handed us the burden of Perestroika, I would probably never have known the many different shapes and forms human beings can take. This is serious, you understand. For me this is one of the most difficult moral tests of Perestroika: the specific way people behave, what they say and what they do. What they were yesterday and what they are today. What they are when they are with you, and what they are with other people. What they are when it is their advantage, and what they are when it is not. Sometimes I even see, or rather feel, that they are not faces but masks, but masks of the real world, not the fantastic world of fairy tales. And, do you know, the masks I see will suddenly disappear and I can see quite clearly the faces of the people who informed on my grandfather in the 1930s. And of those who destroyed him. And of those who, with their tails between their legs, would not approach a dying woman, just because she was from the family of an 'enemy of the people'. Nikolai Gubenko, minister of culture, actor, and director, once said to me: 'Do you know what I dream of doing? I would like to make a film called 'How I was a minister'. I believe there will be more than one film, but not fictional, not the result of someone's sick fantasy or inflamed imagination. They will be documentary films telling the truth about the people of Perestroika. Fortunately, the documentary material for them, both official and unofficial, written, and oral, well known and so far, little known, is more than sufficient. I think most often and with most regret, of course, about those who were comrades and colleagues of Mikhail Sergeyevich and called themselves 'brothers-in-arms'.

— *No, I would drop that expression.*
— Well, why... [she shrugged her shoulders] – that's what they called themselves. And they put a lot of effort into Perestroika. The ordeals that each of them went through in their careers were not

easy. But did they all turn out to be up to the task; could every one of them say, hand on heart, that we were, we are, and we shall continue to be part of the campaign for Perestroika, working for our common cause? I re-read this handwritten letter from Stanislav Sergeyevich Shatalin to Mikhail Sergeyevich, and I so want to believe what he writes! The letter was written a year ago.

Dear Mikhail Sergeyevich!
I learned with bitterness and an indomitable desire to fight on about what took place at the Plenum. You know that I don't like paying compliments to my superiors. But I want to tell you that I respect you and am sincerely fond of you and am ready to go with you to the end. Don't pay any attention to the 'right-wingers'. By virtue of a profound historical misunderstanding, they consider themselves to be communists, but they are in fact political opportunists who have no right to speak in the name of the people. Life will discard them, and the people will talk of them with scorn. Pay no attention either to the hysterics of the 'Left-radicals'. Not in the plebeian sense, but in the real sense of the word, I am perhaps one of the most 'left' people in the USSR. But you are carrying out on the whole the only realistic programme for the salvation of genuine socialism and of our country. If you want to know my opinion about ways of investing your programme with a more consistent character, I will be glad to oblige. Make a show of calm and decisiveness at the Congress of Deputies. It is your main support. Lenin was not afraid to conclude the treaty of Brest-Litovsk. React philosophically to the irresponsible decision of the Lithuanian

Communist Party. On January 3rd I shall return from a trip abroad (I am preparing a major long-term project on East-West relations), and I am ready to perform any tasks you may give me. May these words help, however slightly, to improve your mental equilibrium. Convey my sincere greetings to Raisa Maksimovna. I wish you and your family a happy New Year. We have no choice: we shall prevail.
Yours ever, Academician Stanislav Sergeyevich Shatalin.

Here's a photograph with us all together. The photographer was the corresponding member of the Soviet Academy of Science Georgi Khosroyevich Shakhnazarov. According to him the great merit of the photo lies in the fact that nobody has another like it: news photographers are not as a rule invited into such a narrow circle, even in the time of Glasnost. Yes, today Perestroika is probably going through its period of greatest strain. Various contradictory and totally opposed processes and forces have become interwoven. And in the centre of this gigantic whirlwind is the President of the USSR and General Secretary of the Central Committee of the CPSU and the person closest to me. Will we be able to come out of the whirlwind with honour; will we be able to create a life worthy of modern man, to revive the best that is in us and preserve the best that is around us? Mikhail Sergeyevich lives in a state of incredible tension. Six years of daily, selfless work, in the fullest sense of the word. The years have merged into one endless working day. I never see him back home before ten or eleven o'clock at night. And he always arrives home with a pile of papers. He often works till two and sometimes three o'clock in the morning. On foreign trips his programmes are extremely compressed and intense. Talks, the signing of documents, dozens of meetings, and events – everything worked out to the hour, to the last minute of his stay in the country. Members of delegations, newspaper men and other people accompanying him on trips know it very well. He never manages to sleep more than four or five hours a night during such trips. In addition, one has to bear in mind his physical state because of the changes of climate and the different time zones. Moreover, Mikhail Sergeyevich has never allowed himself the luxury of having, not just a day or two, but even a few hours for him to adapt to new conditions after a long flight.

— I have noticed that foreign trips now take place mostly on a Saturday or Sunday. Previously the time taken by such trips was measured in days; now they are measured in hours. In Spain he spent thirty hours; in Italy six or seven.

— That's correct. But the amount that is squeezed into such visits increases in geometric progression. Even during his holiday, he practically never succeeds in cutting himself off from work. It is on holiday that he always writes his main forthcoming speeches. That was how he wrote his book on Perestroika. And, most important, never for a minute, wherever he is, does he lose contact with Moscow. I calculated that in August 1990, in the twenty days' holiday he managed to get in Yalta, he had an average of seventeen urgent, pressing, telephone calls every day. It was then, just before the end of our holiday, that Mikhail Sergeyevich said to me: 'We've

got the most difficult time ahead of us. There is going to be political fighting... political squabbles... it's very alarming... You see,
it will inevitably affect the economic situation and the solution
of our economic problems. Our super-problem today is that we
mustn't give in to the conservatives: we would never get out of that.
But we mustn't surrender the fate of the country and its future to
cowboys. They would ruin everything. We shall carry on step by
step. Perhaps not every step will be the right one; they won't all hit
the target. But they have to be taken!' I know the pain and concern
that he is going through. It is not easy; it is never easy for an honest
man. It is doubly so for a man who has taken upon himself such a
burden of responsibility for his country and his people. A man who
is aware of his debt to people's faith, a humanist, and a democrat
by nature, equally exposed and receptive to people's happiness and
sorrow.

— *Your husband has enviable self-possession. What is his secret?*
— People often speak of his self-control and his tolerance. But
for other people – and there are some like that – it has nothing to
do with self-possession but rather 'a lack of decisiveness'. Those are
the people who, with provocative intentions, declare that policy is
not made with shaky hands. Those are dangerous people, thrown
up to the surface by our stormy times. But let us return to your
question. I once heard Mikhail Sergeyevich reply to that question
himself. It was in Finland at a lunch given by Mr Koivisto. In a sort
of joking way Mikhail Sergeyevich then gave three 'reasons'. The

first was that he had to thank his parents for having handed down to him the genetic capacity for self-control. As the second reason he named me. I have to thank Raisa Maksimovna, he said, for her help, support, and loyalty. The third was his faith in the correctness of the path he had chosen and the aim he had set himself. I believe, Georgi Vladimirovich, that the third reason is the most important: his sense of the justice, importance, and necessity of what was started in 1985. What can deprive a strong man of his courage is, in my view, above all the loss of faith and doubts about its truth. I think that's it.

— *You know, he repeated practically the same view in a recent very frank and informal interview on Soviet television.*
— Yes, you are right. And I, of course, also watched and heard that interview. I will not conceal the fact that I was very pleased that, among the three reasons he gave for his self-possession he again named me – he didn't forget me. I would add to the factors named by Mikhail Sergeyevich one more which is essential for an understanding, as you say, of his self-possession, tolerance, and self-control. It is very important. For him all people are human beings and personalities. He never asserts his own dignity by trampling on the dignity of other people. That has been a characteristic of him throughout his life. Never in his life has he humiliated the people next to him so as to make himself taller. Never. And it is because of that that you hear him say things like: 'You can't agree with everything he says, of course, but he's a working man', 'he

has his own opinion and so forth. Or 'one must, of course, give it some thought', 'there is something reasonable in all that'. Or 'in principle we could accept it'. This is not a case of diplomatic etiquette, and certainly not of timidity, indecisiveness, or uncertainty. And not even of any special upbringing. It is an inborn respect for human beings, about which I have spoken. You know, in the family he listens to everyone as an equal, from the eighty-year-old to the three-year-old. I have no doubts about Mikhail Sergeyevich's moral strength. My worries concern something else, and I think millions of women, wives and mothers, will understand me. I am extremely worried today about his health. I would like to bring this meeting to an end, Georgi Vladimirovich, by answering your question: what do I understand by happiness? It is very simple and very complicated. It is an eternal question, one as complex and as many-sided as life itself. I know one thing: you can't be happy if you are alone – if nobody needs you. I have in front of me a message of congratulation on the occasion of Women's Day, the 8th of March, which I have just received.

Dear Raisa Maksimovna,

However hard it is for you and Mikhail Sergeyevich in these desperate times you may rest assured that the efforts made in the last six years to transform and improve our country have given it a simpler, more sincere image, in harmony with the concepts of honesty, morality and humanity. It is difficult, even impossible in the course of six years to bring the process of Perestroika to completion. But I know that all your thoughts, and all your feelings and all that you have done together in these years had only one aim – to serve the country.

Nikolai Gubenko.

The second is a note from Georgi Khosroyevich Shakhnazarov.

Dear Raisa Maksimovna,
I send you my heartfelt congratulations on the 8th of March. An amazing fate has befallen you – both a happy one and in some ways an unkind one. But you are taking both its gifts and its blows with great human dignity. If marriages are really made in heaven God tried to give Mikhail Sergeyevich a companion in life in accordance with the mission he was destined for.

Yours sincerely, Shakhnazarov.

Perhaps that is happiness, Georgi Vladimirovich? Or... Here is one of the gifts that I hold very dear – Vanity Fair by Thackeray. It's a first edition, published in London in 1848. It was presented to me by Mrs. Margaret Thatcher. This work of an outstanding novelist ends with the question: 'Which of us is happy in this world?'

The work was finished. I was escorted downstairs, right to the front porch where a car was awaiting, and I kissed my hostess's hand. She remained at the porch where there was also a feeling of spring. The house behind her was lit up only in places: no expensive illuminations. Before walking to the car, I tried to impress the picture on my memory: the house, the glass door and the woman standing on the threshold.

Yes, I had read that in the West Raisa Gorbacheva had been described as 'the Kremlin's secret weapon', thus suggesting that personal charm is also capable of producing entirely tangible political dividends. But I cannot get out of my head the scene I witnessed outside the miners' club in Donetsk: in a friendly way Raisa Gorbacheva takes by the hand a woman, apparently a working woman, who wants to say something but just can't push her way through to where the top people are and leads her into the circle of heated political and industrial discussion. I can't get it out of my head probably because that scene was repeated so often before my own eyes. Not only in Donetsk, not only in Sverdlovsk, or in Nizhny Tagil. And so I am now thinking on my way back into Moscow: and in the Kremlin itself? Whose 'weapon' is she in the Kremlin itself? – for it is certainly a fact that even there she is not just a porcelain figure.

Today, when I know more about Raisa Gorbacheva than anyone else outside her immediate circle, the answer to that question is clearer to me. However elegant, and even refined, she may be in the corridors of power, humanising them in her way and making them more attractive, smarter and even more interesting for the public at large, she is invisibly accompanied, it seems to me, by the hardships of her childhood, the blind cripples singing not very soberly on railway platforms after the war, and by the woman from a miners' area harassed by our current humiliating shortages and disarray. If Raisa Gorbacheva is known in the West as a 'weapon of the Kremlin', it seems to me that in the Kremlin itself she is a 'weapon' for those who have no weapons. May God grant it! I recently read somewhere a very interesting report.

A group of specialists made a study of the contemporary popular idea of female beauty – only I don't know what kind of specialists they were – in female beauty or statistics. They collected the facts together, studied them and arrived at some generalisations that were really startling. The ideal turned out to be the average. A face made up of exactly the average nose, the most ordinary lips, eyebrows, and so forth. Symmetry rules, not only over the real world, but also over our imagination, it appears. The less individuality there is the greater the attraction. Is there anything wrong with individuality – at least in the popular idea of beauty? In Russia, out of a sense of self-preservation, the wife of the top leader usually did not step a millimetre outside his shadow. The more she kept in the shadow the better. Raisa Gorbacheva deliberately keeps away from any part of the official power structure: if she plays any part, it is only in social work and even then, not in a prominent role. I cannot say that she ever oversteps the political boundaries set by her husband or speaks out of turn. She does not, and she is extremely careful in that. It seems to me that even the rhythm of her speech, especially on television, is conditioned not only by her many years' work as a teacher but also by a strict inner self-control.

The boundaries coincide, and all the same you can see a quite obvious, strange luminescence round the edges. True, I would not call this the Raisa Gorbacheva phenomenon but the Gorbachevs' phenomenon. She permits herself an individuality, expressed primarily in a sense of her own worth, while he treats that feeling with invariable quiet respect. That is their phenomenon – the phenomenon of the preservation of individuality. I have noticed that she doesn't like the empty chatter of society. She keeps the thread of any conversation firmly in her hands. She reacts sympathetically when you hit upon the right word or some worthwhile thought, but when something you say is off target, she reacts with even greater sharpness. Altogether the woman whose book you are now reading is not one of those with whom you can relax mentally when you are talking – it is as well to keep the mind in good working condition. She is also a woman who does not turn her eyes away from the truth: to know nothing, see nothing, hear nothing. She does not turn away, and she prefers to call a spade a spade. I am not sure whether, for all the President's democratic ways, there are many people in the top Soviet establishment who are telling him the direct truth. But that she is one of them, of that I am convinced because I heard it said more than once. Even though it is probably more painful and more difficult for her than for anybody else to voice that straight truth. There may sometimes be salvation in a lie. It seems to me that she believes that only the truth, however bitter it may be, can be salutary. That corresponds more with her character and her past.

My Hopes

I am writing these concluding lines of the book late in the evening.
Vremya, the main news programme on Soviet television, has just
ended. It included an item having direct relation to my last meeting
with Raisa Gorbacheva. Directing my attention to a pile of letters and
telegrams sent to her husband on his sixtieth birthday, she had said:

— And one fellow, a pensioner and beekeeper from Ukraine,
apparently sent Mikhail Sergeyevich a ton of honey as a gift.
— *Why 'apparently'?*
— Well, I received notification – we had to take delivery of a
ton of honey. I thought: they've probably made a mistake. Instead
of a kilogram someone has written a 'ton'.
— *Let's tell the story of the honey in the book – it's interesting.*
— I'm not sure about that; in any case we ought to make quite
sure: maybe it really was some kind of mistake.

Judging by the report that appeared in the Vremya programme,
it was not a mistake. Raisa Gorbacheva took the honey to an old folks'
home. She sat there among them, chatting, replying to questions and
for good company drank tea with the honey that had been redirected
to the home on her husband's instructions. I know that another presi-

dential gift had found a place in that Moscow home for the elderly: a luxurious television set that Li Peng presented to Mikhail Gorbachev in Peking and which Gorbachev ordered to be handed over to the old folk. I had learnt earlier that day that there had been no mistake about the honey when I happened to run into the person whom the President had instructed to deliver some of the honey to a children's home that treated children who had cerebral illnesses and had been rejected by their parents at birth. The 'presidential honey' was in fact divided into three parts: for the children's home, for the old folks' home, and for the Moscow children's Republican hospital, of which, as has already been said, Mrs Gorbacheva is a patron. In general, the conclusion of the book and a postscript to it should by rights be written by the author herself – Raisa Gorbacheva. But I am writing these lines especially since seeing on the screen the concentrated and self-controlled features of the person I had only recently been talking to, and hearing her, in words so unusual for her and for Soviet television in general, send Easter greetings to the old folk. These are difficult, even bitter, times for the President. Perhaps the Ukrainian beekeeper is a distant descendant of that same Rudy Panko about whom Gogol wrote his unforgettable Evenings on a Farm near Dikanka *and in his simplicity does not himself suspect how symbolic his sincere gift was. Raisa Gorbacheva has already explained why she decided to produce this book. The book is an explanation of her own self and, while addressing herself to the foreign reader, she of course sees out of the corner of her eyes our own, Russian reader. Who knows – perhaps it is actually a try-out before writing a book directed exclusively at the Soviet public? She wants to*

be understood in her own country. I saw, when she decided to write this book, that Raisa Gorbacheva had to step beyond the limits of her own character, her own reserved nature, and ultimately of tradition.

Unless my memory lets me down, only one Soviet 'first lady', that being Nadezhda Krupskaya, has ever undertaken anything like it. She acted contrary to tradition, although it is precisely for ignoring some of this country's oldest traditions that she is most often criticised. To.be understood means to a certain extent to be supported. I am impressed as a person by the sincere impulse that motivates Raisa Gorbacheva. Moreover, I am profoundly convinced that, for all Mikhail Gorbachev's exclusivity, he is not an accidental but a completely logical and necessary figure in our contemporary history. And his exclusivity is probably in the fact that he has detected with unusual sharpness the general direction in which things were moving – from a world that is breaking up and divided and fraught with the prospect of self-destruction to the concept of a single world – and the latent readiness of society to move in this direction; he injected into that movement an exclusive tempo – with all the associated consequences. He did so also because he realised that he had very little time left. As I was re-reading V. O. Klyuchevsky I came across the fact that Peter the Great, the most resolute and dramatic reformer of Russia, ruled the country for thirty-six years. He became Tsar in 1082 and ruled from 1689 to 1725. That's how many years it appears are needed in Russia for achieving cardinal reforms! Gorbachev realised that he would not have thirty-six years of rule, if only because it was not for that that he made a final break with Stalinism. All of us in this country are waiting for him to produce results – 'here and now'. As the father of four children, despite the general and quite natural impatience, I would agree: let our children enjoy the results, so long as they come. Regard this as the pardonable digression of a reporter in the unfamiliar field of political generalisation. Now I hand over the microphone to Raisa Gorbacheva:

— So, Georgi Vladimirovich, today we have our sixth and final meeting, as you and I agreed. Were they conversations, interviews or just time for recollections? I don't know. You will remember that I did not agree at once to do them. Why? I have spoken about that at the beginning of the book; that was where we started. Mikhail Sergeyevich and I are very fond of ballads. Perhaps that is typical of our generation – I don't know. Amongst the ballads we like most is one of which a recording can often be heard in our home, an old Russian love song by A. Abaza to the words of Turgenev. It is almost the only love song Turgenev wrote. It is sung by Nikolai Gedda – 'A misty morning, a grey morning, the mournful fields covered in snow.' It's a beautiful love song! As for Gedda's voice, I don't even know what adjective to choose: beautiful, enchanting, magical or amazing. A love song puts you in the mood for recollecting. His hero himself recollects. But, Georgi Vladimirovich, our life with its daily affairs, problems and cares, and our hours, days, and years full to bursting – has no time for reminiscences. I have heard Mikhail Sergeyevich say many times: 'I always wanted, and I still want to write. But there has never been time for it and there still isn't.' As for me, I was beset by doubts: ought I to give interviews and talk about myself – why? Or talk about Mikhail Sergeyevich? But no one can talk about him, what he has been through and is still going through, better, and more truly, than he can himself. About what he has done and how and why. But in life there is on every side a 'division of labour': some people do things; others write about them and criticise. Everyone has his own destiny. But that is by the way. And now, Georgi Vladimirovich, I do not regret having had these talks with you. I don't regret it, although these four months – as far as I recall our first meeting was some time at the end of December last year – these four months have proved to be for me physically, intellectually, and emotionally difficult. It was also because they coincided with a grave, perhaps the most difficult, period in the life of our country and in Mikhail Sergeyevich's work. And because, for the first time in my life, I came to a halt, so to speak, and relived my own life. I have been trying to recall facts and events from my past.

And, quite unexpectedly for me, out of some quite unthinkable depths of my memory, these episodes, happenings and facts from my past began to roll out like little beads and link up, string themselves together and turn into a very long, endless thread of reminiscences. Such an experience probably happens in every person's life. I have discovered that there is a great deal more that I want to talk about: about my family, about the people with whom my life is linked and about what I have seen. And about the letters that people send me. Previously it never occurred to me to talk about these things. And again. It turned out emotionally not to be so easy to deal with this avalanche of reminiscences. I really did seem to be living through it all over again. As I told you, I wept as I recalled this or that event and my heart ached. I lived through it all again in those four months. Finally, I tried to understand and work out the meaning of what happened and what is happening now. That is also very important for me. These four months included so many extraordinary events and so many very important decisions. So many changes took place in the country and in ourselves. It was a truly critical and crucial period. Perestroika is not a barren fig tree: there is fruit on it. But there are also bad things that it has exposed or perhaps itself caused involuntarily. I dream of the time when they will no longer exist, when Perestroika will begin to yield tangible and rich harvests, so that everybody will feel – and this is the most important for me – that they are inwardly more at peace with themselves, that it is firmer underfoot, and better both at table and at home. I want my husband, along with his supporters and associates, to carry what they have started to a successful conclusion and to see for themselves the real fruits of the tremendous transformation they have undertaken. I want particularly to say something about my husband's colleagues, about the people who initiated the changes with him and who are now still at his side, battling along together through all the obstacles, mistakes, and prejudices.

There are among them people whom I know well and there are others whom I know less well, who are younger and who set out later on this thorny path so necessary for the country and society. But I am grateful to every one of them for the active help they have given my husband and their loyalty to the common cause. I wish all of them well. I wish them and their families not to give up and not to lose the strength of spirit that is nourished by the importance of the cause they are serving. The stabilisation of the market for consumer goods, of the monetary system, the land reform, the beginnings of phasing out state control and free enterprise are gathering force. If they are not upset by political cataclysms, we have the right to expect change for the better. And the sooner the better! On the 13th of March 1991 our country held the first referendum in its history. Eighty per cent of the Soviet citizens registered on the electoral roll went to the polls to answer the question: 'Do you consider it necessary to preserve the Union of Soviet Socialist Republics as a renewed federation of equal sovereign republics in which the rights and freedoms of persons of any nationality will be fully guaranteed?' To this, 76.4 percent said: "Yes, let there be a great, renewed, democratic Soviet Union.' I believe and hope that Soviet people will have the strength, self-control, and patriotism and – I consider this very important – the common sense to overcome all the difficulties and obstacles on the path to such an end. I would like the Soviet Union, while passing through the crucible of renewal, to remain a union – of peoples, republics, and ideals. We cannot allow to be cast to the winds the priceless, centuries-old moral and social experience of so many scores of languages and peoples living together and collaborating. It seems to me that that experience will still be of value to everyone, the whole of human civilization.

Who knows – perhaps it is precisely that centuries-old mutual attraction and interpenetration that constitutes what in olden days they called an 'emanation of the spirit' – from every one of the peoples inhabiting the Union – including the Russian people? My hope is for peace. There is nothing more frightful or more inhuman than war. The calamity of war, wherever, whenever and upon whomever it descends, is a tragedy for the whole of humanity. Only a few years back practically every time Mikhail Sergeyevich met with the people you could hear the cry: 'So long as there's no war!' And in the 1960s and 1970s even I, still a very young woman sociologist going with my questionnaires from one village house to another, would be asked anxiously, especially by mothers of children: 'And there will be no war?' I would ask them about their pay, their work, their children, their families, and their needs, about how often they visited the cinema, the club, or friends – the questionnaire included such questions – and they would reply: 'So long as there's not a war!' Nowadays such cries and such fundamental questions are not heard. The threat of a worldwide conflagration, threat of annihilation, that was felt keenly for decades by every home in our country and every family, has been averted. For my country, which has for centuries been at the junction of two worlds, that is a change in its perception of the world and its attitude towards it: from a constant state of anxiety to the acquisition of a sense of security. The world is no longer split in two. For Russia, for the Soviet Union and for all the peoples on this Earth peace has become more durable. I am proud of this because, after all, it is to a large extent thanks to the political efforts and statesmanship of my husband. I am proud of the Nobel Peace Prize he was awarded. I am, of course, worried, very worried, lest there should develop a confrontational situation within our country. Such a conflict, destructive and senseless, could develop into a tragedy not only for our people but for the whole of humanity.

In a peaceful future lies the happiness and wellbeing of the people of this Earth, the happiness of our country, our children, and grandchildren, including the President's family too. March has just come to an end. It is a special month in Mikhail Sergeyevich's life. In March 1985 he was elected General Secretary of the Central Committee of the CPSU. In March 1990 he became the country's first nationally elected President. On the 2nd of March he celebrated his sixtieth birthday. We received several thousand warm and much appreciated congratulations and good wishes from all kinds of people and from every corner of the country.

Dear Mikhail Sergeyevich.

Congratulations on your birthday. I wish you from the bottom of my heart the very best, good health and happiness, and steadfastness. After all, it is so terribly difficult to be the President of our unfortunate country. We are endlessly grateful to you for your incredible achievement in ridding us of fear and giving us hope and freedom. We grew up under Brezhnev and regarded everyone at the seat of power with revulsion and hatred. But we have faith in you. And when the nationwide presidential election takes place, we shall vote for you.

With the most profound respect – Lev Isakovich Sigal,
Marina Valentinovna Morozova, Moscow.

Good day, Mikhail Sergeyevich.

Don't be upset because you have reached sixty. It is not very much. Every day that you live can be compared to years. The good seeds you have sown with your heart and mind in our sinful land will inevitably yield a good harvest and much joy. Where can I send you some white dried mushrooms?

The Chakushkin family, Cheboksary.

Dear Mikhail Sergeyevich.

Sincere birthday greetings. Courage to you, dear fellow, in the struggle for justice and happiness for the people.

Communists, members of the Komsomol and Pioneers, the
teachers, and the whole staff of school No. 64 in Stavropol.

Dear Mikhail Sergeyevich.

I offer you my heartfelt congratulations on your sixtieth birthday. First of all, I wish you good health and strength of mind. Don't give in, and don't retreat. I can see that you are having difficulties. Your political opponents, and not only the political ones, hide themselves behind democratic phraseology and are fighting a fierce battle with you and your team. They do not use only political methods. Unfortunately, they have succeeded in literally fooling a section of the population of our country, using for their mercenary ends the economic difficulties and the conflicts between the nationalities which, I am sure, arose through the fault of those 'democrats'. Once again, I wish you good health, success, and happiness in your private life.

Your firm supporter, Kozlov, Smolensk.

Dear Mikhail Sergeyevich.

We congratulate you from the bottom of our hearts on your sixtieth birthday. We wish you good health and success in your laborious efforts to revive our Motherland. Genuine workers are wholly on your side. We support you and have faith in you. You should know that you are our hope. We embrace and kiss you. May God help you.

Alla Karabanova and Nina Nazarova,
telegraphists at the Central Post Office, Moscow.

Dear and deeply respected Mikhail Sergeyevich.

Sincere congratulations on your birthday. The very best and soundest of health to you. Please hold on in the face of lies and extremism. Sincerest compliments for your patience and courage. Remember that your nobility of character is our human hope. We support you with all our hearts.

M. Shask, Leningrad.

Dear Mikhail Sergeyevich.

I congratulate you on your birthday. I wish you good health and success in your difficult task. I would like you always to be president and to fight for peace. Come and be our guest in Petrozavodsk and we can go fishing together.

Misha Torchik, nine years old, Petrozavodsk.

Dear Mikhail Sergeyevich.

We congratulate you on your birthday and wish you success in your difficult work.

Students at Lvov State University.

There are two more letters, to which I would like to draw special attention:

Dear Mikhail Sergeyevich.

I send you warmest greetings on your birthday. In my old age fate gave me the possibility of meeting you, a person at the very centre of world events. This was exceptionally valuable for me. I regard it as a gift. Lite has mixed up a great deal (but not everything!). It is difficult to shield oneself from its winds, we are all exposed. Born in the provinces of Russia, continue to believe in the man of the soil. He is closer to heaven, and therefore stronger, than men of the air. I send you heartfelt greetings and wish you health, strength of will and long life to carry out the task that has been placed on you.

With deep respect, Georgi Vasilyevich Sviridov
[the foremost Soviet composer].

To the President of the USSR, M. S. Gorbachev.

Deeply respected and dear Mikhail Sergeyevich. Permit me to congratulate you sincerely and from my heart on the sixtieth anniversary of your birth. I pray that the Lord may increase your strength and that your heart should always retain its wisdom, full of peace and love. May your work as head of the great Soviet state be blessed and may you succeed in strengthening the unity of our peoples in all their variety and the enrichment of each other's life. I believe that with God's help the great cause that you have initiated for the renewal of our Motherland on democratic, law–based, and moral principles will arrive at its beneficent conclusion despite all difficulties. I assure you that our prayers and our efforts are an inseparable part of this great historical process. Please convey my sincere congratulations to your partner in life, Raisa Maksimovna, and all those close to you.

With deep respect, Aleksi,
Patriarch of Moscow, and All Russia.

We also received a great many flowers on his birthday. Splendid roses, magnificent orchids, messengers from the heart, pinks, tulips from the steppes. Beautiful blue irises – the colour of hope. Patches of crimson anthuriums and yellow, lilac, and white freesias. By tradition, Georgi Vladimirovich, I give Mikhail Sergeyevich violets on his birthday. The violet is a delicate, graceful flower that smells of the open air and the spring. It is for us a symbol of youth and reminds us of the first year of our married life when, for the first time after our marriage, Mikhail Sergeyevich and I travelled down to his native village. Have you come across that southern tradition – the little garden in front of the parents' cottage and the scent of night violets growing in it? From that time the violet became my invariable present. On behalf of his mother and mine and on behalf of our children, grandchildren, brothers, and sisters, and on my own behalf, of course, I said to Mikhail Sergeyevich on his sixtieth birthday: 'Thank you for the fact of your being, for being what you are, and for the fact that we are beside you.' I hope that his health will not abandon my husband or let him down. After all, he has just turned sixty. I hope that my children and grandchildren will keep well. I hope that fate will grant me too the strength to be with them as long as possible and alongside my husband, helping him and sharing every heartbeat. We have had everything in our life – joy and sorrow, tremendously hard work and colossal nervous strain, successes and failures, poverty, hunger, and material well–being. He and I have gone through it all while still preserving the original basis of our relationship and our devotion to our ideas and ideals. I believe that strength of spirit, courage and firmness will help my husband now to withstand the unprecedented ordeals of the most difficult stage in our life.

I hope.

Moscow
December 1990 – April 1991

THESE DAYS WERE HORRIBLE

From the Diary of the President's Wife

Raisa, What Hurts My Heart

Foros: 73 Hours Under House Arrest

August 19th–21st, 1991 – These were tragic days in the history of our state, the days of Perestroika. August 18th–21st – These were days of imprisonment, the internment of the President of the USSR and his family in Foros.

On August 20th, 1937, the Troika of the NKVD Department of the West Siberian Territory decided to shoot my grandfather, a man whose only occupation in life was working as a farmer. He was charged with the following: counter-revolutionary agitation aimed at corrupting the collective–farming discipline, discrediting the policy of the party, government, the Stakhanovite movement, and the defence loan. The accused, citizen, Pyotr Stepanovich Porada, as it appears from the protocol of interrogation, did not plead guilty: he never broke labour disciplines anywhere, he was never a part of any gangs, counter-revolutionary organisations, uprisings, and he did not conduct agitation against the Soviet regime. In the end, the Soviet government gave him some land. Though what's also true is that in 1932, the government had already taken away everything: the house, the land, and the family… The decision of "Troika" was carried out, and only decades later was there rehabilitation.

In September, at a meeting with a group of newspaper editors, Mikhail Sergeyevich mentioned my notebook whilst answering questions. Yes, it was the one about me in Foros. However, quite frankly, it wasn't exactly a diary: there were no careful, day-to-day entries. What I kept were quick, small, brief notes made at different times, on different occasions. The only exceptions were on August 18th, 19th, 20th and 21st, when I kept more detailed notes. The Foros notes have already come to my aid three times: when I gave my interviews to the *Trud* newspaper and the *Vremya* programme, and when I, as a witness, testified to prosecutors. Now I think that these notes in the notebook may be of some interest in recreating the overall picture of the events in August.

August 3rd, Saturday

We're going on vacation after all. Mikhail Sergeyevich had decided: while the Union Treaty is being prepared for signing, that we should go on vacation. If we don't go now, who knows when we will be able to go next. Rest is important after all! We packed for the trip with Irina. However, I did not feel particularly happy. There is some anxiety in my heart. I'm always waiting for something... At 19:00, Mikhail Sergeyevich returned from work. He confirmed that tomorrow we will fly to the Crimea. Adding: "It will last as long as is possible..."

August 4th, Sunday

We flew from Vnukovo–II. Everyone who usually saw us off gathered in the airport pavilion. Boldin and Pavlov were the last to arrive after us. The conversations we had were mainly about the forthcoming signing of the Union Treaty. Mikhail Sergeyevich said that he would definitely participate in its signing. Irina and I noticed that Yanayev had eczema on his hands. Among our loved ones there was a person who also suffered from this kind of disease for a very long time but was cured rather quickly, quite unexpectedly by means of traditional medicine. On the plane, we agreed that as soon as we return from the vacation, I would talk with Yanayev, share the address of this person, and advise to turn to him for help. Landing at a small military airport near Sevastopol. We met with the leadership of Ukraine, Crimea. They invited us to dine with them. A traditional meeting. But this time there were many new "details" that were discussed, of course, none of this was accidental. Our greeters, excluding the military and the Chekists, wore short-sleeved summer shirts. When we met them before, on official business: they only wore suits. Usually, the first words spoken at the table are by Girenko, secretary of the Central Committee of the Communist Party of Ukraine. This time however, Kravchuk spoke first. Instead of greetings and wishes for good health, Leonid Makarovich spoke at length about the place of the President of the USSR in the country, as well as the attitude of the left and right towards him. In the end, only recommendations for the President followed.

Then there was silence at the table... The conversation switched to the situation in the Crimea, in Ukraine, in the party. The always-confident Girenko was visibly depressed and could not hide his inner irritation. The commander of the Black Sea Fleet, Admiral Khronopulo, loudly and cheerfully made a toast to the health of the Supreme Commander of the Armed Forces of the Soviet Union and assured those sitting at the table were ready "at any hour, any minute, to fulfil all his orders." And somehow unexpectedly: the young, recently elected secretary of the Crimean Party Committee, L. I. Grach said kind, warm words about our family, about me. A natural reminder that the President came on this vacation to rest...

August 5th, Monday

It's hot. The air temperature is 30°C, the water in the sea is 25°C. The trees – pines, thuja, juniper, birches – dried up and crusted. Flowers too. There are signs of a drought. A line of mountains in the haze. Above the sea, on the pier, the beach – there are seagulls. Nastyonka pesters the adults for attention: "What is the Black Sea like? The sea is blue though... can't you see?" We were approved of our daily routine: in the morning – we do gymnastics, swimming, medical procedures.

In the afternoon Mikhail Sergeyevich works. In the evening – an hour's walk, and then again, some more swimming in the sea. Another hour or two later – depending on the circumstances – there is usually work and a cultural programme: a film, TV, a walk or some meetings. Sleep is the highest priority. Irina, Anatoly, Ksenia, Anastasia all have their own programme – as they said, it's a lot more "free", less creative, but much better for their bodies. I read an article by A. Latynina in the Literary Magazine. Meanwhile, Mikhail Sergeyevich read Avrekh's book "P. A. Stolypin and the Gate of Reforms in Russia."

August 6ᵗʰ, Tuesday

It's a little cooler. Cloudy. We are on a walk. Walking is easy and pleasant. "I will write–" Mikhail Sergeyevich says, "–a book or an article, whatever happens, it'll discuss: was a restructuring necessary? Are we headed for disaster? Have I sold out to US imperialism? I think it will work out..." And one more thing: "Tension is growing in the country. It worries me. It is necessary to move to reforms faster – but it isn't working. The anti-crisis programme is stalling. There is a power paralysis. I hope for the Union Treaty. The talk in the press about the 'strong hand' resonates in society – a very serious symptom. I want to write about all this in an article." And then: "Apparently, on the 19ᵗʰ, I will fly out to Moscow to sign the Union Treaty and hold the Federation Council... Dementei called today, he expressed the wish that Belarus participates in the signing on August 20ᵗʰ.

August 7ᵗʰ, Wednesday

There are much fewer vacationers and visitors in the Crimea today than in previous years at this time. It is a lot more difficult to shop for meat products in Yalta. There are few vegetables and fruits – and this is the season for them too. Everything is expensive in the city market... More expensive than in Moscow. Anatoly has some "water-themed" hobbies: water-skiing and watching the sea. He studies the sea surface with binoculars. Mikhail Sergeyevich reads several books at once. Today, he's reading one donated by the author, an American political scientist named Robert Tucker, called "Stalin. The Path to Power." The female half of the family are diligently "tanning" on the shore.

August 8th, Thursday

Mikhail Sergeyevich talked on the phone with S. Niyazov and A. Mutalibov about the Union Treaty. He told me: "Today, the most important thing is to preserve the union state." In the newspapers: discussion of materials of the Russian Communist Party Plenum are happening, B. Yeltsin's decree on departisation of enterprises, institutions, and organisations. Several speeches and interviews by N. Nazarbayev. For some reason, while walking, we remembered the war years. Mikhail Sergeyevich said that then, as a 10-year-old boy, he was assigned the first job in his life – a postman. He worked for two days, then they replaced him. They put a woman with children in his place. She needed to feed the children somehow. He remembered how he worked for several days in a construction team with other "boys." An adult man was watching them. He remembered how this man used to swindle the boys. They would sit down at the dinner table, and he would begin to tell jokes, tossing something out of the ordinary. Whilst the boys were laughing, this 'joker' would fish out all of the pieces of meat from the shared bowl, leaving the boys with nothing but the remaining liquid...

1942... On July 31st the last retreating units of the Red Army passed through Privolnoye. And on August 3rd the Germans entered the village. The family house was located on the very edge of the village. Three boys, three close friends – silently huddled up, standing against the wall of the hut. They decided: to not be afraid, not to hide… Across the road, Grandfather Andrey did not let the Germans into his hut. There, a young, beautiful female soldier, the 24-year-old Aunt Sania – their father's sister – gave birth to a blue–eyed girl, a sister…

August 10th, Saturday

Group weighing. That's how I would sum up the first five days. The whole family, with the exception of Nastya, were on a diet. First, a 45-minute swim in the sea. In the evening we had guests: Leonid Makarovich Kravchuk and his wife Antonina Mikhailovna, a teacher at the Department of Political Economy of Kiev University. They are also in the Crimea on vacation. The atmosphere at the table was relaxed, very 'holiday-like'. They made toasts. They talked about anything and everything: about the meeting between Leonid Makarovich and George W. Bush, the positions of republican leaders 'on current painful problems', about politics and morality, 'party bureaucracy', about the situation in the student environment, about teaching staff, about my book that is being prepared for publication…

The evening was nice. We all dispersed quite late. Our family went out for a walk under a dark starry sky, which happens only in the south. The silhouettes of mountains. Lights. A searchlight beam in the sea. A conversation began about how leaders are born, to what extent this is determined by the personal qualities of a person, and to what extent by their situation and circumstances. There is evidence in history of how the environment and situation demand for certain personality traits that, under normal circumstances, are considered as weaknesses or even shortcomings.

August 13th, Tuesday

I. Karimov called Mikhail Sergeyevich: the leaders of the Central Asian republics are gathering in Tashkent. They decided to discuss economic, interethnic issues of the region. I am currently reading Roman Gul's story about Dzerzhinsky in *Moscow Magazine*. It's terrible: the Red Terror, the White Terror... Cruelty gives rise to more cruelty. The willingness of people to do these things enthrals me. Where does this violence root from? Who should be held responsible? The tyrant, Sharikov – 'human trash with a dog's heart' – who was brought out by special experiences in the name of improving the human race. And who 'brought out' those who carried out the bloody nightmares of those past years, and those who these days, call for revenge, is this not terror?

August 14th, Wednesday

Mikhail Sergeyevich had a long conversation with B. Yeltsin about the forthcoming signing of the Union Treaty. The position of Mikhail Sergeyevich: to maintain the Novo-Ogarevsk agreement. Ksyusha broke away from the 'swimming' ring. He started his first solo swims. The rest of our group had arrived. In the evening we met with fellow countrymen. Mikhail Sergeyevich asked about the changes in the Stavropol region, and about those with whom he had worked for many years.

August 15th, Thursday

Mikhail Sergeyevich has an exacerbation of lumbar sciatica, a backache. As always – unexpectedly: while walking, when climbing a mountain. They did some physiotherapy; they applied some ointment.

August 16th, Friday

It is difficult for Mikhail Sergeyevich to walk. He works in the office all day. They gave him a drug blockade.

August 17th, Saturday

On the evening of the 19th we fly to Moscow, on the 20th the signing of the Treaty happens. On the 21st – the Federation Council. Mikhail Sergeyevich says that 'a big, difficult, but absolutely necessary conversation is going ahead at the Federation Council. You may have to stay in Moscow longer.' We went out to the territory of our dacha, we walked: this medical procedure helps the body heal. He told me that he had invited N. V. Bagrov, the Chairman of the Supreme Council of Crimea, to fly to Moscow with us.

August 18th, Sunday

We went to the sea in the morning. We swam, Mikhail Sergeyevich sat and read. Now he is in the office – working. I check the mail, I read the newspapers. What is happening around the Union Treaty! Some are saying: that a bureaucratic, unitary state is being restored. Others are saying: the country is dying, crumbling, being torn to pieces, the provisions of the Treaty are vague, indefinite, unclear. Why have such a treaty? A message: The Central Committee of the CPSU proposed to expel A. Yakovlev from the party. He referred the question to the primary party organisation for consideration. Everything was done without the knowledge of Mikhail Sergeyevich. Aleksandr Nikolaevich filed an application for withdrawal from the party.

19:00 I must continue to take notes... Somewhere around five o'clock Mikhail Sergeyevich suddenly came into my room. Alarmed. "Something bad has happened," he says, "Maybe even terrible, Medvedev has now reported that Baklanov, Boldin, Shenin, Varennikov have arrived from Moscow." – "Who is he, the last one?" I ask. "The general, Yazov's deputy... They demand a meeting with me. They are already on the dacha's territory, near us. But I didn't invite anyone! I tried to find out what's wrong. I picked up the handset – one, two, three... All phones have been switched off. Do you understand?! All telephone communications – government, city, internal, even the red 'Kazbek' – all have been turned off! We're isolated! Is this some kind of plot? An arrest?" Then he said: "I will not go on any walks with them, strike any deals. I will not succumb to any threats, or blackmail." He paused and then added: "But all this can cost us dearly. Everyone, the whole family. We must be ready for anything..." The children were called. For some reason I asked for tea. Galina Afrikanovna – the cook, brought it to us. Naturally, no one began to drink it. They told Irina and Anatoly about what had happened. We learned from them that a few minutes ago the radio in the house went silent and the TV stopped working.

Then, as if appearing from thin air, Plekhanov stood at the central entrance of the house. He asked: "Where is Mikhail Sergeyevich? His comrades have come to see him." Anatoly replied: "I don't know. I think he's home." The children and I supported Mikhail Sergeyevich and his decision. Our opinion was the same: "We will stay with you." Mikhail Sergeyevich's meeting with the visitors took place in his office. For the whole time Anatoly, Irina and I were nearby, near the office doors. Are they arresting him? So suddenly? Will they take him away...? The 'visitors' left the office at about 18:00 without Mikhail Sergeyevich, on their own. Varennikov passed by without paying any attention to us. Boldin stopped in the distance. Baklanov and Shenin (I was sitting, the men were standing nearby) came up to me. They said: "Hello." Baklanov held out his hand. I did not answer the greeting, did not shake their hands. I asked: "Why did you come? What's happening?" I heard one phrase uttered by Baklanov: "There were necessary circumstances." Then they turned and together, the three of them, left.

Mikhail Sergeyevich exited the office. He held a piece of paper in his hands and handed it to me. He said, "The worst has come to be. An emergency committee has been set up. I was demanded to sign a Decree on the introduction of a state of emergency in the country, to transfer powers to Yanayev. When I refused, they offered me to resign. I demanded to urgently convene the Supreme Soviet of the USSR or the Congress of People's Deputies, so that I can resolve the issue of the need for a state of emergency and my presidency there. They said that I was arrested or would be arrested, but I didn't understand, Yeltsin… Here, on the piece of paper, there are names of the other members of the committee…" He was outraged, not only by the ultimatum of the visitors, but also by their impudence and intrusion. At a meeting with A. Chernyaev, he said that he called them "self-destroyers" and "murderers". "The country is in a difficult situation… The world will turn away… An economic and political blockade… This will be our tragic end." Medvedev also left with the "delegation" – the head of Mikhail Sergeyevich's personal bodyguard. Did he actually leave? Or was he taken away? Information from the security officers was contradictory. The main thing is that he did not express any protest, he did not go to the President or get into his car and leave. He only asked someone to collect his things and send them to Moscow…

They also said that Plekhanov wrote an order for his removal. No one was let out of the dacha after work. The only ones left today are, A. S. Chernyaev – Assistant to the President; Olga Vasilievna – Stenographer and Assistant secretary; Doctors; Service Staff. All of them – including those from the local service staff – are women who have families at home. All of their cars were sealed shut. They said that the plane on which Mikhail Sergeyevich was supposed to fly to Moscow tomorrow had been sent back. We are trying to hear something, to catch something with the help of a small Sony pocket transistor. What a blessing to have it with us! In the morning, while shaving, Mikhail Sergeyevich usually listens to *Mayak* on that same transistor. I took it with me to the Crimea. The stationary receiver available here in the residence does not receive reception on any band. The little Sony one is working though. But there are no special messages. Everything is as usual... We agreed that Anatoly will hide the transistor. And no one should know that we have it. Nobody. I will make more detailed notes. I can't sleep... I am tormented by the bitterness of the betrayal of the people who worked next to Mikhail Sergeyevich. In the afternoon, Yanayev asked Mikhail Sergeyevich on the phone when he would arrive in Moscow tomorrow. I found out the exact time of arrival is on the 19th. It said that he will meet the President at the airport.

By association, footage of a recently seen newsreel pops into my mind: Khrushchev's 70th birthday is being celebrated. The St. George Hall is full of tables... Brezhnev is presenting an award... such sweet-tongued words... saying that Khrushchev will be removed in a few months. What is happening now in the country, in Moscow? In the President's dacha near Moscow? And the people who are here with us... Who and what will they do in this situation? Oleg Anatolyevich – stationed here at the dacha, Plekhanov left him in charge of being the President's personal bodyguard – he said: "Mikhail Sergeyevich, we are with you." But will the guards protect us to the end, or will they follow the instructions of their leadership? What will those traitors do? Did Mikhail Sergeyevich become dangerous to them recently or was he always dangerous? In recent years, several people reported on documents fabricated in 1983–84 by the investigating authorities in order to accuse Mikhail Sergeyevich of bribes. Documents were handed over to the reception room of the Central Committee of the CPSU, from which it is clear that the investigators demanded that the defendants give false testimony. This was done, no doubt, on the orders of people 'of the highest rank in the country.' There is anxiety for my husband, for the fate of my children and grandchildren. It torments the soul.

August 19th, Monday

At about 7 o'clock in the morning, Anatoly and Irina caught a message on the transistor (the wavelength was not *Mayak*, it seems it was the World News Service or the BBC): a State Committee for the State of Emergency has been created, a state of emergency has been issued in certain regions of the country. They convey the call of the committee to compatriots, an appeal to the states of the world, the content of the decree was on the allocation of 15 acres of land for each person... And "due to the illness of the President of the USSR and the inability to fulfil his functions, vice–president Yanayev takes over his powers." So, all the documents were ready... Early in the morning, somewhere around 5 o'clock, Anatoly said that several large warships approached our bay. The guard ships approached the shore unusually, stood for about 50 minutes, and then moved away into the distance. What was that about? Was it a threat? Enforced isolation, even from the sea? There is no mail, no newspapers. They said: "And there won't be any." A field communications officer has been detained since yesterday here on the territory. The radio is silent, the TV is off. Anatoly is trying to make an antenna for a stationary receiver with the men from the security. Boris Ivanovich – who was also there – found a piece of wire. However, nothing can be achieved. Through the senior security officer, Mikhail Sergeyevich sent a message to Moscow, addressed to Generalov. It was a demand: to restore telephone communication, deliver mail and newspapers, to switch on the TV and to immediately send a plane so that we can return to Moscow, to work. Unfortunately, on the territory of the residence 'new faces' have shown up, men carrying machine guns.

A. Chernyaev came. We went out to the balcony to talk; we're afraid of anyone listening in. Security officers do not rule out such a possibility. Anatoly Sergeyevich complains that he does not have the essentials with him, not even a shaving kit. Everything remained there, in the "South" – the sanatorium where he and the stenographers were located – the referent Olga Vasilievna and his secretary Tamara Alekseevna. Here, in the service house of the residence, they come to work every day. He said that he spoke with Generalov and demanded that he be released: "I am a People's Deputy of the USSR. And I'm not interned. Why are they keeping me here?" We walked across the territory, to the sea. It was necessary for everyone to see – both 'our' people and those who were watching us from the rocks and the sea, that Mikhail Sergeyevich is healthy, and in normal condition. Ksenia and Nastya cannot share an umbrella – who should carry it? Nastenka came to me: "Granny, Ksenia is annoying me. She doesn't let me play or sleep. Nothing scares her! I should have been the only one born, do you understand?" Boris Ivanovich and Igor Anatolyevich talk about the news they heard through an old receiver with a makeshift antenna attached: the Emergency Committee has been created, Yanayev has new powers, every citizen of the country will now receive 15 acres of land as property. It is reported from abroad: that Yeltsin has not been arrested. "And just yesterday…" says Boris Ivanovich, "Generalov told me that he had been arrested, and has to stay in the dacha." In general, information about ongoing events is very different depending on where it's coming from. It's hard to understand… It's reported that one of the Russian deputies has been arrested…

Here, at our residence, we also have some news: a fire engine and a watering truck have been placed on the helipad. Before the entrance, right across the road, there are trucks. Submachine gunners have been placed: at the garage, at the gate, on the helipad. All these people were new, unfamiliar. Oleg Anatolyevich and Boris Ivanovich declared again: "Mikhail Sergeyevich, we will be with you. We'll be here to the end." It is quiet on the sea: no pleasure boats, no passenger ships, no dry cargo ships, no barges are visible… Near the only ship anchored to a post, as always, there was one 'guard'. Usually, people were visible on the deck. They would do all kinds of things: sometimes they bathed, sometimes fished. There is not a single person on deck now. Tatyana Georgievna – a nurse – is indignant: "Wow, these 'friends' and 'supporters' – they are traitors. Even Olga, when she saw Boldin, who is her boss by the way, said that in times of trouble, there is no worse person than him in this operation. After all, Pugo was resting in the 'South' sanatorium. He left yesterday, should have been earlier. They say that he and his wife were poisoned. No one is allowing Raisa Maksimovna to leave the territory. Nobody. It is evident that no one will know the truth: That Mikhail Sergeyevich is healthy." Mikhail Sergeyevich and I are at home, in his office. Anatoly and Irina came running. There is news: the TV is on, there is a musical broadcast. Additional "guards" appeared at the sea. They keep at a distance from the coast, but they were still visible. The transistor news broadcasted the BBC wavelength: B. Yeltsin condemned the conspirators. He calls for opposition to the newly minted power. On Kazakh television, N. Nazarbayev addressed the people of the republic, he called for calmness, restraint, and observance of order. There was not a word about the removal of the President of the USSR...

At **17:00** the Senior Security Officer reported: that military signalmen were taken out of the territory.

At **17:30** Mikhail Sergeyevich invited A. Chernyaev. He told me that he had instructed him to immediately retransmit his demands to Yanayev for the restoration of government communications and the provision of an aircraft for a flight to Moscow. In case of refusal or silence, convey the requirements for a meeting with Soviet and foreign journalists. After Anatoly Sergeyevich left, he asked me to write down the Political Statement that dictated:

"1. The decision of the vice-president to assume the duties of the President of the country under the pretext of illness of the President of the USSR and the inability to perform his functions is a fraud, since I am in a normal state, even rested, and was going to leave today, August 19th, to sign the Union Treaty and hold the Federation Council. Therefore, this decision cannot be regarded as anything other than a coup d'état.

2. All decisions taken by the vice-president and the State Committee for the State of Emergency (GKChP) on this basis are illegal.

3. The escalation of measures related to the illegal introduction of a state of emergency may result in a further aggravation of the entire situation in the country, a split, confrontation in society and unpredictable consequences."

4. I demand that the implementation of the adopted decisions be immediately suspended, and that Comrade Lukyanov, as Chairman of the Supreme Soviet, urgently convene the Congress of People's Deputies of the USSR or the Supreme Soviet of the USSR to consider the current situation in the country's leadership."

A press conference of members of the State Emergency Committee was on TV. What treachery, what lawlessness, what vile lies! It is clear that they will do anything: even the worst. To lie before the whole world, declaring the incapacity of the President... The question of the fate of Mikhail Sergeyevich, they have already decided our fate. At night, the external security of the house was strengthened. Now the President's personal security officers will have to practically work around the clock. We agreed that Mikhail Sergeyevich, the children and I were to switch our lifestyle, and start saving more food, to use only the older food, that which is available in stock and purchased before August 17th. We put together a bag of fruit for the kids. Irina, just in case, hid hers in a closet under the air conditioner. We collected all the medicines and pills that we personally have. We decided to use only them.

We didn't sleep at night...

(With our video camera we recorded the Appeal, the Statement of Mikhail Sergeyevich to the people. In order to try and 'release' the information. If it fails, we hide, try to save ourselves. No matter what happens to us, people should know the truth about the fate of the President. We found a room, which, in our opinion, was not visible either from the sea or from the rocks. We closed the curtains. When it was about 4 o'clock in the morning we began looking through the footage, muffling the sound, downstairs – on the basement floor – the door suddenly slammed. Urgently everything was turned off. Anatoly disappeared with the film in another room, Mikhail Sergeyevich and Irina went downstairs and checked all the doors. Everything was closed. Mikhail Sergeyevich went outside. There was a double post at the door. Irina and Anatoly processed the film until six in the morning. They looked at the film through the viewing window of the camera and cut with nail scissors the end of each of the four recordings. The cassette was dismantled, and the tape was cut. Each recording was rewound on a thin paper roller, packed with "adhesive tape", wrapped in paper. Then they were hidden in well-known dachas. The cassette was then reassembled so that it was not obvious that someone had taken it apart)

August 20ᵗʰ, Tuesday

There is still no mail, no newspapers. But the Sony transistor continues to work. At the entrance to our bay, several guard ships would stay around all the time. Mikhail Sergeyevich tried to convey his demands to Moscow again: to restore telephone communication, to read the newspapers, to immediately get a plane to return to Moscow, to work. He adds a new requirement: to report any act of gross misinformation about his health on radio and TV. So far, apart from Generalov's assurances that all demands are being forwarded to Moscow, there are no other results. Mikhail Sergeyevich issues a warning: in case of failure to comply with the requirements, he will take extreme measures. Outwardly, we try to behave normally: we follow the doctor's orders, we went out to the territory of the dacha, to the sea. We all stuck together – Mikhail Sergeyevich, Irina, Anatoly, me and my grandchildren: anything could happen. We gave each other moral support. Not only us as family members, but everyone who ended up here with us, and who in fact, were also interned. I am especially worried about the women: I hope they can worry less, hold on and believe we can get through this. And, of course, so that the granddaughters wouldn't understand anything, so as to not trouble them. The senior security officer and the doctor express concern about the family's food: "the food is delivered from outside," from "someone else's car," and that "there is a danger." It means that they evaluate the situation in the same way as we do. We are now making a general decision: to live on the supplies we have and in the canteen of the guards.

Once again, I carefully discuss everything with the cook – Galina Afrikanovna. We also agreed: we will eat only boiled food.

I talked with the senior personal guard and asked: "Oleg Anatolyevich, can we 'release' information whilst bypassing Generalov?" (I didn't say what exactly I was talking about). He replied, "No, you can't. We are completely blocked from the sea. On land, we are surrounded so that you can't even crawl through..." Only my notebook remained with me. We tried to use one real opportunity: Olga Vasilievna's small child, who was left at home in Moscow because he had fallen ill. His father had a heart attack before, so she is worried. Mikhail Sergeyevich instructed A. S. Chernyaev to categorically raise the question of sending Olga Vasilievna to Moscow before Generalov... Mikhail Sergeyevich and I are discussing the situation. Why are Lukyanov and the Supreme Soviet silent? Why is Ivashko silent? And the leaders of the republics? After all, today is the day of the signing of the Union Treaty. The most terrible assumption: did the country really accept the State Emergency Committee? L. M. Kravchuk spoke on Ukrainian television yesterday. He called for "calmness, prudence, observance of the law, prevention of confrontation." Not a single bad word about the President... Do Mikhail Sergeyevich's demands convey? How can we push and 'release' our information? They don't let anyone out of the dacha. Maybe try to 'break out'? Our 'combat unit', according to Oleg Anatolyevich, is 'not very significant', but still armed enough...

Radio from the West broadcasts the messages: a state of emergency has been declared in Moscow; troops have been brought in;

both Moscow and Leningrad do not support the conspirators. A demand is being sent to clarify Gorbachev's situation – where he is, in what condition? They also report on the possible termination of economic assistance to the USSR. We have news on our end: someone tried to break into the territory of the residence from the outside. They didn't succeed, we didn't let them in... Generalov suddenly began to appear in the office building, where the security officers were. However, for two days he practically did not visit them... And most importantly, Generalov conveyed Mikhail Sergeyevich's demands to Boris Ivanovich Yanayev: he said that the demands will be fulfilled. At the same time, Generalov explained that he was transferring everything to Moscow through Plekhanov. I also received an answer through him. The senior guards fear an increase in activity at sea. Oleg Anatolyevich does not recommend taking children to bathe in the evening and even letting them outside the dacha. Ksenia and Anastasia said: "A strong wind is expected – you can't go out. Stay indoors." Feeling that something is about to happen. Some of the guards were brought into the house. Igor Anatolyevich and Nikolai Feodosevich, as well as some doctors, will also be in the house with us. Irina took Ksenia and Nastya to her bed. Anatoly lay down to sleep next to them on the floor. It's three o'clock in the morning...

August 21st, Wednesday

Morning information: there are clashes in Moscow. There are victims – wounded and killed. Has the worst really begun... Mikhail Sergeyevich demands to immediately speak to Yanayev: to stop the use of troops, return the troops to the barracks. At about 10 o'clock in the morning, two groups of ships appeared at sea, on the horizon. At the entrance to the bay there were three 'guard ships,' doing the usual. But there were also five additional ships that were heading towards us. These were landing ships, on air cushions. They were heading straight for the shore, towards us. But, not even having reached the 'guard ships,' they sharply changed their course, turned towards Sevastopol and disappeared behind Cape Sarych. What were they doing? Was it a blockade? Is it possible that someone has finally come to arrest us? To help us out? I have no doubt that they know that the President is alive and well. Oleg Anatolyevich and Boris Ivanovich do not advise anyone from the family to leave the premises today. They fear that a shootout may be provoked and the President's life endangered. Some newspapers from the day before yesterday were brought into the house. There were no official reports – neither on TV nor on the radio – about the state of Mikhail Sergeyevich's health. The madness: the President is "sick and incapacitated" and nothing truthful is being reported. At the same time, television informs about the wellbeing and health of Prime Minister Pavlov. Today is the birthday of Marina, the mistress of the Foros dacha. She is a sweet, young woman. There are tears in my eyes. For three days now she has not been released from the dacha. We congratulated her and agreed to bake a cake.

20:00. I'm in bed. I'm feeling better. Mikhail Sergeyevich is in the office. Lord, the worst seems to be over! Irina and Anatoly, swapping with each other, leave the room and return back with a pile of news: "Dad is talking on the phone with Yeltsin, Nazarbayev, Dementei, Kravchuk, Karimov, Panyukov, Moiseev, Dzasokhov. He refused to talk to Kryuchkov and Ivashko! The delegation of the Russian parliament is flying out of control! He's talking on the phone with Bush! The plane of the delegation of the Russian parliament will be received in Belbek... In the office of Pope Chernyaev. For the first time in three days, barges and civilian ships appeared on the sea... People in camouflage suits crawled to the dacha. The guards radioed: "Turn back. Otherwise we will shoot." They turned, crawled in the opposite direction... Somewhere around three o'clock in the afternoon Irina and Anatoly heard a message from the British BBC radio station on the Sony transistor: Kryuchkov agreed to fly to Crimea, Foros, with a group of people, the "delegation". In order to personally make sure that Gorbachev is really seriously ill and incapacitated. We took this as a sign of the worst. In the coming hours, action can be taken to make the vile lies a reality. Mikhail Sergeyevich gave an order to the guards to block the entrances, the entrance to the house; do not let anyone into the house without his permission; be on constant alert; use weapons if necessary. Security officers with machine guns stood on the stairs of the house and at the front door. The children, Ksenia and Anastasia, were locked in one of the rooms. They asked Aleksandra Grigorievna to be with them.

I had a sense of impending danger. What will they do? One thought kept constantly bouncing around in my head: we need to hide Mikhail Sergeyevich. But where? Everyone knows every last bit of the dacha and its territory like the back of their hand. And suddenly, in an instant, I felt that I was going numb, my arm sagged, and I wasn't able to say anything... I started feeling very ill. It flashed through my mind: a stroke.... Though I was relieved, thank God that everyone was nearby: my family, the doctors – Igor Anatolyevich, Nikolai Feodosevich. Everyone was in the house. They put me to bed, gave me medicines: it was a hypertensive crisis. Nikolai Feodosevich said: "Raisa Maksimovna, hold on. Their main goal now right now is to unsettle Mikhail Sergeyevich and you." At about 5pm Oleg Anatolyevich knocked on our door and quickly entered the room: "Mikhail Sergeyevich, cars have arrived at the territory – two ZILs and a Volga. The ones who arrived were: Yazov, Kryuchkov, Baklanov, Ivashko, Lukyanov and Plekhanov. They asked to meet with you." He added: "What are their plans? Why did they come?" Mikhail Sergeyevich said: "To take me into custody. Tell them my demand – I will not accept anyone until government communications are turned on." A few minutes later, Oleg returned with the answer: "This will take too long, they said. Enabling communication will take at least 30 minutes. Those who have arrived are asking for a meeting now." Mikhail Sergeyevich said: "They can wait. I will not conduct any negotiations until all communications are turned on."

At **17:45** the connection was turned on. After 73 hours! The isolation was over! And the house arrest too! Irinka entered: "Plekhanov and Ivashko tried to get into the house. Boris Ivanovich stopped them at the entrance: "Our order is not to let anyone in.

We will shoot!" Plekhanov said: "I knew it... that they'll be point-ing guns at us." They turned around and walked back. Dad is still talking on the phone." Mikhail Sergeyevich came in. He asked me how I feel. He said that he decided not to talk (despite repeated attempts on their part) with any of the conspirators. He immedi-ately spoke with Boris Nikolayevich Yeltsin: "Mikhail Sergeyevich, my dear friend, are you alive? We have been standing at death's door for the last 48 hours!" He talked with the other leaders of the republics. George W. Bush and Barbara sent their regards to me and said that they had been praying for us for these last three days. He showed a note signed by Lukyanov and Ivashko: "Dear Mikhail Sergeyevich! We have an important request. Can you receive us now if possible. We have something to report to you." He said: "In general, I'm not planning on accepting Kryuchkov, Baklanov or Yazov. I have nothing to talk about with them now. Lukyanov and Ivashko... Maybe I'll accept their request later. I am still waiting for the Russian delegation." The delegation arrived. Rutskoi, Silaev, Bakatin, Primakov, Stolyarov, Fedorov, the deputies, the press... Everyone is in the house. From below, on the first floor, joyful, excited voices are heard... I asked Irina to bring me the women who were here during these last few days, in the house, with us. We hugged and cried. I thanked them for all they have done for us and shared with us. Anatoly entered: "Mikhail Sergeyevich gave the command to get ready. We're flying away. Leave your belongings here. They will be packed and sent on the next flight, on which all our Moscow people will be sent."

August 22nd, Thursday

We left the Foros residence at 11am on August 21st. My last impressions were before my eyes: the excited, agitated faces of the 'rescuers' and 'recluses', as someone aptly noted, we were the "new Soviet prisoners." But now, fortunately, we were former prisoners. Ksenechka was in the car next to me. She hunched over, pressed herself against me: "I was afraid, Granny... I was afraid when I saw people with machine guns... I was completely frightened when my mother ran into the room and said: "Quickly... we are going... we are flying home to Moscow." I wanted to sleep so much!" It's dark outside the car window. The arrest ended; our vacation was cut short four days ago. It was cut short suddenly, and out of nowhere. In recent years, Mikhail Sergeyevich, for one reason or another, interrupted his vacation. But even so... Will I ever return to Tessel, to the Foros dacha? Probably not, it's not something I want. No matter what fate decides: whether Mikhail Sergeyevich will be the President of the country or not, or whether the Foros dacha will remain the residence of the President in Crimea or not. Too many moral and physical torments are connected with that place... Three years ago, my daughter was here on the verge of death. We took off from the airfield in Belbek, on the plane of A.V. Rutskoi. We were placed in a separate small room. Mikhail Sergeyevich invited A. Rutskoi, V. Bakatin, I. Silaev, E. Primakov, A. Chernyaev, I. Borisov, O. Klimov and B. Golentsov. Nastenka fell asleep on the side seat next to Irina, Ksenechka curled up on the floor. But, as they say, in tight quarters, as long as you're comfortable. The main thing is that we're all together... Kryuchkov is flying in the same plane, sitting in a separate compartment.

We had a conversation, we talked about everything that happened these last few days in Moscow, in the country, in the Crimean residence of the President, what we experienced, how we survived. We talked about our time, about the people in it. Aleksandr Vladimirovich talked about the protectors of the White House, how he taught people to hold the chain in hour hours, about the security officers who flew with him to save the President. None of them refused, they did not stay at the Moscow airport, although he knew about the possibility of a tragic outcome of the flight. Vadim Viktorovich and Evgeny Maksimovich told how they prepared the text of the statement, which they made on August 20th. They showed me the text, I left it with me: "We consider it unconstitutional to introduce a state of emergency and transfer power in the country to a group of people. According to the information we have, the President of the USSR M. S. Gorbachev is in good health. The responsibility that lies with us as members of the Security Council obliges us to demand the immediate withdrawal of armoured vehicles from the streets of cities, to do everything to prevent bloodshed. We also demand that M. S. Gorbachev's personal safety be guaranteed, and that he be given the opportunity to speak in public immediately." This statement was refused to be signed by a member of the Security Council, Minister of Foreign Affairs of the USSR – A. A. Bessmertnykh. The plane landed in Moscow at 2am, at Vnukovo–II. There were many people meeting us at the airport. Mikhail Sergeyevich was surrounded by a dense ring. Irina and I immediately left to get into our cars with the children. These kinds of things give me chills. I feel very uncomfortable and lose myself…

August 24ᵗʰ, Saturday

Moscow says goodbye to Vladimir Usov, Dmitry Komar, Ilya Krichevsky. Hundreds of thousands of Muscovites are at the funeral procession. I believe their grief and pain is shared by millions.

August 26ᵗʰ, Monday

I'm not feeling myself. I try to follow all the doctor's orders. Irinka is also sick. I relive what happened over and over again. In my mind, one after another, details pop up that I somehow didn't pay attention to before. Before Plekhanov's departure from Foros (he flew there with us on August 4ᵗʰ, stayed for two or three days and flew to Moscow), in a conversation, Mikhail Sergeyevich asked: "How is the situation in the Crimea?" – and he answered: "In general, it's fine. But we have slightly increased security at sea, added a group of scuba divers." Was it really due to the need to protect the President? Or the implementation of a specific plan to isolate him? In the same conversation, Plekhanov urged a leave of absence for Medvedev. Although, in the opinion of Mikhail Sergeyevich, there were no objective reasons for this. On August 13ᵗʰ and 14ᵗʰ, Anatoly noticed that the 'guard ship' No. 026, which usually stood at the entrance to the bay, had been replaced by another, a different type of 'guard ship'. It was a large ship that could previously only be seen with binoculars on the horizon.

Every day, in the morning, Anatoly met with Medvedev on the tennis court. On August 18th, when they parted, Anatoly asked: "Vladimir Timofeevich, will we play tomorrow?" (On the 19th, Mikhail Sergeyevich was scheduled to fly to Moscow, and Anatoly decided to clarify if they would meet after that, and when). Medvedev replied: "Actually, I don't know ... Mikhail Sergeyevich has sciatica, after all." Anatoly was surprised by this, and at breakfast he asked us: "Have you changed the day of departure to Moscow? Was it moved to the 20th?" When on August 15th Mikhail Sergeyevich urgently needed additional medical care, Dr. Liev, who was supposed to provide it, arrived only two days later. The reasons for the delay were still unclear. The presidential dacha near Moscow was also 'on the defensive' on August 19th, 20th, 21st. The officers of the President's service who remained in Moscow – some of them interrupted their vacation due to the situation – armed themselves on their own initiative and took up the defence of their 'duty'. Vladimir Anatolyevich Bondar says: "We were amazed when we learned that Medvedev was in Moscow. He didn't come to us. He appeared late at the airport, when Mikhail Sergeyevich arrived, and on the morning of the 22nd here, at the residence near Moscow.

It turns out that he was not even disarmed in Crimea. We asked him to hand over his weapons. Oleg Anatolyevich says: "If Medvedev had given us a signal in Foros on the 18th, the entire 'delegation' would have been arrested." Personal protection officers of the President, who did not betray him, remained next to him at a difficult moment. They were young, strong, handsome men. Handsome not only outwardly, but also by the nobility of the human spirit, and their duty as officers.

August 27ᵗʰ, Tuesday
For the fourth day I have been reading, reading over and over again, the letters of Mikhail Sergeyevich. All of them. I say goodbye to them. I destroy them one after another. My heart shrinks, tears cover my eyes... The words of our life, our destiny. They are written to me and belong only to me. I do not want other people's unkind hands to ever touch these papers. I don't want someone to mock the words, thoughts and feelings that are dear to me.

* * *

The putsch failed. The democrats are celebrating their victory, talking about the consolidation of forces, about freedom, the renewal of society, and the implementation of long-awaited reforms. But what is happening to us today? There is an aggravation of national, economic problems, and society is increasingly splitting. Not only were these "putschists" crushed, but so were the communists, the KGB members, the 'partocrats' and their sympathisers. There is a fierce struggle for the seizure of 'power', 'spheres of influence', 'property'. The ties and traditions that have developed in the country for centuries are being torn apart. The state is being destroyed. People who were always grovelling in search of a new 'owner' or 'patron' were rushing about, without shame or morality. One after another, articles are printed in the media about the need for a 'good dictator', a 'good dictatorship'. The position of the President of the country is called into question. Some people do not stop at open slander and lies. "You know," the President told me, "I don't care about insulting nonentities. It has been like this in all critical eras, when not only new forces entered the arena of history, but also a lot of garbage was brought out. The main concern is how to avoid starvation in the country, how to use forces for the sake of the main thing, in order to continue what has been started – the reforms. New challenges... they are ahead of us. And, probably, they are the most difficult, the most serious, and require the most attention.

"Komsomolskaya Pravda (TVNZ)"
December 20ᵗʰ, 1991

I HAVE NEVER BEEN IN THE SHADOW OF MY HUSBAND

Interview

Raisa, What Hurts My Heart

Interview with R. M. Gorbacheva, in correspondence with Maria Fedorina of 'Moskovsky Komsomolets'

— *"You were at the very pinnacle of power. You have experienced the heaviness of the ascent and the bitterness of the descent. Which path is more difficult to overcome?"*

— "Firstly, I was not at the top of power – I was close to power. At the pinnacle of power was Mikhail Sergeyevich. And I was just there, sharing his fate. Although they say that the one who is near the top feels the abyss more sharply."

— *"You were the first wife of a Soviet leader who managed to come out from the shadow of your husband and become a real first lady. How did you do it? How hard was it to break the stereotype?"*

— "In all of our life together, I have never been in the shadow of my husband. We met when we were at university, got married early and have been together ever since. And my relationship with Mikhail Sergeyevich is not only a mutual feeling, but also a feeling of support and respect. These relations of ours did not change depending on his positions, and we never came up with something special for this or that occasion. Whatever relations we had is what still remains. Was it difficult to become the first lady? Well, we weren't taught on this subject. Basically, I always lived, acted and did things out of love, based on personal experiences and, of course, always with the consent of Mikhail Sergeyevich.

My advisor has always been and remains only him. The fact is that throughout the civilised world there are wives of heads of state, and their position, rights and duties are strictly outlined. In our society, one fate was prepared for me – the lack of the right to an official, public existence. This situation was formed even under Stalin and became very firmly established in our Russian politics. And so, I was not just the first lady, I was the first lady of our country. This is where the complexity lies. And some of my special individual abilities played a decisive role. Just my appearance next to Mikhail Sergeyevich caused a very mixed reaction in society.

I have thousands and thousands of letters (and I still receive them) in which I am thanked for the fact that I worthily bear the image of a Russian woman. But I also have detractors. Many accepted my existence cautiously, almost like Perestroika. There are a lot of myths and conjectures about some of my extraordinary predilection for villas, dachas, luxurious outfits and jewellery. It was beneficial for someone to spread these fictions. In the fight against Mikhail Sergeyevich, I was used as a trump card. And now they are still using me. Only not as a tool in the struggle for power, but to justify what is happening now. How hard was it to break stereotypes? We lived, worked, did what we saw fit. These last six years were very suppressing. But now I can say that neither my friends nor my detractors should be ashamed of me and my role. I regard the fact that it has become a tradition in our country to have our own first lady as a positive factor, because the appearance of a woman in politics as the wife of the first person of the state, endowed with certain rights, contributes to the emergence of a respectful attitude towards a woman in general, a woman as a wife, and a woman as a mother."

— *"Did you have any stylists?"*

— "We didn't have any stylists. We didn't even know the word at the time. All the stylists I know entered our life and political careers after Mikhail Sergeyevich. Just like that make-up, both physically and politically, I would ethicise "straightening" and that's about it. We didn't really have stylists. In our case, the main thing was what Mikhail Sergeyevich proposed and did. This, of course, does not mean that I did not look after my appearance and the appearance of my husband. And our main assistant in these matters was and is our daughter Irina."

— *"In this regard, did you have a desire to persuade your daughter to work in the presidential field?"*

— "No, never. What for? Not only did Mikhail Sergeyevich not take anyone from his family into power, but he also did not drag anyone on his tail from Stavropol. Before him, all the other leaders dragged their own people when moving to Moscow. And Yeltsin brought a lot of people from Sverdlovsk."

— *"Did the 'Kremlin Wives Club' exist in the era of the Politburo?"*

— "When I found myself among the Kremlin wives, this was not the case. Women met only at official events. Any individual contacts, especially in a personal narrow circle, were not encouraged. Only the Brezhnev family could afford this. When Mikhail Sergeyevich became General Secretary, I considered it necessary to somehow bring women together, to overcome the atmosphere of alienation. I organised something like a club. We got together, invited artists, scientists, government officials, diplomats, and discussed various issues. We prepared the government's receptions for March 8th. It happened, and they went together to enterprises, to museums."

— *"Did you manage to overcome the formality of relations in this way?"*

— "To some extent, yes."

— *"There were many rumours about your influence on your husband. Do they hold any truth?"*

— "The rumour that I influenced the adoption of political and personnel decisions is a myth. You would have to be completely oblivious to the Russian system or pretend that you do not know, in order to admit that someone other than the Politburo and the General Secretary could make decisions. That's one. And second. Whoever spreads this rumour must not know Mikhail Sergeyevich at all. Another thing is that our life has developed in such a way that we always discussed what worried us. Remember the years of Perestroika, what global changes were going on and how hotly they were discussed in the country. We discussed them of course, just like they did".

— *"But did he listen to you?"*

— "Of course. After all, if I were not Gorbachev's wife, I would still be his supporter, you know. The fact is that I belong to that part of the intelligentsia that has supported and continues to support the ideas of Perestroika. This does not mean that we did not argue on certain issues. We have argued. And he listened to my opinion, but he always made decisions himself, as he saw fit."

— *"What about everyday matters?"*

— "I listen to him and then make decisions myself. By the way, Mikhail Sergeyevich is quite picky when it comes to everyday matters. I remember when I would come home from work, I would often find notes on the stove like: "Zakharik, (that's what he calls me in our family) you forgot to salt the borshch." And that's it. In general, when it comes to food, we are unpretentious. We just love to eat delicious food, like everyone else in Russia: pies, borshch, sweet dumplings, savoury dumplings. We aren't unfamiliar with these aspects. Not only in the sense of high values, but also when it comes to normal desires: to eat, to have fun, to buy a beautiful thing, to furnish an apartment nicely. I don't see anything special in this. This is natural, but on the condition that all this must be done with the money you earned yourself."

— *"Korzhakov wrote in his book that you selected candidates for the presidential guard based on photographs. Is this so?"*

— "Like Catherine II's handsome guards? Something like that? Was Korzhakov offended that he was not among them? I am not personally acquainted with General Korzhakov, Boris Nikolayevich's chief bodyguard. I skimmed through his book. The general impression is political disassembly. The most vivid impression came from the final words: 'Before, Boris Nikolayevich, we thought that we were deceiving the people for the sake of democracy and reforms. Today I realised that only your family and a handful of people who have privatised power need this lie.' As for the formation of the guard, this was the business of the head of the presidential guard. We got acquainted with the photographs after the recruitment of new guards was conducted, and we looked at them to remember what they look like."

— *"There have been many legends about your outfits. How was your style developed? Is it true that some of the outfits were subsequently sold?"*

— "When it comes to the outfits, it is very important to understand that in those years a lot was connected with the official life of Mikhail Sergeyevich. And they have their own rules, their own laws. Official receptions, meetings and dinners are usually shown on television. And this implies, according to the protocol of each country, that long dresses, gloves, hats, tailcoats, etc. were necessary. These are clothes that I don't really need in my ordinary life. I myself love trousers and sweaters, skirts with a jacket and coat. But on those occasions, I had to dress like the wife of the head of state. And since the wardrobe needed to be changed every so often, I bought everything with my own money, earned by us, and I eventually had to sell what I no longer needed. I gave those outfits to a charity shop."

— *"Where do you prefer to get your clothes?"*

— "As the wife of the head of state, I considered it my duty to wear only national clothes. Now it doesn't matter to me where I bought them, but back then, I only wore national clothes. And basically, everything was sewn for me at the Fashion House on Kuznetsky Most. These were made by Tatyana Konstantinovna

Makeeva, Elena Nikolaevna Sterligova, Irina Vladimirovna Krutik-ova and the atelier master Lidia Grigorievna Magieva. And today, once again, I want to say a huge thank you to them."

— *"And when you were abroad, not for official receptions but for yourself, where did you prefer to buy things?"*

— Nowhere. I repeat, while I was the wife of the head of our state, I wore only national clothes. I had a case in 1985 in Geneva, at Mikhail Sergeyevich's first meeting with Ronald Reagan. At dinner, George Schultz came up to me, pulled my sleeve and asked: "Where did you get this? In Paris?" I said: "No, in Moscow." Schultz was very surprised. But that's his problem...

— *"Did you have a discussion with the wives of Western leaders about who prefers to get clothes from where?"*

— "No, this wasn't something that was accepted. They didn't ask me, because maybe they knew that I was wearing Russian clothes. We talked more about cultural issues, about children, and discussed charitable and humanitarian aspects.

— *"There were rumours about your friction with Nancy Reagan..."*

— "Once, there were rumours in the American press that we had some kind of friction. However, this was nothing more than a rumour. I had equal and friendly relations with most of the women I met. Although with some of the wives of leaders I have stronger relations. For example, with Kadar's wife, Sonia Gandhi, Jaruzelski's wife, Mrs. Mitterrand. I have great sympathy for Queen Sophia of Spain.

— *"With the election of Mikhail Sergeyevich as head of the country, you had to change your way of life, many habits. Did you have to give up something that you later regretted?"*

— "Of course, life changed a lot when Mikhail Sergeyevich became General Secretary. My circle of contacts has expanded enormously, the number of acquaintances has increased, and responsibility has increased. The time for our personal rest, for meetings with friends, for walks, reading books, going to the theatre has been significantly reduced. Life has become much more stressful. I stopped working professionally. The amount of time when we can be in the family circle, together with Mikhail Sergeyevich, has sharply reduced. What do I regret? If I may say so, it is a loss of freedom in my private life. For years I was, and still am, in plain sight under the scrutiny of strangers, other people's gazes. It's not easy – it's very hard to first be surrounded by people you trust, and then you find among them both informers and traitors."

— *"Which parts of Gorbachev's presidency do you remember most pleasantly, and which have been the most unpleasant ones?"*

— Still, fate favours me, even if not everyone understood me, accepted me, and some people even now are slandering me. I am happy that I was with Mikhail Sergeyevich and was not just a witness, but a participant in those events that changed the world and continue to change it. The most pleasant thing is communication with people and the support for Perestroika (Mikhail Sergeyevich travelled a lot around the country), which we felt from millions of people, that hope that Perestroika gave rise to. We still receive many letters in which people write: "Mikhail Sergeyevich, our lives brightened with your presence." This was the nicest thing left from those times. And as for the most unpleasant things, we all managed to survive them together: Chernobyl, the earthquake in Armenia, the tragedies in Vilnius, Baku and Tbilisi. And the dramatic events of 1991.

— *"Gorbachev repeatedly said that the putsch had the strongest influence on you. What did you really feel while sitting in Foros?"*

— "In Foros I had a breakdown. We were in isolation for 72 hours, we were under arrest for 72 hours, men with machine guns sat on the stairs for 72 hours, who said they would protect us to the end. I did not sleep for these 72 hours, I was even afraid of taking sleeping pills – I thought that it was at this time that they could do something to us, because they had already announced to the world that Mikhail Sergeyevich was ill, incapacitated. I thought about Mikhail Sergeyevich, about all of us, about the children who were with us. I was simply tormented by the thought of being betrayed by the people we trusted. There was another terrible coincidence: it was on August 20th, 1937, that they shot my grandfather, without a trial, accusing him of Trotskyism. But he, a peasant, did not know anything about this – neither who Trotsky was, nor what Trotskyism was. After Foros I experienced more than one "putsch". As for my health, it is now worse than before Foros, but thank God, it's better than it could have been.

— *"Again, in Korzhakov's book, an opinion is expressed that your unfriendly relations with your inner circle predetermined his betrayal in Foros. Do you agree with this?"*

— "The simplest explanation is that betrayal always comes with power. Remember the 'Ides of March', when Caesar gets twenty-one blows, and the last blow comes from the man he trusted the most. Khrushchev had traitors; Mikhail Sergeyevich had traitors. If we take the case of the GKChP, these are the people who started the reforms with Mikhail Sergeyevich. And in the course of these reforms, they found themselves on the other side of the barricade. But they betrayed not only Mikhail Sergeyevich – the GKChP also betrayed the country. And no matter how his former "comrades-in-arms" reviled him, the fact remains that it was not petty passions and selfish interests that owned his thoughts and actions."

— *"Would you live more peacefully if Mikhail Sergeyevich had not become the head of state?"*

— "Probably, but I don't think about that."

— *"You have created your Club. Do you plan to enter the socio-political arena on your own?"*

— "Personally, I don't plan to. I'm not going to get into politics. A group of very interesting, smart, worthy women has gathered around me. We have held our first meeting. Representatives of many women's organisations were invited. We discussed the question: 'Why is the voice of women not heard in society?' For there can be no normal society where women do not have civic consciousness and their voices are not heard. We decided: we will discuss the painful problems of our society, as we understand them. Expressing our position. Support public initiatives, specific projects, proposals aimed at solving these problems. Currently we have taken up the question: what are we doing for the future of our children?"

— *"Have you ever thought about doing commercials? Were there any such proposals?"*

— "No, there were no offers for me personally. There are a lot for Mikhail Sergeyevich."

— *"Is he going to be in advertising?"*

— "No, I don't think so. This is not really his field of interest. His participation in the advertisement shown on TV was forced due to the fact that in 1992, if you remember, President Yeltsin took away the premises from the Foundation. Mikhail Sergeyevich wants to find a place for the archive and library of Perestroika. And he accepted this offer, signed the contract. All money, up to the last dollar, will go to fund these things. So, this step is somewhat forced."

— *"Did you dissuade him from filming?"*

— "I was against the fact that he starred in commercials. But at the same time, I understand him."

— *"Do you personally know Yeltsin? How do you assess the role of his family in shaping today's Kremlin policy?"*

— "Only superficially. I've had occasional meetings with him and his wife at official events during the presidency of Mikhail Sergeyevich. Judging by the press and publishers, the role of the Yeltsin family in shaping the current policy is very significant. But personally, I can neither confirm nor deny this."

— *"In your opinion, how useful is it for the country that the family influences the development of Presidential decisions?"*

— "The family, of course, has some influence on the leader. It certainly has always been and is the case. However, even more influence is exerted by advisers, ministers, assistants, members of parliament, the media, etc. The main thing is who is at the head of the state. Because all decisions are theirs."

— *"Going back to the questions about your outfits, where do you prefer to get clothes these days?"*

— "I buy ready-made things. Things that I like. Sometimes in Moscow, sometimes abroad. My daughter often helps out. I trust her taste completely. The most important thing is that whatever I'm wearing suits me, that it is right for me, and not me for it. I have just ordered two suits from 'Paninter'. I've already had a fitting – I liked it. And it's not too expensive."

— *"Is it a financial issue?"*

— "Thanks to the earnings of Mikhail Sergeyevich, we are, of course, quite well off. And I can afford to buy what I need and like. But the main thing is not just to throw money away, but to get decent things with it."

February 1998

She Is the First Woman in Many Years Whose Life Was So Public.

*Interview with I. M. Virganskaya
for the newspaper 'Kommersant',
August 2001*

— *"Irina Mikhailovna, do you often remember those three days in Foros?"*

— "You know, a lot has already been erased from my memory. You can endure everything that has been endured over the years by only removing certain events from your memory. This is a kind of defensive reaction. There were no less terrible things than those of Foros. When Dad retired, the almost endless Foros topic began to surface. Foros was a visible event, and what happened afterwards remained invisible to the people. And so, it was not perceived as it happened in August '91. Mum [Raisa Gorbacheva] even wanted to write a book about the years after she retired. It was about daily life in Foros – an abyss of betrayal, slander, isolation and much more."

— *"But back then, in August 1991, were you scared?"*

— "It was a huge shock. We were all together: the children, my father and my mother. They could have done anything with us. Most of all, we were afraid that Dad would be taken away from us or us from him. I'm really happy that our stay there was so short – only three days. Because if it dragged on even a little bit more – for a week or ten days – there would be no way out of this situation, except for some kind of physical violence. And then: the people who decided to stay with us – would they have survived those days? After all, everyone had families in Moscow."

— *"How did your children react to this situation?"*

— We isolated them. They sat in a separate room and understood practically nothing.

— *"The main argument of the State Emergency Committee was that the President was ill and could not perform his duties..."*

— "If a temporary case of sciatica is all you need to be removed from power, then yes, I guess their reason wasn't wrong"

— *"Have you tried to leave Foros?"*

— "How could we leave when everything was blocked? What, should we have climbed the fence? The cars were stolen, and the garages were blocked by machine gunners, there was also a car with machine gunners on the helipad. So what? Should we have broken through all this? It would have been such a gift to the putschists though, because in this case they probably would have said that they didn't know who was breaking through and where."

— *"Your mother once said that she was afraid that Mikhail Sergeyevich could be poisoned, and you were wary of food. Was there a reason for this?"*

— "The history of our country is multifaceted, and it is familiar with stories of poisoning. But what was our life like? All service personnel were from the KGB. Even the products were from there. All were subordinate to one person. And when for no reason at all the head of your own guard and a co-conspirator of the putschists comes to you, what else can you think? We did not know how all those people around us would behave. They were all in the service of the KGB. So imagine whatever you want."

— *"So, the fact that the guards were loyal to the President was a lie?"*

— "No, no, the personal guards, except for the head of personal protection Medvedev, remained faithful. But their situation was also difficult. Imagine, the head of security, that is, their immediate supervisor, is getting ready and leaving. Basically, throwing them away, and what are they left to do? Either they must follow the instructions of the one who replaced Medvedev, that is, Generalov, or they must decide to stay and obey only the President. They decided that during these three days they would stay with us."

— *"Is it true that Medvedev left because it was time for him to go on vacation?"*

— "Lies. He didn't go anywhere. He was supposed to fly with his dad to sign the Union Treaty, and there was no talk of a vacation at all."

— *"What did you feel when the putschists came to you for the second time? Did you know why they came?"*

— "No. Because we already had information from radio broadcasts about the situation in Moscow. Although there was a terrible moment when it was announced that the Russian delegation was allowed to fly to Foros, we were afraid that something might happen. Because our father was declared sick, but he was healthy. And, logically, one might have thought that he could be made sick on purpose."

— *"Did your father take the betrayal of his entourage hard?"*

— "He was worried. He is generally quite an emotional person. He is often reproached for talking a lot, but he talks a lot because he wants to convince people. His mother often told him: 'You still won't be able to convince everyone.' But it seemed to him that if you explain something to a person properly, they will definitely understand. This is his position. This is his passion, combined with the conviction that people need to be explained what to do, and not driven like a herd, so that they can make their own decisions. Hence the manner of speaking for a long time."

— *"Why is it that the whole world is grateful to Gorbachev for the changes that have taken place, but his own people are not?"*

— "The world accepted what was done because, first of all, the Cold War and the wild confrontation were over. And when it was all gone, they accepted it with gratitude. As for our people, they are used to living in such a state and so appreciate it to a lesser extent. There was a totalitarian state, we were completely isolated from the outside world. Probably some people liked to live like that, but others did not. And it was necessary to give people the right to choose how to live and where to live. After all, it's human rights, not a state right. In addition, our society had other problems. The following years were very difficult. It was necessary to survive, it was necessary to somehow earn money and feed the children. But the people live these days. And everyone can be understood. Therefore, I will not judge anyone strictly. We are who we are. Although I remember when my dad first became General Secretary, he was told: "Mikhail Sergeyevich, end the war in Afghanistan, and we will erect a gold monument of you." Well, it ended. Where is his monument? Inherently, humans can be quite ungrateful. In general, we are rarely grateful to each other even in ordinary everyday life. But still, it seems to me that the attitude of society towards my father has changed lately. And it didn't happen with the change in regime. Apparently there was some eventual understanding."

— *"And you didn't tell your dad, say, in 1993, when the Soviet Union had already collapsed and incomprehensible reforms began: 'Dad, what have you done?'"*

— "No. Because he did something completely different."

— *"But one follows from the other. If there were no reforms from Gorbachev, maybe Yeltsin wouldn't have done what he did?"*

— "Well then, the main culprit for this must be the God who created us. People always make their own choices. Yes, and in 1985 there were many options, as well as in '91. And each of them, Gorbachev and Yeltsin, made their choices.

— *"Why do you think people's discontent often spilled out not on your father, but on your mother?"*

— "This is also natural. She was the first woman in many years whose life was so public. And who in Russia loves beautiful and smart women?"

— *"After such a betrayal by your inner circle, did you become disillusioned with people?"*

— "Was betraying us the only thing they did? And what about the huge part of the intelligentsia, which suddenly forgot everything? And what about the huge part of the press, which, having gained freedom of speech, also forgot everything? After all, there was a moment when there was a ban on Mikhail Sergeyevich. So, is it just them? The circle made up of these people is very wide. And a certain disappointment always haunts me. There are days when you are disappointed in everything. And there are days when you are not disappointed in anything. Personally, I have become much more careful around people, but this does not mean that I hate them. I just became careful. And if we're talking about my father, then he has an indestructible faith in people."

— *"Does he know how to forgive?"*

— "Yes. He has forgiven many people."

— *"What about the Gekachepists?"*

— "That I do not know. I think it would be too much to forgive the main group of people who were closest to him and who stabbed him in the back. There is still some measure of forgiveness. But I wouldn't be able to do it.

— *"In general, was it hard to be the daughter of the General Secretary? Were you also closely monitored?"*

— "So what if I was? I have practically lived like this my whole life, ever since my father became the First Secretary of the Stavropol Territory Committee.

— *"So you're used to it?"*

— "Well, I don't know I'd call it that? I am currently happier than I was in those years because I have more freedom."

314

— *"How do you feel about the period right after Foros?"*

— "I believe that the turning point began not with Foros, but in 1985. Those reforms that began in 1985 marked all of the turning points that followed. And those ten years that have passed since 1991, I evaluate ambiguously. For that period, which is usually called the "Yeltsin period", people had high hopes for him. And he justified himself in some way. At least in that it gave rise to some primitive forms of a market, but in parallel with this, it also gave rise to corruption, criminalisation, impoverishment of the population and, in general, reduced the role of the state to nothing. But the state is comprised of totalitarian functions; it is also the social protection of the population, the protection of human rights, etc. All this was destroyed. Therefore, I have an ambiguous assessment."

— *"Now a new era has begun, a new person has come to power. Are you waiting for anything?"*

— "I have not yet formed a definite opinion. On the one hand, certain hopes have appeared again, because I am a young, educated person. Although, apparently, he is still associated with the previous regime – otherwise he would not have come to power so easily. But this is a different generation. With a large age difference from previous rulers, with a different experience. There are hopes, of course. But I can't say anything definitive yet."

— *"Has the attitude towards Gorbachev changed for the better since Putin's arrival?"*

— "Yes. Apparently, that personal conflict that was between my father and Yeltsin is gone. Although Mikhail Sergeyevich had more political confrontation, while Boris Nikolaevich's personal confrontation prevailed. And Vladimir Vladimirovich, apparently, does not have it. In general, I believe that political decisions should always be above personal interests. When personal interests over-shadow the state, then the true tragedy begins.

On August 17ᵗʰ, the conversation with Irina Virganskaya continued by phone.
— "I am simply shocked by A. Kolesnikov's note from Mikhail Sergeyevich's press conference. It's not just the offensive tone. And not in the way Mikhail Sergeyevich's statements were taken out of context, 'edited' and commented on. But with the last phrase, the author essentially approves of the coup – the main thing, it is said, was that Gorbachev was toppled.

Does the newspaper share this position?"

She Made this Path.

Interview with I. M. Virganskaya by BBC Russian Service
December 9th, 2010

Seva Novgorodtsev: Today, the BBC Russian Service had a guest – the daughter of the first and only President of the USSR, Mikhail Sergeyevich Gorbachev, Irina Virganskaya. We have already talked about the fact that in March next year a jubilee will take place in London: celebrating Mikhail Gorbachev's 80th birthday. Family, friends, many well-known public and political figures have been preoccupied with preparations for this event for several months. But, as my colleague Anastasia Uspenskaya found out from Irina, this is not just a holiday for the Gorbachevs. This is a very important mission that the family took on many years ago.

M. Virganskaya: Mikhail Sergeyevich will be 80 years old. It was not we who made the decision, and we are not the creators of it. I had to come up with something to pay tribute to him. I won't say that we are the only ones doing this. A lot of people are involved. And there will be a variety of activities. This is a fairly large series of events. But here in London, I'm a part one of them. The concert at the Albert Hall. This is a gift for him. There will be many friends, many acquaintances, politicians…

Anastasia Uspenskaya: But this is not a surprise for him? I understand that he knows that it is being prepared.

I. M. Virganskaya: Naturally. It is necessary to obtain from him the consent that he approves of this in principle. So, in some way, he is involved. He does not ask about the details of the process. But just a concert is not typical for us. With us, almost any action should be accompanied with some kind of public event. Therefore, it was decided that this concert would be necessarily charitable. Our family is on a mission. There comes a point when you have to choose: either you continue, or you are no longer able to follow your path. The beginning was laid by my mother many years ago: back in the Soviet Union the word "charity" was pretty much non-existent, and they didn't really know what it was. She, having visited a hospital for children with leukaemia, was so traumatised by what she saw that she began to help these children. We invested personally. We were a part of the Nobel Peace Prize. For years she did this, even after the resignation of Mikhail Sergeyevich. And we always tried to find money – we moved the project to create bone marrow transplantation centres forward, which did not exist in Russia at all before. And then, in 1999, a tragedy overtook us: my mother herself died of leukaemia. My dad and I, who stayed together with her during the last two and a half months of her life in the hospital, around the clock, in turn, we went through that hell with her, we simply could not refuse. Although now charity has already become a part of Russian life. But so far, unfortunately, it cannot be said that I have never been in the shadow of my husband. In our society, charity is especially respected or supported. This requires tradition.

Anastasia Uspenskaya: You said that you often visit London.

Does this mean that you work closely with British charities?

I. M. Virganskaya: First, Britain still occupies a special place in Europe in terms of charity, paying special attention to private charity. There are excellent examples of such private initiatives here. The local society is the readiest for it. It is well received and accepted. That is why we needed an English partner for such an event.

Anastasia Uspenskaya: Is there any statistics on how many people managed to help?

I. M. Virganskaya: I can tell you one thing: when Raisa Maksimovna started, 95% of children would die of leukaemia. Now the survival rate is around 80 to 90%. That is a huge leap forward. Mother was, in fact, the one who punched her way through. The way for new technologies, for training doctors and nurses, for protection... It is necessary to invest a lot in equipment, drug programmes, technologies, medicines, so-called protocols.

Anastasia Uspenskaya: The surname, Gorbacheva – does it open a lot of doors for you?

I. M. Virganskaya: No. Not every door opens for me. But the fact that people usually trust me a lot more – this is true. Maybe I cannot open certain doors for various reasons, more often, of course, political ones. But do they trust me? Yes. In general, much more than anyone else.

Seva Novgorodtsev: Thank you, this was Irina Gorbacheva.

RAISA MAKSIMOVNA'S CLUB

Contribution to the Creation of Civil Society

From the speech of R. M. Gorbacheva at a meeting of the Club

They say the ice has broken. Today's meeting is a logical continuation of the first one held by our Club on October 30th, 1997. Let me remind you that at that time we discussed the topic: "Modern Russia – the View of a Woman." We tried to comprehend the position of a woman in today's society, the problems that concern her, and the opportunities that women today have for self-realisation. At the first meeting, we agreed that society cannot be considered normal if the voice of a woman is not heard in it. It is hardly possible to count on the formation of a civil society in the country if there is no civil consciousness of both men and women. We decided to continue these meetings, formalising their topics. There were many responses to our first meeting, many proposals for cooperation. The composition of our Club has replenished. During this time, we tried to determine more precisely its place and role, to understand what the Club's contribution, albeit small, to the formation of civil society in the country, could be. We decided to bring up for discussion the most painful, most pressing issues both for Russian society in general and for women in particular. Express your opinion, your position on these issues. Stimulate public interest in them and support public initiatives, projects and proposals related to these issues. The wider the field of activity of public organisations, private organisations, different groups of people, the more real the opportunities will be to understand and solve certain problems.

We Should Not Become a Country of Victorious "Indifference"

The topic of today's meeting: "Our children: the image of the future and the practice of education." As we know, there are a great many problems of childhood in the Russia of today, and all of them are acute and painful. But no matter what position society is in, it cannot ignore the future, which is embodied through its children. Whether we are talking about an individual family, the state or the public, we have no right to withdraw the troubles of childhood, to ignore those who need it in the first place. We should not become a country of victorious "indifference" – where no one cares about anyone. It would seem that everything is clear. It's hard to argue with the facts. There are very important documents on the problems of childhood. The UN Convention on the Rights of the Child, World Declaration for the Survival, Protection and Development of Children. The Russian Federation has developed the Main Directions of the State Social Policy for the Improvement of the Situation of

Children until the year 2000 – that's the so-called national plan of action in the interests of children.

There are many structures, commissions in the executive and legislative authorities, at the federal and regional levels. Thousands of working educators, teachers, doctors, cultural figures, journalists and people who just, at the call of the soul, have connected their life activity with the fate of childhood. Enthusiastic people, Altruistic people. Everything is there, but what are the realities? What is happening in our reality? And this is where opinions differ. Some believe that yes, there are difficulties, there are costs. But when were there ever not! Arguments about the moral crisis of the younger generation, they say, have no real ground under them. This is one of the myths of our time. There is no reason to talk about the conflict of fathers and children. There is another assessment. There are millions of disadvantaged children deprived of shelter in the country; the homeless, orphans, drug addicts, the mentally ill, the mentally handicapped, the handicapped, children not attending school; children associated with crime. It is believed that the system of pre-school education and upbringing is being destroyed. There is a commercialisation not only of education, but also of children's recreation, treatment, teaching. Everything suddenly became paid: choir, dance clubs, sports clubs, etc. – everything has a price, and hefty prices at that. And the salary of the vast majority of families is low, if not negligible. And besides, most of it has not been issued in months.

With the poll data provided, we can see that most high school students now consider getting dollars and money in general as their goal, their ideal. But not through labour, but through theft, blackmail, banditry and bribery. As you can see, the difference between these opinions and assessments is very serious. In order to somehow define the scope of our conversation, we chose three key questions from a variety of questions.

1. What is specifically being done for our children today?

2. Fears and dangers. What do we fear the most when raising children?

3. What models of happiness and success do we offer our children today?

Here in the hall there are deputies of the State Duma, the Moscow City Duma, employees of the Moscow government, the Ministry of Culture of the Russian Federation, scientists, experts from research institutes, centres, universities, highly qualified teachers, writers, journalists, representatives of children and international organisations. There are people who make a living on the concrete, real issues of today. Many expressed their desire to speak at our meeting. We are happy about it. We hope that they will share their thoughts, their experience, that they will find people here who are close to them in terms of the nature of their activities and position. And perhaps they will find those who are willing to become sponsors and provide material support. And, of course, we hope that the journalists present will help convey to our citizens everything interesting and useful that will be said here. And then

new points of comprehension and new forms of action of the phe-
nomena discussed today can arise in society. <...>

So That Our Voice can be Heard

(From a closing statement at a meeting of the Club)

I think we've had a useful conversation today. The working group of our Club will try to summarise all of the materials and speeches, analyse and think over the specific proposals and conclusions of the meeting participants. Of course, dear friends, we all know that socialism cannot be built in one country, just like capitalism cannot be built in one single city. And we will not solve the problem of childhood in isolation from other problems. However, there are glaring issues that require priority attention and priority decisions. I liked the idea expressed in one of the speeches that an intellectual is, first of all, a person capable of empathy. It certainly is the case. But I would not want Russia to be a country of intellectuals who only empathise and suffer. Still, an intellectual should be someone who is able to create something. Therefore, we will not deprive the intelligentsia of the right to some constructive thoughts and actions. I spoke about the small contribution that we, I hope, can make in order not to be a society of universal 'apathy'. Today, our society is practically only 'surviving'. Something must be done so that this state of survival does not become our permanent state. The task that the Club takes on is to wake up the society and give rise, perhaps in the exchange of opinions, to some new semantic points, and hence new actions in solving the problems that we are discussing. I think our Club has one problem currently. We need the help of the press. We can't do much without them. Many interesting, informative proposals and projects have been voiced here today. But it is necessary that all these points reach the citizens. Otherwise, we will remain a party club, of which there are plenty already. We hope that the press will support us and talk about us and our affairs so that we are known, so that our voice can be heard.

Moscow, February 18ᵗʰ, 1998

Raisa, What Hurts My Heart

LETTERS
AND ARTICLES

Published before September 20ᵗʰ, 1999

Raisa, What Hurts My Heart

Gayaz ALIMOV

Lady Dignity

*Thousands of letters and telegrams come
in support of Raisa Gorbacheva*

An amazing discovery of the last few days: hardened in the eternal struggle, Russia has been honoured to show the greatness of its soul. It seemed to us that the Gorbachev couple was not loved in Russia, that they had been forgotten, thrown into the dustbin of history, to be forgotten. And we have changed. We have become human. We, it turns out, have not forgotten how to sympathise with the grief of others. Evidence of this is in the thousands of letters and telegrams that came from Russia to the German clinic, where doctors are fighting for Raisa Gorbacheva's life. It turns out that the country has not lost itself. It seemed to us that with deafening speed it was descending into a cold place of commercialism and selfishness. And then suddenly, there was a breath of national warmth of human understanding. People from everywhere write to Raisa Maksimovna. From the most distant countries. And we became, albeit on a sad occasion, witnesses of the respect between two people who love each other – Raisa and Mikhail, for it is perhaps one of the most famous Russian families in the world. In our country, Raisa Maksimovna was disliked. Nobody accepted her as soon as she appeared in public alongside the young and powerful General Secretary. However, it seems that this was not an appearance, but a phenomenon. The Soviet female personalities rejected her only because she was different. She is not like the others: she was fragile and graceful, with an exquisite taste for beautiful clothes, she has become a symbol of a country liberated from dullness. She was not understood. Or maybe, they did not want to understand her. Perhaps, when this family was in power, an endless number of demands were made towards her. But they were not able to break and subdue her.

Bill Clinton and his wife Hillary sent a warm letter to Raisa Gorbacheva literally the day after her hospitalisation. These were their words: "We admire the nobility and dignity with which you constantly accompanied your husband in his great affairs." More letters were sent by German Chancellor Gerhard Schroeder, the former German Foreign Minister Hans-Dietrich Genscher, former US President George W. Bush and many other statesmen. The flow of letters and telegrams from Russia did not stop. And the most interesting thing is that most of them were from women. They wished Raisa Maksimovna a speedy recovery. There was a call to the clinic from the administration of the President of Russia. Of course, with an offer to help. But how I would have liked if Boris Nikolaevich managed to find the strength to personally call or write to his predecessor. Just as a man and a human being, to say two words of support. And that would be enough. But alas... The other day we saw Mikhail Gorbachev on television. The man has aged twenty years in front of our eyes. Everyone is equal in the face of adversity. Someday a great saga will be written about Raisa and Mikhail – a saga about love.

'Izvestia', August 6th, 1999

Rudolf KOLCHANOV,
Correspondent for the newspaper 'Trud' in Bonn, a friend of M.
S. Gorbachev at the Faculty of Law of Moscow State University, who
studied with Mikhail Sergeyevich in the same group.
(Note: Kolchanov's speech is represented with italics)

My Dear Friend

(Meeting with Mikhail Gorbachev in Münster)

The first one I saw was Irina, the daughter of the Gorbachevs. She looked immeasurably tired, with greying hair, but her face had not lost its charm. She was returning from night duty in her mother's ward.

"How was your mother tonight?"

"It's very difficult for her. Painful. I was terribly afraid..."

A few minutes later I greeted Mikhail and we hugged.

"Many of our classmates call me in Bonn these days, they're wishing Raisa a speedy recovery, they sympathise with you, empathise with you, they hope and believe in heavenly justice, which, nevertheless, more often than not goes past good, kind-hearted people."

"We receive about five hundred letters, telegrams, faxes, every day in Münster through a popular newspaper with a wide circulation. I thank all my fellow countrymen, and thousands of foreigners, for the sincere words of sympathy and support at a difficult time for our entire family..."

"Irina is here with both her daughters. Did they get to see their grandmother? After all, the rules in the ward are sterilely strict – there aren't any flowers here, nothing extra at all, every centimetre of the place is carefully processed to avoid the slightest infection."

"All of us who are here in the ward are subjected to the same treatment. But the eldest granddaughter still visited the ward."

"Maybe it wasn't worth it?"

"Raisa really wanted to see her."

"The German press, referring to the opinion of reputable doctors, wrote that the disease was severely neglected. How could this happen, was it not possible to recognise before it got so bad?"

"It's not quite that simple. This form of leukaemia appears really quickly, explosively. Raya complained about her back pain. She was given painkillers, she immediately felt better, we walked with her after that. But you see how it all turned out."

"When the diagnosis was made, did you tell her about it directly, how did the German doctors behave?"

"I spoke to her very frankly, choosing, of course, to express carefully but almost openly. Doctors spoke with her in streamlined formulations."

"With your frankness, did you count on the strength of her character?"

"Exactly. And I wasn't wrong. Last night she was very ill, I feared the worst, but she, as always, behaved with amazing courage, stamina and self-control. She is a strong person, worthy of the highest respect. I don't know how to explain it, but if I would describe it with one word, I would be 'admiration'. I bow to my wife and am happy that she gave me so many happy years..."

"The first stage of chemotherapy is over. What's next, what is the treatment programme?"

"In short, the next most important stage is spinal cord puncture. After that, in a couple of days, a lot more about the disease will become clearer. It is clear what kind of expectations that I, Irina and her granddaughters have.

"Your round-the-clock support in the ward, I hope, is not due to a lack of attention by the staff?"

"We can't complain about that. In this regard, everything is organised perfectly in the clinic. And the attending physician, Professor Buchner, is a world-famous luminary."

"When you are alone with Raya, what do you talk about with her, if you don't mind me asking?"

"What can we really talk about right now... the moment between the past and the future?"

"Maybe, to digress a little, let's talk about politics?"

"I'd rather not talk about that right now."

We didn't talk about politics. We chatted about this and that for a few more minutes. Then Mikhail quickly got ready and went to support the person dearest to him.

And I, with several of my colleagues, went to "catch" the elusive Professor Buchner, out of journalistic necessity. While waiting for the doctor, I managed to get my hands on a document – "Medical Bulletin", whose contents I will quote in full:

"Mrs. Raisa Gorbacheva has been staying in our clinic for 18 days due to an acute form of leukaemia. She is in a critical phase of therapy. The patient is very debilitated from leukaemia and chemotherapy. Many clinic specialists are involved in the treatment of Mrs. Gorbacheva. It will be possible to talk about the results of the first phase of treatment only after some time has passed."

We asked questions to the attending physician Professor Buchner, about what is allowed to be revealed currently.

"The bulletin talks about a 'critical phase of therapy', can you please explain what this means?"

"It takes four to six weeks of therapy to stop the progression of the disease. Until it ends completely, we cannot breathe a sigh of relief. The first phase of therapy for such a disease works approximately the same way. The disease still cannot be stopped – to this, in addition, side effects associated with the therapy itself are added. As you know, not only sick cells are affected, but there is also a negative effect on other cells and organs."

They have developed a large-scale strategy on how to deal with emerging complications.

"What is your main goal at this stage of this treatment?"

"To achieve remission and stop the development of the disease. In our opinion, a second stage of chemotherapy will be required.

"From your experience, what is the percentage chance of achieving remission with such diseases?"

"Mrs. Gorbacheva has a very serious form of leukaemia. In principle, we have achieved remission in seventy percent of similar cases. The chances of a complete cure are about fifty-fifty. We believe that our efforts will lead to success, but it is still too early to relax and believe that the main problems have been solved. ...The first stage of chemotherapy is over. The fight for life and health continues."

'Trud', August 13th, 1999

Diaries. Interviews. Letters

Fiammetta KUKURNIA,
Correspondent for the Italian newspaper "La Repubblica" – for
the "Obshchaya Gazeta"

(Note: Kukurnia's speech is represented with italics)

Mikhail Gorbachev Signs the Most Important Document of his Life

I came to Münster in those days when a scandal broke out and newspapers all over the world were talking about the gigantic network of corruption that swallowed up Russia, and, it would seem, it wasn't without the participation of its leading circles. But here, in this green town of northern Germany, another face of Russia appeared before me. A Russia of decent people. A Russia of those who know how to love, respect and who know what honesty and devotion are – both in grief and in joy... Mikhail Gorbachev returned to his hotel at eleven o'clock in the evening. Exhausted and tired from the weight of waiting for fifty-two agonising days. He is wearing the same jeans and T-shirt. His eyes are red, they are the eyes of someone who doesn't sleep. And it seems to me that I have never seen him so sad and lonely before. He warmly hugs me and quietly says:

341

— "It's very difficult at the moment."

Tonight, Mikhail Sergeyevich does not want to have supper. He doesn't even try to get some rest. I have a lot of hard work ahead of me, all night. Gorbachev says that doctors are preparing Raisa Maksimovna for transplantation. This is a new technique of transplantation through the blood. Raisa Maksimovna has a sister – the kind and gentle Lyudmila Maksimovna. She has been in Münster for several days now. Everyone knows that brothers and sisters are the best donors. Nevertheless, in this case, there is a possibility of rejection. The possibility of it happening or not will become clear only after the operation. Science cannot yet give an accurate prediction.

Tonight, Mikhail Sergeyevich must read and study the papers that the doctors have just given him. He must try to understand between the lines of the sterile language, to know what the medicine is, what are the dangers and what are the real possibilities. Only then will he put down his signature. The morning sun rises, it's warm and sunny in the outgoing summer. At half past eight in the morning, Mikhail Sergeyevich is ready to go to the clinic. He crosses the park on foot, then, as he has done every day, goes through the corridors full of grief. He approaches the ward of his wife, takes off his overclothes and shoes, puts on a white coat and, finally, crosses the threshold of a sterile room where the other half of his soul is. We walk along a long park alley, followed by a bodyguard, like his shadow and friend. Bicycles rush past, and from time to time someone stops to say hello and support him with kind words. They speak both German and Russian, unceremoniously, as if they have known each other all their lives.

— "Like in my village Privolnoye," he says.

But in reality, nothing can distract him from the heaviness that lies on his heart. I am very worried. After such tension and fear, we now face the most difficult stage before us. No one can predict how it will turn out and how long it will last. We are waiting for a transplant. Lyuda came here to be a donor. But she couldn't even see her sister. They are not only sisters, but also great friends, which means that it would be a huge stress for Raisa Maksimovna to see Lyuda here. The sister managed to approach the ward and silently look from afar, but only once. Dear Lyuda. But what do the doctors say? What are the chances? There is only one hope: transplantation. But there is a risk, and a very serious one. Doctors don't talk about success rates. They say there is hope. And we hope. Their research proves that there is a possibility of remission of the disease after surgery. If only she could muster even a little bit of strength so that she could perform this operation... Irina should be back soon. She left for Moscow to collect the children for the beginning of the school year. Everyone is trying to persuade Mikhail Sergeyevich to take a break and go home for a few days when Irina arrives. I confess that I am also trying to tell him to think about himself. But I immediately feel ashamed. He looks at me in bewilderment, as if I had betrayed him.

— "My place is here, next to her. We have lived our life together, both in struggle and in joy, we must overcome this together.

She would do the same for me."

A long silence follows…

— "There are moments in life when we better understand what is most important to us. For example, when children get sick, you want to be in their place. The same thing happens when a loved one suffers: they are a part of your life, especially if it's a woman, a partner. In a moment of such misfortune, we regained the cordiality of our country, as if our grief had erased a misunderstanding. No, I can't go anywhere, my place is here. We'll come home together when we get better."

He has reddened eyes. I don't know whether it was from a sleepless night, or from tears.

September 9, 1999

Editors of "Novaya Gazeta"

He and She

All people have feelings. But not everyone can be great. And if there are, then not everyone lets the whole world know. Apparently, a real great feeling is one that only He and She knows. Otherwise, it's art. Or an artificial feeling. Everyone was talking about the Gorbachevs' relationship. They used all kinds of words, except the word "love". Now all those words are forgotten except for one. And the most accurate one. When Mikhail Sergeyevich gave an interview on NTV, he did not utter a single 'strong'" adjective. He also held back on verbs. Only his voice and eyes betrayed him. Lord, is it possible to have politics close to your heart? It turns out you can. Women have always envied Gorbacheva. Secretly. Now that envy has become bright and clear. If happiness is real, then they do not envy it, because it warms everyone. It's good that they spoke about it simply and warmly. Now not only Mikhail is praying for Paradise. But so are we. If tears appeared, if they talk and chat about it, if the pain of one materialised in the minds of hundreds and thousands... She is used to hate. He stands for... do you need all of the accusations repeated? She stands for the party leadership of the President, for appearing on the political stage in beautiful outfits. And then – the news of her illness. And on the screens – he was there. Not as a politician, not as an ex–President. He was in his highest position: A Loving Man.

We believe that after all they will return. To another country. Russia has become different because it has comprehended something new in love, fidelity and beauty. Not all people have feelings. But let them be with everyone whom we allowed to power.

P.S. The doctors told us: it was Raisa Maksimovna, who, without advertising anywhere, helped the 1st Republican Children's Hospital, personally and seriously, a place where children with similar diagnoses are treated. "The hospital is world class. We can only wish that she had the same."

August 9ᵗʰ–15ᵗʰ, 1999

ARTICLES
OF SAD DAYS

(Published on and after September 20ᵗʰ, 1999)

11 Hours 28 Minutes
ITAR–TASS (Urgent)

Moscow, September 20ᵗʰ (correspondent: ITAR–TASS)

The life of Raisa Gorbacheva, the wife of the first President of the USSR, Mikhail Gorbachev, ended today at the university clinic in the German city of Munster.

Cause of Death

Raisa Gorbacheva suffered from the most severe form of leukaemia – blood cancer. According to the medical bulletin, signed by the attending physician of Raisa Maksimovna from the University Clinic of Internal Medicine in Münster, Professor Büchner, the chromosomes of the patient's leukemic cells were completely reborn. Therefore, the initial chemotherapy was only partially successful. A planned bone marrow transplant (Gorbacheva's sister became the donor) was postponed due to a severe infection in the patient's body. She was transferred to the intensive care unit. However, at this point, the leukaemia began to progress again. This led to a violation of blood circulation in all of the internal organs, which caused the death of Raisa Maksimovna.

Parting

Boris Yeltsin offered his help and support to Gorbachev at this difficult moment. By his order, a coffin with the body of Raisa

Gorbacheva will be delivered from Germany, on board a TU–134 aircraft of the Rossiya airline, to the capital's Vnukovo–2 airport on the evening of September 21st. As 'Izvestia' was informed in the Gorbachev Fund, the farewell to the wife of the first President of the USSR will take place on Wednesday, September 22nd, in the building of the Russian Cultural Fund.

Raisa Gorbacheva will be buried at the Novodevichy Cemetery in Moscow on Thursday, September 23rd. All those who come to the funeral from abroad will be able to obtain a visa directly at the Sheremetyevo Airport.

'Izvestia', No. 176, September 21st, 1999

Loss

They were always together: at official meetings, at social events, in all of the official and home photographs, Raisa Maksimovna is next to Mikhail Sergeyevich… The spectrum of people's attitude to their 'No. 1 Woman' was great: from adoration and admiration to hatred. There were no indifferent people. Hatred for the transience of time has passed, but love has remained. The Gorbachev Foundation still receives bags of letters from all over the country and from abroad, addressed to Raisa Maksimovna. There are different ways to assess what Mikhail Gorbachev did for the country: some blame him for all of the troubles of today, some regret that there was not enough time to complete what was started… History will put everything in its place. But we lived in the 'Era of Gorbachev.' And who knows what this era would have been like if Raisa Maksimovna had not been next to Mikhail Sergeyevich all these years.

They were the brightest couple in the entire Soviet history, and even in the post-Soviet period. While Mikhail Gorbachev expanded the world lexicon with the concepts of 'Perestroika' and 'Glasnost', Raisa Maksimovna introduced the concept of 'First Lady of the State' into Russian everyday life. The appearance of the wife of the Soviet President had no less effect for Russia than the destruction of the Berlin Wall for the West. Gossip immediately spread that Raisa Maksimovna influences all decisions made by the head of state. The people simply could not realise that a normal family was very important for the head of the USSR, a reliable foundation that supports him, without which it would have been unthinkable to withstand, especially during the inhuman amount of work during the 'Perestroika' years. The Gorbachevs themselves never asked themselves the question "Who Influences Whom", at the Komsomol wedding there was no oath "to be together in sorrow and in joy until death do us part," – they have simply always been together since their student days, from the day they met while studying at Moscow State University. To the very end.

"We were young, energetic," Mikhail Sergeyevich recalled in his interview with 'MK' a year ago. "When Raisa Maksimovna was doing her sociological surveys, she ran around in rubber boots through the mud in several villages all at once..." Years later, the manners and outfits of a former girl from the city of Rubtsovsk in the Altai Territory, who ran through the mud of rural roads in search of material for a diploma, would become the subject of discussions throughout the world press. How does she do it, what world celebrities sheathed the First Lady of the USSR? "As the wife of the President, I have always considered it my duty to dress only with Russian fashion designers," Raisa Maksimovna especially emphasised. Probably, only she could make them sew like that... Neither before nor after, no one could compare with her. Always strict, toned, dressed with impeccable taste, great hair, even in recent years, when she was already very sick and appeared less and less in public...

Being the wife of the head of state and after Gorbachev left the presidency, Raisa Gorbacheva did a lot of charitable work. With her help, the Cultural Foundation was created – the first public charitable organisation in Russia. The new buildings of the 'Gorbachev Foundation', the 'Perestroika' museum with a library – Raisa Maksimovna paid great attention to everything. Now the building is completed, the packed things are waiting to be moved – they were delayed, waiting for the return of Raisa Maksimovna and Mikhail Sergeyevich from Germany... A long list of institutions: hospitals, orphanages, boarding schools, committees of veterans, creative teams – they helped everyone: some with money, some with equipment which assisted studies... It's a terrible coincidence that Raisa Maksimovna always paid her main attention to the Research Institute of Paediatric Haematology at the Children's Republican Hospital, the priority charitable project of the Gorbachev Foundation was participation in the work of the international association 'World Haematologists for Children' and the program 'Children's Leukaemia in Russia'. Millions of dollars were spent on the fight against a terrible disease: royalties for books by Mikhail Gorbachev and Raisa Maksimovna herself, sponsorship money. More than eight million dollars spent for the purchase of medicines and equipment for the 'Centre for Bone Marrow Transplantation' – the first medical centre in Russia where such operations were performed. At the expense of the Foundation, many doctors were trained abroad. How many lives were saved thanks to this help... The doctors, alas, were powerless to help Raisa Maksimovna herself.

When we asked Raisa Maksimovna for an interview a year ago, it was clear that it was not easy for her to speak. Especially about what affected the fate of her loved ones, her family, people whom she and Mikhail Sergeyevich considered friends. Raisa Maksimovna never recovered from the events in Foros. What has become history for us, remains an unhealed wound for her. Tears stood in her eyes as she recalled the events of that terrible August. "The betrayal of our closest friends, those with whom everything started, whom we trusted..." It's unfortunate that we were not allowed to continue, we were stopped halfway. And yet – we fear for the family. The family has always been the main thing in the life of Raisa Maksimovna. Her 'girls' – that's what she called her daughter Irina and her two granddaughters. Every weekend, if there were no foreign business trips, the whole family would definitely gather at the Gorbachevs' dacha... Largely thanks to his wife, Mikhail Sergeyevich continued his active political life in recent years. Now it will be difficult. It will be very difficult just to exist, without Raisa Maksimovna... We all believe and hope that Mikhail Sergeyevich, Irina Mikhailovna, the entire Gorbachev family will find the strength to endure the pain of loss. The Moskovsky Komsomolets team expresses its deepest condolences to all the relatives and friends of Raisa Maksimovna Gorbacheva.

"Moskovsky Komsomolets",
September 21ˢᵗ, 1999

Gayaz ALIMOV, Yuri BOGOMOLOV

Last Autumn

She's gone. A woman who was just being a woman and a wife turned the world upside down. Our Soviet, concrete and grey world. But not only ours. The entire world suddenly saw a completely different woman – one that is graceful, elegant, well put together. With everything she did, you could not help but love her. And by God, by the General Secretary of the Central Committee of the CPSU as well. Gorbachev himself was seen as a saviour. From long despair. He managed to justify our hope, which became more and more impatient over the years, for the best. And he was able to breathe a fresh, cleansing wind into the sails of a decrepit, falling country. Raisa was next to him. A fragile woman who brought out envy in others. She was not perceived accurately, perhaps also because she was independent, and was not some kind of appendage of supreme power. Raisa Maksimovna has become our history to the same extent as Mikhail Gorbachev. And she is a sign of the current era. The first sign of the 'Perestroika' that began in 1985: at the General Secretary of the Central Committee of the CPSU, speaking before anything was put down on paper. Second, his wife is a pretty woman, and the fact that she is next to him at official receptions and on business trips. This immediately Europeanised her in the eyes of the world community. Yes, and we – as a community – have become Europeanised in our own eyes. We must recall the Soviet tradition, established by comrade Stalin, by virtue of which the wives of the country's leaders remained outside their public life. They were off-stage characters. They were established for everyday life and leisure.

The Gorbachevs broke that tradition. The significance of this mini-revolution can be appreciated if we remember that, in general, the Soviet mentality assumed the erasure of the border not only between the city and the countryside, but also between a man and a woman. In favour of the man, of course. Not without reason, the role of the 'mystery woman' left the Soviet cinema of the thirties. A woman in the cinema was allowed to become a member of the government, but on the condition that she ceased to be a woman. She was allowed to become on a par with a man, but on the condition that she outrun him on a horse. Raisa Maksimovna did not stop her galloping horse, did not enter a burning hut, did not compete with anyone – she remained herself and was her husband's true friend and companion. That was a feat. Today it would be a sin not to remember that in the mass subconscious, he aroused as much respect as irritation. This is because the Gorbachevs made their own mini counter-revolution, but we as a whole did not. The woman who elevated our Motherland has left. In the eyes of not only our country, when Russia was under the name of the USSR, but also in the eyes of the whole world. She was like a flash of a new star. She flared up and shone; unfortunately, it was not for long. But the stars have such a divine feature – even when dying, they leave their mark. She was loved and hated. She was often misunderstood. But no one has ever remained indifferent to her. She was not like everyone else. She didn't look like anyone. And, of course, they envied her. She has been unconscious for the last few days. But in moments of clarity, seeing her Mikhail next to her, she once said only three words: "Whilst he's near..." This Russian family, having lost the heights of supreme power, remained worthy, resistant to shocks, grief, insults. Raisa Maksimovna and Mikhail Sergeyevich were together until the last second. And now Gorbachev is alone. It's not just his personal loss. We all lost her, a bright and unique woman. We will always remember who she was. And with her appearance she opened another Russia to the world. A Russian with a female spirit – a loving, devoted and faithful spirit. Farewell, our First Lady... Farewell and forgive us.

'Izvestia', No. 176,
September 21st, 1999

UNTIL
THE FATED DAY...

From the Letters

That came on the eve of September 20th, 1999

Dear Raisa Maksimovna, Hello!

It is with great sadness that our family learned of your illness. We often, and with gratitude, recall the participation shown by you, Raisa Maksimovna, and Mikhail Sergeyevich. Thanks to you, we managed to send our only son Valery to Germany for treatment. In 1990, he was diagnosed with acute leukaemia. With your help and with the help of German doctors, the disease was defeated. Now our son is healthy, he studies at the Moscow State Social University. A low bow to you and Mikhail Sergeyevich for what you have done for us! With appreciation and gratitude, the Uvarov family.

P.S. There are four of us now. Valera has a little brother Maksim.

Uvarovs:
Larisa Nikolaevna,
Yuri Arkadyevich,
Valery and Maksim,
Odintsovo, Moscow Region.

Raisa Maksimovna and Mikhail Sergeyevich Gorbachev!
Our dearests! Be strong in spirit. Win with love! Understand and accept this challenge. We love you and pray for you.

Alla and Andrey Fomina,
Kira Anatolyevna Barabanova,
Cheboksary.

Dear Mikhail!
Mila and I were very upset when we learned about Raisa's illness. We hope that her condition will improve, and that she will find health and peace with you, her daughter and granddaughters. Warmest regards.

Yours sincerely
Brian Mulroney, *Montreal*

Dear Mikhail Sergeyevich!
I was informed that your wife fell ill and has been in a clinic in Germany for a long time. I am very worried about this. I can imagine how much you are worried.

Sincerely,
Nakasone Yasuhiro, *Tokyo*

Dear Mikhail Sergeyevich!
I was deeply moved by the news of the illness of your wife Raisa Maksimovna. I recall with pleasure our meetings and conversations, in which Raisa Maksimovna often took part. She was

always interested in the state of affairs, actively supported the conversations. Your business stays in Vilnius in those turbulent days of January 1990 left a great impression on me. Although discussions on solving existing problems took up a lot of time, communication with you and Raisa Maksimovna was always pleasant and interesting. I hope that soon everything will work out for you, that there will be an opportunity to meet with you, Raisa Maksimovna, and have a joint conversation on various topics.

Sincerely,
Algirdas Brazauskas,
Vilnius

Dear Raisa Maksimovna!
In these difficult days, I decided to write you a letter of gratitude, admiration and support for you. You are a model of elegance and femininity for me. I really never cease to admire your mind and strength of character. You, along with Mikhail Sergeyevich, had to experience so many difficulties, but you never betrayed yourself. Your relationship with Mikhail Sergeyevich is for me the ideal of relations between spouses, an example of love, sincerity, and mutual understanding.

With respect and love,
Galina Nikolaevna Sokolova,
Moscow

Good afternoon, Mikhail Sergeyevich and your whole family!

The one writing to you is a grandmother of a grandson, who in 1987 was sentenced to acute leukaemia. At that time, I was working in the Irkutsk region, and when I received a letter from my daughter, a day was enough for all the hairs on my head to turn grey. This was my first grandson; he was my entire life. Briefly there was local resident, who after seeing me, advised to give him some grass that grows in their region. I immediately sent her to get it, and we gave Janik, the grandson, water all the time. The grass is called "bone-eater" by the common people, I don't know its proper name. We did everything possible, and now my grandson is alive and well – he served in the army, got married. But they say that he survived thanks to a 'grandmother's heart.' I found the address where the grass was sent to me from, please have a look at it and give Raisa Maksimovna lots of water, because we also went through everything – chemotherapy and such.

Galina Arsentievna Smolyanova,
Krasnodar

'Moscow News',
September 21ˢᵗ–27ᵗʰ, 1999

To the President of the USSR Mikhail Sergeyevich Gorbachev – I pray to God for the recovery of Raisa Maksimovna. You saved my son. Thank you, sir. You are a wise teacher

Anna Ivanovna Gorlach
Arkhangelsk Region, August 5ᵗʰ, 1999

SORROW
AND MEMORY

Raisa, What Hurts My Heart

David Chikvaidze,
Head of the Secretariat Office
Director General of the UN Geneva Office

I Trust You!

December 25th, 1991. Mikhail Sergeyevich has just made a statement about the termination of his activities as President of the USSR. After seeing off the main guests, journalists and other visitors who flocked to the Kremlin from all over the world to witness this unprecedented event, my colleagues and I began to disperse. I went downstairs to my office, leaned back in my chair, and stared at the wall. The events of that day, the previous months, the memories, thoughts about the future, everything swirled in my head in a chaotic, uncontrollable cycle. About an hour later, still in a state of numbness, I opened the centre drawer of my desk and sorted through the contents without much purpose. In a folder, I found a photograph of Raisa Maksimovna and Barbara Bush, taken by the official photographer of the White House during the opening ceremony of the sculptural composition 'The Way for the Ducklings' at the Novodevichy Convent, where B. Bush donated to the children of the Soviet Union during the visit of the US President to the USSR a few months earlier.

I turned to the computer and began to write a letter: "Dear Raisa Maksimovna! May God bless you and Mikhail Sergeyevich with health and long life, but this evening I keenly feel what the Americans felt when they learned about the assassination of John F. Kennedy." My short but emotional letter asked for a signature on the attached photograph: "The boy in the striped shirt standing next to you as part of a group of children is Sasha Chikvaidze, that's my son." I was sure that Raisa Maksimovna would remember the first and last name; Sasha Chikvaidze. My father was a classmate of Mikhail Sergeyevich at the law faculty of Moscow State University. A few days later I received the photo through a security officer with the caption: "Sasha! R. Gorbacheva. 1991".

Our family, as well as the majority of the Soviet people, accepted the election of M.S. Gorbachev as General Secretary of the Central Committee of the CPSU with joy and enthusiasm. But nothing compares to the feelings I experienced on December 7th, 1987, after long weeks of working as part of an embassy team preparing a visit to the United States. For the first time in my life, I saw M. S. and R. M. Gorbachev descending the gangway at Andrews Air Force Base near Washington. It was pride in its purest form, pride for the young, energetic President, for the elegant and charismatic First Lady, for the country! In the 'electrified', solemn, even festive, atmosphere that reigned at the moment the Andrews base flooded with spotlights, the American analogue of Vnukovo–2, hope was also clearly felt. The hope that the USSR and the USA will finally be able to put their relationship on a balanced, good–neighbourly, mutually beneficial basis and not be subject to emotional "ebb and flow".

Gaining experience at the "top meetings" in Washington and New York, I did not suspect that after the end of my business trip to the USA, from October 1990, I would start working in the "newly minted" Protocol Department of the Administration of the President of the USSR, that was created shortly before, I would share general responsibilities for the reception of foreign delegations and preparatory work on the road with my colleagues. Increasingly, they began to send me to work with Raisa Maksimovna, which in professional jargon we called "according to the women's program." This was a special responsibility, since the "women's program" itself, as a rule, was complex, filled with meaningful and high–profile elements. First of all, this was determined by the personality of Raisa Maksimovna herself: a highly professional, elegant modern woman, with a sharp intellect, encyclopaedic knowledge, diverse interests and attention to detail. She was a woman with a kind, open smile, an ability to carry herself with dignity, without aplomb, which attracted not only people, but also cameras. A certain difficulty in working out the program of the First Lady, in comparison with the program of the President, was that the latter was the object of painstaking work "through diplomatic channels" and was the result of long political negotiations, where everything was verified, agreed and not subject to fundamental changes at the final stage. But the "women's program" was a much more "creative" process and made it possible to optimally "bring" it to the level that best met the goals of the visit. Sometimes this desire of ours caused certain difficulties in negotiations with the host country. So was the case during the preparation of the first ever visit of the leader of the USSR to Japan in April 1991. But, thanks to the wisdom of Raisa Maksimovna and the flexibility of the advanced groups on both sides, everything was settled, and a visit to the school was included in Raisa Maksimovna's program. For Raisa Maksimovna, the issues of childhood and children's health were above others, primarily in her own country, but also during her visits abroad.

Raisa Maksimovna was a demanding, but at the same time a benevolent and kind person. This was clearly manifested in the moments of "overlays". One of them just so happened during that same visit to Japan. Due to the lack of mobile communications at that time, all commands, changes in the program and urgent information were transmitted through the special Soviet switch-board. Despite the transmitted information about the change in the program, the team did not reach the press pool, which, having filmed an element of the President's program, were supposed to join R. M. Gorbacheva's cortege. Despite this serious incident, Raisa Maksimovna ordered not to "look for the switchman" and even more so to punish. I was very grateful to her for this, because apart from me there were no candidates for the role of "switchman" in that situation. In general, I have never seen Raisa Maksimovna scold anyone in public. A deeply intelligent woman, she did not humiliate herself or anyone else with such behaviour, one look from her was enough. Raisa Maksimovna enjoyed great respect and authority in the world. In 1989, a group of women led by Ingrid Hills, an American public figure from San Francisco, created the 'Friends of Raisa Gorbacheva' society in recognition of the important contribution of R. M. Gorbacheva to the development of democratic principles in the Soviet Union. Raisa Maksimovna met with the group during a visit to Washington in 1990 and during the visit of Ingrid Hills and her colleagues to Moscow in the spring of 1991, where they discussed the project of financing by the Friends group a position for Soviet economic researchers at the Institute of International Studies at the University of California at Berkeley. The program ran until 1993.

The last time I saw Raisa Maksimovna was in the summer of 1992 at a reception on the occasion of the opening of the new building of the German embassy in Moscow on Mosfilmovskaya Street. When Mikhail Sergeyevich and Raisa Maksimovna entered the hall, those present fell silent a little and parted in the centre, standing up somehow in a half turn. Once in the second row, not far from the entrance, I ducked and greeted "my President" and "my First Lady", despite the fact that at that time he was already working in the protocol department of the President of Russia. After exchanging warm greetings with me, Raisa Maksimovna turned to Mikhail Sergeyevich: "Mikhail Sergeyevich, I would like to look at myself in the mirror to make sure that everything is in order." Taking the liberty, I said: "Raisa Maksimovna, you look great!" She looked at me with surprise and, smiling, said: "I trust you!" And to Mikhail Sergeyevich's obvious relief, she added: "I changed my mind, Mikhail Sergeyevich." This is how I remember Raisa Maksimovna.

November 14th, 2021

Oleg KHLEBNIKOV,
Leading Editor of 'Novaya Gazeta'

In Memory of R. M.

These are jealous times,
where temper is unsociable...
You didn't like that she – was with him?
Well now, he's alone

Maybe they will be forgiven even now
with an ailment of fidelity.
After all, when on the rise, we were overtaken by
the fear of separation.

And that separation awaits everyone –
the important, the one.
Forgive their happiness of mortal sins,
this sinful country!

Look who you have lost
and to whom – a widow –
you gave yourself up by the right of simplicity –
a crime worse than theft.

Listen, are there really doubts
in this chosen destiny?
How will you forgive, love and honour,
those who are strangers to you...

'Novaya Gazeta', No. 35, September 23rd–26th, 1999

Fragments of Letters

That Came after September 20th, 1999

It is with deep sorrow that I learned of the death of your wife Raisa. In such moments of pain, words are powerless. I want to express my most sincere condolences to you on my own behalf and on behalf of the French people.

Jacques Chirac

Raisa Gorbacheva was a highly educated, eloquent and charming woman. She and her husband were an inseparable couple, and Raisa's continued support greatly contributed to President Gorbachev's political accomplishments and the great reforms he introduced in the Soviet Union.

Margaret Thatcher

I am deeply saddened by the news of the death of your beloved wife. Please accept our most sincere condolences. I hope the devotion of your family and friends will give you the strength to bear this loss. I pray for you.

Pope John Paul II

The Italian people will remember Raisa Gorbacheva with warmth and love.

Azeglio Ciampi, President of Italy

Raisa Gorbacheva evoked deep respect and admiration in our country. Her human warmth, as well as the courage shown in recent weeks, deeply touched the people in Germany. I wish you, dear Mr. Gorbachev, strength and God's blessing at this difficult time.

Johannes Rau, President of Germany

Raisa Gorbachev was an outstanding personality whose determination and strength helped the former Soviet President Mikhail Gorbachev in his political life and the politics of change. I personally and the German people are deeply grateful to Raisa Gorbacheva for everything she has done for us. Today, Mikhail Gorbachev is not alone in his grief.

Helmut Kohl

Dear Mikhail Sergeyevich!
The artist Sergei Yursky is writing to you. This tragic day of your life has become a day of mourning for me and for my wife Natalya Tenyakova. Since 1985, when I first got to know you and the unforgettable Raisa Maksimovna, I have been a fan of your family. I am absolutely sure that for many centuries that Russia has existed you are the only real human ruler. I was always touched and admired that at all the twists and turns of journey you always managed to sincerely preserve and emphasise your unity with your wife and the importance of that unity. We met once, for a bit, but I closely paid attention to all of yours and Raisa Maksimovna's

appearances on the television. Today I, like thousands of others, mourn with you. We heard the news from Germany with personal anxiety and personal hopes. And now this is our personal grief. We have but blessed memories of the wonderful woman, Raisa Maksimovna! Be strong, dear Mikhail Sergeyevich, people really need you. Sincerely and respectfully.

Sergei Yursky, Natalia Tenyakova

Dear Mikhail Sergeyevich!
Bolshoi Tovstonogov Drama Theatre is shocked by the news of the death of Raisa Maksimovna, an outstanding personality, and for us, a friend, a wonderful and sincere person, our meetings and communication with whom will remain in our memory forever. We mourn with you, dear Mikhail Sergeyevich. It is without saying, but you are always welcome and a dear guest in our theatre.

Kirill Lavrov and the Whole Team
Bolshoi Tovstonogov Theatre

Dear Mikhail Sergeyevich!
We mourn with you. Stay strong. Your family is with you always and through everything.

Vladimir Gusinsky, Igor Malashenko,
Oleg Dobrodeev, Evgeny Kiselev

Dear Mikhail Sergeyevich!
I am deeply saddened by the death of your wife Raisa Maksimovna Gorbacheva. On behalf of the government of the Russian Federation and on my own behalf, I express my most sincere con-

dolences to you and your family. Always, in grief and joy, she was not just a wife, but first and foremost, a devoted friend. We will always remember her.

Prime Minister of the
Russian Federation
V. Putin

Dear Mikhail Sergeyevich!
Realising that no words can free you from the gravest shock of these last few days, we still cannot but repeat to you: we have always been with you and will always be with you. Eternal memory to a bright person and beautiful woman, Raisa Maksimovna Gorbacheva. With love.

Leonid and Nina Filatov

Dear Mikhail Sergeyevich!
Raisa Maksimovna is part of the history of the USSR, the famous Perestroika, these bright renewed days. With her departure, something very good, beautiful and significant is cut off. This loss is irreparable, and grief is inescapable. I often think of her. Her face, her manner of speaking, laughing – all this has long since been stored deeply in my heart. I would like to be with you at such a difficult time, to support you, to assure you that we all still love you. Today it is not customary to confess one's love to politicians, but life is too short to conceal the impulses of the heart. Please

accept my condolences, dear Mikhail Sergeyevich. Always yours.

Rodion Nakhapetov
September 22, 1999

Mikhail Sergeyevich Gorbachev,

I think that this is a mournful day for all of us, the day of our pain and sorrow. This day will not be able to obscure the impact of this amazing, beautiful woman, who so organically combined intelligence and kindness, unusual cordiality and firmness, amazing responsiveness and a sincerity that's hard to find in modern times. She always knew how to remain a brilliant, elegant, graceful woman at all times, a person at all times. She will remain with us forever. I bow my head low.

Vladimir Spivakov

Dear Mikhail Sergeyevich!

The 'soldiers' mothers' of Russia are very sympathetic to your grief. We mourn with you. Those of us who have been to the Raisa Maksimovna Club remember her as kind, hospitable and very attentive to people. I don't want to believe that she is gone. We can well imagine how difficult it will be for you without your loved one. After all, many of us have lost sons and know how it feels – the loss of a dear and close person. We wish you courage and strength to endure this terrible grief. There are a lot of 'soldiers' mothers' in Russia, and they all sincerely sympathise and condole with you.

Members:
Union of Committees of Soldiers' Mothers of Russia
Regional Movement of Soldiers' Mothers "Solidarity"
Association of Soldiers' Mothers of the Chelyabinsk Region
Nizhny Novgorod Regional Committee of Soldiers' Moth-
ers
Volgograd regional organisation "Mother's Right"
Committee of Soldiers' Mothers of Sochi,
Miass City Committee of Soldiers' Mothers
Committee of Soldiers' Mothers of the city of Sarapul,
Tyumen Regional Committee of Soldiers' Mothers
Tomsk Committee of Soldiers' Mothers
Representative of the COP UKSMR in Murmansk and
many members of other organisations of soldiers' mothers.
September 22ⁿᵈ, 1999

Dear Mikhail Sergeyevich!
Our condolences. We grieve – the death of such a wonderful
woman that Raisa Maksimovna was, many St. Petersburg residents
experienced this as a personal drama... Mikhail Sergeyevich, please
write a book about Raisa Maksimovna, write about how difficult
it was for her to be the First Lady, how she studied it, how she
wanted to represent the country in the best light, to spread good
and beauty – after all, many simply do not know this! Many people
think that her life is just "cheese in butter", that she only took from
life and gave nothing away. We are waiting for this book – "The

First Lady of the Russian Land." Take care of yourself, we need you!
But Raisa Maksimovna did not die, her voice, her image is always
with us! With deepest respect.

Galina Aleksandrovna *Morozova and others*
September 22, 1999, St. Petersburg

To Mr Mikhail Gorbachev,
Dear Michael!

With a heavy heart, I send my sincere condolences to your
family regarding the death of your beautiful wife Raisa. Being one
of the few people who had the honour of knowing her personally,
I, like many other Americans, understood what a bright personality she was. I believe that women like your wife were a rarity in
the modern world. Her charm, sensitive heart and mind were an
example for everyone. Your wife also possessed great courage and
fortitude. I can only try to imagine how brave and determined a
person must be in order to follow one's principles and feelings, even
if they do not coincide with the opinion of the majority. And I will
always remember the time when I had a chance to communicate
with her. Maria and I hope you find comfort and peace in your
memories of her. Please remember that you are not alone in these
tragic days. We think of you and pray for you and your family.
With deepest respect.

Arnold Schwarzenegger,
September 23, 1999

To Mr. Mikhail Gorbachev
Moscow
Dear Mr. Gorbachev!
We were deeply moved and saddened by the news of your wife's death. Your wife's visit on 13th June 1989, to the cemetery of the former prisoner of war camp, Stalag 326 Stukenbrock-Senne, made this place famous throughout Germany and made a significant contribution to the creation of the Archive Documentation Centre, which opened in 1996. Since then, a permanent exhibition has been operating here, teaching about the life and death of Soviet prisoners of war in this region. One of our main tasks is to consider the clarification of the fate of more than 300 thousand prisoners of war who passed through this camp. Please accept the assurances of our sincere sympathy. The name of your wife will always be inextricably linked with our work. On behalf of the board of trustees.

Werner Busch, Dr. Reinhard Otto
Board of Trustees of the
Documentation Centre "Stalag 326 (VI–K) Senne"
September 27th, 1999
Mikhail Sergeyevich Gorbachev,
Academician Goldanskie Vitaly Losifovich,
Advisor to the Russian Academy of Sciences,
Institute of Chemical Physics,

Dear Mikhail Sergeyevich!

Having returned from abroad, we send you an expression of deepest sorrow and sympathy for the unforgettable Raisa Maksimovna, the most remarkable woman of Russia, forever imprinted in our history. We will always be your faithful friends and champions of yours and Raisa Maksimovna's great cause. We hug you tightly.

Goldanskie
October 28ᵗʰ, 1999

Honoured and Dear Mikhail Sergeyevich!

In the richest of the Russian language, I cannot find the words that could convey the severity of the blow that fell on your family and on everyone who loves you. This is what I am, a sinner. I will never, until the last hour, forget the attention I received from the unforgettable Raisa Maksimovna and from you. It was for me, and me alone, an attention I'll remember through my entire Soviet life. When I found out about what had happened, at that time I was conducting Mahler's 3rd Symphony in Holland. I dedicated the last part of this brilliant work to the blessed memory of Raisa Maksimovna. Tears were running down my face. The Dutch were crying too... stay strong. And know: millions of people are with you! And are devoted to you!

Evgeny Svetlanov
October 1999

Parting Words

Raisa Maksimovna. First Lady of the country, public figure, loving wife and mother. A bright image that has left its unique mark in the history of recent decades. Raisa Maksimovna introduced the whole world to the new image of a Russian woman – purposeful and independent, charming and educated. Nature endowed her with a penetrating mind and a sympathetic nature. Therefore, she perceived everything that happened so sincerely, so close to her heart. And she lived her life honestly, in one breath. She got the extremely responsible and extremely difficult role of the wife of the President of a huge country at a time of a historical turning point and difficult trials. And she coped well with it. Her openness fascinated people and broke the ice of prejudices and old grievances. The news of her tragic death shocked the whole world. Raisa Maksimovna, her noble and spiritual appearance will forever remain in our memory.

Naina Yeltsina

Maria Rozanova

Only Great Women Can Evoke Such Great Feelings...

28.9.99. Ninth Day

Dear, dear, dear Mikhail Sergeyevich! I wanted to call you and suddenly realised that I could not talk, I could only cry. Back when they buried Sinyavsky, I didn't shed a tear, at the cemetery I found the strength to smile and almost laugh. I invited everyone to go into the house (fortunately, it was only ten minutes from his grave to mine) to "drink, eat and tell jokes that the deceased was very fond of." But when I watched you at Raisa Maksimovna's burial, I sobbed, quietly howling: "Andryusha, Andryushechka..." For a terrible thing happened before my eyes – "one rule" was broken, the main law of the fairy tale collapsed – "they lived happily and died on the same day." And it's always easier for me to be inside the horror than to look at it from the side...

Words of sympathy now are empty and meaningless. You yourself know, you yourself saw how the world around your house shook up, when Raisa Maksimovna fell ill and when she died, and for the ninth day now, I have been talking to you all the time, and with whomever I meet, everyone empathises and sympathises with you. But I want to tell you something completely different.

Once upon a time you were a big boss. The most important person. And suddenly they began to rock your chair, your throne. And they spoke all sorts of words and performed various actions. Some I liked, some I didn't. Sometimes I, with my big foul mouth, honoured you to the very last word, but there was one point where you struck my imagination. That point was with your wife. You know as well as I do, that the rumble of indignation came about because of "Raika" ("and why is she interfering", "and why is she poking her head where it doesn't belong"), but it was she who taught me to love you. Because when in disputes about her, I always say this first: "He loves her, and how wonderful it is!" And they objected to me: "So what if he loves her, I also love my wife" (and in fact, although our time is vile, but not everyone has forgotten how to love yet), then other words were formed later: he not only loves her, he is not afraid to show this love to everyone, he is not afraid of your gossip, your prejudices (you know how to our great people – beating, means to loves, and if teaching, then with a yoke), your condemnation. He is not a coward, and if he does something wrong, then he's a pioneer, he didn't study Perestroika anywhere... But where did this Russian-bred (see above) pioneer learn to aim so high, so beautifully, so brave, like a prince to love? It means that he has a great order in his soul, God laid a lot of things there. And she? What is she? She is just a great woman. Because only great women can evoke such great feelings...

Margaret Thatcher on Raisa Gorbacheva

She Entered Our Lives and Became a Symbol of Hope for Change, for a Better World.

...It was late autumn 1984 in Chequers. That day I saw how confidently Raisa Gorbacheva entered the great hall of the country residence of the Prime Minister of Great Britain. I had a premonition that the day would come when the powerful ice that had bound relations between Western European democracies and communist countries for forty years would finally melt. Raisa was completely different, not like those we used to associate with the Soviet system. She was a self–confident, bright and lively woman. Perhaps she was a bit like a teacher. She was dressed amazingly – her excellent taste was felt. She showed up that day in a beautifully tailored grey pin-stripe suit. I remember that I looked at her with envy: I also wanted such a suit. And after just a few minutes of conversation, it became clear that Raisa is a highly educated woman who can perfectly carry on a conversation with the British ministers whom I invited to Chequers. Seeing such dramatic changes in the Soviet elite, one could assume that the whole Soviet system was not far off.

I invited Mr. (not yet President) Gorbachev to the UK, because at that time he was one of the candidates for the highest post in the state, which was led by old, sick leaders, and I wanted to have a reserve for the future. I chose Chequers for our first meeting because I believed that in such an informal setting, we would have more opportunities to look at each other, understand the political lines of our countries and, accordingly, develop a vision for the future. And I wasn't disappointed. It didn't take long to realise that both Mr. Gorbachev and Raisa were something completely new, something that had never been seen before in our unpromising relationship with the Soviet Union. They had both a fresh look and openness in the discussion. There was nothing like it before. Simply put, they were an example of a completely new style, although adherence to certain old communist ideals continued to be felt. That time, Raisa and I did not get to talk because Mr. Gorbachev and I had official business to attend to. While we were working, my husband Denis showed Raisa the library – it is magnificent in Chequers. There she looked through the original letters of Napoleon, written during his exile on the island of St. Helena. Raisa chose books on the shelves, which made it immediately clear that she was an erudite person with a degree in philosophy. Denis, who himself is an excellent connoisseur of history, was simply shocked by her solid knowledge and well–aimed remarks.

This was my first meeting with Raisa. Then there were many other meetings both during the time when I was prime minister and after that. Many of them were on unofficial, "family" occasions: at a table in a small dining room on Downing Street, at dinner before visiting the Bolshoi Theatre in Moscow. One incident is particularly memorable when Raisa and President Gorbachev gave a dinner in our honour at a historic old mansion in Moscow. After dinner, we sat in front of a huge fireplace and spoke frankly about our work, about our hopes, about the aspirations of our countries. After this conversation, I began to respect Raisa even more. She had firm and independent views; she was always ready for energetic polemics. I myself am not a stranger to all these qualities! Definitely, her family suffered greatly in the 30s during the forced collectivization. Her grandfather died during the liquidation of the kulaks – then tens of thousands of such people died. But no matter how it affected her attitude towards communism, she remained a true patriot. She always defended the Soviet Union and the achievements of Soviet science, especially in the field of space research and education. She was very proud of her daughter Irina and granddaughters.

Raisa was charming and knew how to use that. She intrigued the British media with her elegant outfits, which were never deliberately flashy. She knew how to behave in public. I remember that one day, while I was having a meeting with President Gorbachev, our Minister of Education, Kenneth Baker, took her to a village school. He was delighted with how easily she communicated with children and with teachers. It immediately became clear that she herself taught a lot. In the Western democratic system during the election campaign, these qualities would provide her with great advantages. But most striking was her relationship with President

Gorbachev. It was a relationship of truly close people. They told me about how they met back in their student years, how they stood together in lines for tickets to the gallery of the Bolshoi Theatre. During the trying and difficult years of Perestroika, she constantly supported and encouraged President Gorbachev, although she never hesitated to argue with him at the "family council". It was felt that they were connected by bonds of loyalty and support. It was the same with my dear Denis. Then, as time passed, we saw with what tenderness President Gorbachev treats her: Raisa began to fall ill after the coup organised by supporters of the old style of communist leadership. All of us, participants in the historical events of those years, have grown old. Memories have faded. But I kept the image of Raisa forever. As I see her now: on that first day in Chequers, with a joyful smile, she entered our lives and became a symbol of hope for change, for a better world. A quarter of a century has passed since then.

From the Transcript of 'An Evening in the Memory of Raisa Maksimovna Gorbacheva' September 18th, 2000

Georgi Vladimirovich Pryakhin,
Writer

She Returns

Speaking today about the fate of Raisa Maksimovna, I would like to recall a popular expression that was very popular among the Moscow intelligentsia in the 60s and 70s. It belonged to one Soviet poet and sounded like this: "We all left from our people; how can we return to them..." In this joke, in my opinion, there is more truth than jokes. So, Raisa Maksimovna, a woman from the very thick of her people, from their very depths, showed in many ways how at some moments you need to rise above some of their ideas and even break away from it, and how, in the final moments, you must definitely return to it. This woman had difficult, but very intimate, blood and, I would even say, somewhat mystical ties with her people, including with the most difficult part of them – the women. I will recall only one detail from her biography. In the early 60s, she studied sociology at the Stavropol Agricultural Institute. With great zeal she went to our villages (I myself am from Stavropol) with a questionnaire. She wore huge rubber boots that were a size 40, so that at least three pairs of woollen socks would fit.

She went with a notebook. It was a very Russian form of sociology, because the respondents were mostly old women (since everything happened at the height of the working day, the rest of the population were on farms or in the fields), they not only answered the questions of the young sociologist, but also asked her very Russian questions. She told me about them. Here are the questions. First, does your husband beat you? Second, does your husband drink? And already after she was leaving, after tea, after pies, already at the gate, the old women asked Raisa Gorbacheva the third question – will there be a war? It was almost a very Rubtsovsk question. Raisa Gorbacheva answered the first two quite confidently. On the third, she found it difficult to answer. Perhaps even then she had a presentiment that her husband's fate would determine the answer to that question.

Raisa Gorbacheva has already entered the people's consciousness, legends and folk art twice. The first time was in 1985, when she was carefully led under the elbow by her brilliant husband. The second was in August 1999, when she went down the ladder in Munster, guided not only by her husband, but also by fate. She flew there, as far as I know, in a private plane, because there is no large airfield in Munster. She descended the ladder to a foreign German land and... returned to her people – but this time, forever. "If I asked God for an easy life, I should have asked for an easy death as well," wrote one of our pre-Soviet classics. By the way, today is the day of the Great Martyr Raisa. In translation, Raisa means "light". As for life, Raisa Gorbachev's life, especially before meeting Mikhail Gorbachev, can hardly be called easy. Perhaps the most important and only point of luck and good luck in her life was a meeting with her future spouse. Here I want to recall the worldly old truth. Each of us, sinful men, husbands (our women are truthfully sinless), are almost equally the product of our own mother and our own wife, whether we like it or not. And thank God, Mikhail Sergeyevich Gorbachev also did not escape our common male fate. Raisa Gorbacheva is back. She came back, maybe belatedly, as it happens in Russia, but she came back. Not to all at once, but to each one individually: insight does not always overtake everyone at once. Now it is clear that the separation from their people, which seemed to be the case since 1985, which actually opened up new horizons for other generations of women, expanded their horizons, provided new opportunities in behaviour, clothing, and simply in self-assertion. Raisa Gorbacheva has returned, just as Vasily Shukshin, Bulat Okudzhava and Nikolai Rubtsov have returned to us. This is characteristic of those people in whom the divine principle is undoubtedly present.

Lyudmila Aleksandrovna Putina

This is a Rarity in our World

Dear guests! Dear Mikhail Sergeyevich! A year has already passed since Raisa Maksimovna left us, but the pain in our hearts that comes from loss is still alive. Of course, our pain is no match for your pain. On this day, one could say a lot of kind, warm words addressed to Raisa Maksimovna. One could talk about what a wonderful woman she was, what an amazing person she used to be. First, they'll say that she is strong-willed, smart, educated, intelligent, and many, many other smart, kind and warm words. But I don't want to talk about that now. For all of us, Mikhail Sergeyevich, you and Raisa Maksimovna were above all, a beautiful couple. A beautiful couple who throughout their lives carried a feeling of great, deep love for each other, a feeling of mutual support, mutual understanding. This is a huge rarity in our world. Not everyone is given the opportunity to find their half in this life, their love, when feeling, mind and heart go hand in hand their whole life. Therefore, the endless pain, grief, frozen in your eyes at the moment of loss, did not leave anyone indifferent, it made our hearts shudder. I would like to assure you that Vladimir Vladimirovich and I greatly empathised with your grief and Raisa Maksimovna is still alive in our hearts. I want to assure you once again that we were with you at the moment of loss, and we remain with you now. And we wish you to keep her in your heart – we have no doubt that you will do so – your dear, beloved Raisa Maksimovna. We will always remember only good things about her.

Vladimir Viktorovich Grigoriev,
Deputy Minister for Press Affairs of the Russian Federation

Today We Have Completely Different Women

I would like to go back to 1991, or rather, to August 1991. At that time, I served in the publishing house of the 'Novosti' Press Agency. And on the 10th of August, Raisa Gorbacheva's book 'I Hope...' was signed for publication. When on Monday, August 19th, at 6 am, if my memory serves me, the first bars of "Swan Lake" rang out, we assembled the main edition, trying to understand what was happening. And the first question that sounded then was how to save the circulation of the book 'I Hope ...'. I tried to find this book in the printing house of the 'Novosti' Press Agency. And the amazing woman Nadezhda Sergeyevna (deputy head of the offset shop) took me to some crazy passage, completely stalker-like in appearance, where piles of papers lay, and all this was covered with the covers of the brochure, 'Where the Threat to the World Comes From.' I asked: "Where is the book 'I Hope...'?" She answered me: "You know, Vladimir Viktorovich, I hid it." – "Where did you hide it?" I asked. "Under the covers of the brochure 'Where the Threat to the World Come From.' So that they would not find it..." – "And who asked you to do this?" I asked. "No one – we just love Raisa Maksimovna and will not allow anyone to offend her."

An absolutely amazing response from the printer, who in general, was an ordinary woman, who in her own way perceived the threat on August 19th, 1991 and hid the print run of the book "I Hope…". I remember it as a real illustration of the people's love. Yes, it couldn't call it anything else. With her elegance, sparkling intelligence, not only men fell in love with Raisa Maksimovna, but, in fact, women as well. Only 15 years have passed – today we have completely different women. They are not afraid to take the leadership of political associations into their own hands and take risks on an equal basis with men. Going back 15 years, I think that many of those present here ask themselves the question: without Raisa Maksimovna, would this ever be possible? I think that she, like Eve from Adam's rib, came out of the love, understanding and warmth of Mikhail Sergeyevich. They were called the perfect couple. I think this metaphor will go down in history. And if Raisa Maksimovna gave a charming female face to the reforms in the country that stood at the threshold, then Mikhail Sergeyevich gave her a decisive spirit of change. Both my generation and the next generation will forever be indebted to this gorgeous couple. Thank you.

Vladimir Petrovich Enisherlov,
Editor–in–chief of the 'Our Heritage' Magazine

We Miss Her These Days

I don't know who had the joyous idea in 1987 to put Dmitry Sergeyevich Likhachev, a persecuted scientist, who was persecuted in St. Petersburg, and Raisa Maksimovna at the head of the Cultural Fund. But it was a truly happy thought. The Cultural Foundation has gained great prestige mainly due to the presence and active work of Raisa Maksimovna and the ideological, scientific and spiritual leadership of Dmitry Sergeyevich. I remember four or five years of my life at the Cultural Foundation, where I often had to visit and help Raisa Maksimovna. I remember her tremendous interest and efficiency. A person close to power appeared in the Foundation, and this helped him a lot. The cultural fund was seething with visitors. People came to the reception with some requests, brought relics of Russian culture. Moreover, they began to be transmitted by Russian people living not only in our country, but also abroad.

By her presence in the Foundation, by her actions, Raisa Maksimovna managed to do a lot for our culture. If you now come to the Museum of Marina Tsvetaeva, which is located on Borisoglebsky lane, to the house that Raisa Maksimovna also helped to defend, you will see an absolutely fantastic collection of more than 50 thousand items of archives and periodicals from Russian abroad. So, two–thirds of all those things – I say this with knowledge of the matter, because I simply brought most of them from abroad – were received thanks to Raisa Maksimovna Gorbacheva. These are the archives of Bunin, Mark Aldanov, Zinaida Gippius, Georgy Fedotov and other prominent figures of Russian culture. All this was purchased from abroad. We received all this after very difficult negotiations with sponsors, with some firms. Raisa Maksimovna never refused us when we asked her to take part in negotiations. She was extremely interested in this matter. That black gap in the cultural environment that has existed in our country for more than a decade has been largely filled by the return of archives and materials of the culture of the Russian emigration, back to the country, all thanks to Raisa Maksimovna Gorbacheva.

I opened the book that was handed to us today. It contains a letter from Prince Vasilchikov from Switzerland. The prince did a lot for our Foundation. He writes about how Raisa Maksimovna met with Sir Philip Oppenheimer, who, unfortunately, is also deceased. And she said to him: "Thank you for helping our culture and returning what we have lost in seventy years." – "And I saw…" the Prince notes, "…how touched Sir Philip was when he heard the words of gratitude and appreciation precisely from Raisa Maksimovna Gorbacheva to the De Beers consortium for helping Russian culture." Somehow (this was probably in 1989) I got a call from Paris from the greatest bibliophile, the owner of the firm, Andrey Savin. He said: "I have a lot of materials related to the Russian emigration. The Americans want to buy them but knowing that Raisa Maksimovna Gorbacheva and Likhachev are in your Foundation, I want to give them to you. I know they won't disappear." And, most importantly, Raisa Maksimovna took great care not only of Moscow museums, where all this was transferred (for example, to the Tsvetaeva Museum), but she also thought about peripheral museums, about peripheral collections, she was in the good sense of the word, a statesperson. I remember the moment when we brought a portrait of General Platov from England, painted on a copper plate, and at the presidium of the Cultural Foundation they decided where to transfer it. This portrait was claimed by the Russian Museum in St. Petersburg, the Tretyakov Gallery and some other Moscow museums. Raisa Maksimovna said: "Let's give it to the Museum of the Cossacks in Novocherkassk." So, it was decided that it is now there. She gave a powerful impetus to the work of the Cultural Foundation. She lived by her deeds and worries, and we all felt it.

The 'Cultural Fund' exists even in our difficult days, it has survived. It would survive no matter what. But this is the great merit of Raisa Maksimovna Gorbacheva. She gave a few words about our magazine. Without that, we would never have stood on our feet in our lives, if Raisa Maksimovna had not helped us with her name, her participation. It was a great happiness to work with such a peculiar and fascinating person who helped to restore our cultural heritage. After all, the most important thing that we have is culture. It seems to me that if we now recall all the good and significant things that Raisa Maksimovna did, then we should not forget about her activities in the Soviet Cultural Fund, not forget that she was a wonderful, very interesting and simple person, whom we lack here today.

Elena Borisovna Vladimirskaya ,
Professor at the Institute of Paediatric Hepatology

Her Great Life

In some, perhaps, the highest sense, Raisa Maksimovna really was an amazingly modest person. She never advertised what she was doing. I don't think many people know what I want to talk about today: about the role of Raisa Maksimovna in what is perhaps one of the biggest achievements of our domestic medicine over the past 10–15 years – namely, in the treatment of childhood acute leukaemia. In 1989, only 4.7% recovered from childhood leukaemia in our country, compared with 75–80% in the entire civilised world. And so, a handful of enthusiasts, led by Professor Rumyantsev, decide to bridge this gap. But how? After all, not only is it very expensive, but it is also a completely different technology, it is a different mentality, which must be learned without fail with the help of the international community. And this requires a leader. We need a person for whom people would follow 'from there', whose name would be recognised. We learned that in many countries such activities are patronised by the wives of the first persons of the state – the first ladies. And then, in 1989, I must say honestly, without much hope, we wrote a letter to Raisa Maksimovna. They passed it on through journalists with a request to become the patron of the International Charitable Association "Haematologists of the World for Children". On the third day Raisa Maksimovna's assistant called and invited Professor Rumyantsev. Raisa Maksimovna agreed to be our patron and leader. Immediately she handed over a charity check for 100 thousand dollars, which was handed to her by some big businessman, I think from South Korea. This money was first used to buy all the equipment for the Blood Bank, without which it is impossible to treat children suffering from acute leukaemia.

And then we did everything together with Raisa Maksimovna. It was hard work. Our doctors and nurses trained abroad. Funds for internships were collected in the name of Raisa Maksimovna and Mikhail Sergeyevich, and later by the Gorbachev Foundation around the world. Purposeful humanitarian aid was carried out not only with medicines, but also with equipment, people who wanted to do something for Raisa Maksimovna and Mikhail Sergeyevich. Sometimes it was a real struggle. I'll give you an example. You probably remember that in the 1990s it was impossible to turn on the TV without seeing a photo of an unfortunate child whose parents asked to raise money for his treatment abroad, namely for a bone marrow transplant. Bone marrow transplantation is an optional measure in the treatment of acute leukaemia, but some-times very necessary. We were ready for this. Thanks to the help of Raisa Maksimovna, specialists were trained. Two million dollars were needed to build the high technology departments. The Soviet Union still existed, Mikhail Sergeyevich was still the President, and after the government allocated these two million dollars, construc-tion began.

After August–December of 1991, there was no Soviet Union, there were no obligations. The firm packed up its things and prepared to leave. Raisa Maksimovna said: "No, we will not allow this to be done." Thank God, there was already the Gorbachev Foundation. Mikhail Sergeyevich and Raisa Maksimovna were getting involved (as I said at the beginning, Raisa Maksimovna was always a bit in the background, but we knew that everything came from her). Mikhail Sergeyevich would write letters, call Yegor Gaidar, the Prime Minister and Fedorov, the Minister of Finance, repeatedly. The Gorbachev Foundation collects a million dollars from all over the world. I know that the personal money of the Gorbachev family was also there. For example, the fee for the book "I Hope…" was transferred in full to the account of our Institute of Paediatric Hepatology, which was already organised at that time. I know that there was money for many of Mikhail Sergeyevich's performances abroad. So, the Fund raised a million dollars. A million dollars had to be transferred through the new Russian government. It was their obligation, but God knew whether they were going to do it or not. And if it were not for Mikhail Sergeyevich, his letters and calls, nothing would have happened. In the end we got this million. And in the summer of 1993, the Bone Marrow Transplant Centre was opened. Our dear, beautiful, charming Raisa Maksimovna and Mikhail Sergeyevich sat on the presidium. The department began to work. If you come to our Centre now, you will see a memorial plaque "Gift of Raisa and Mikhail Gorbachev" on the wall of the department.

Ten years have passed. This activity, work, enthusiasm of Raisa Maksimovna and the Gorbachev Foundation have borne fruit. Now in every region in Russia there is a centre for the treatment of leukaemia with chemotherapy, a standard program for the treatment of acute leukaemia. There are already about a hundred such centres. And now eight out of ten patients with acute leukaemia recover. In 1989, five out of a hundred children recovered. And Raisa Maksimovna stands at the origins of all this. All are mortal. A person's life is not calculated only by the number of years they lived; its value depends on what has been done. If Raisa Maksimovna would not have done anything else in her life, but only this, then her life would have been a great life all the same. Thank you, eternal thanks to Raisa Maksimovna and to an eternal memory to her life.

Mikhail Sergeyevich Gorbachev:
Many thanks to Professor Rumyantsev, who is present here.

Lyudmila Olegovna Telen,
Deputy Editor–in–Chief of Moscow News,
Member of the Raisa Maksimovna Club

She is Still Present in the Life
of the Country Today

I will say a few words only about my personal impressions of
Raisa Maksimovna. I think this is appropriate. For a long time, I,
like many others here, simply watched her from the sidelines. She
was a symbol for me, a legend. Of course, like many, I could guess
that being a beautiful and smart woman is very difficult, and life in
front of everyone is not easy for Raisa Maksimovna. Moreover, she
was not just a beautiful and intelligent woman, but also the wife of
the President of the country. And not just the wife of the President
of the country, but the wife of the President of our country with all
its difficult problems and peculiarities. When I met Raisa Maksimovna personally, I realised that she is much more significant and
interesting than the legends about her. It is even difficult for me to
explain what this significance was. Probably because behind this
external brilliance that we all saw, behind beauty, elegance, intelligence, there was a colossal inner spirit. I saw that she understood
the significance of the role that she had in history and tried very
hard to live up to it. This is very hard work. It is very important

404

that in the Gorbachev family, the memory of Raisa Maksimovna lives not only as a wife, a beloved woman, a mother, a grandmother, but also as a person who tried to do her job, to fulfil – forgive me for high-flown words – some of her historical mission. As long as we all treat Raisa Maksimovna the way we should, she will not pass away. She is still present in the life of the country today, in the life of families and simply, in our lives. And that means she's with us.

Georgy Khosroevich Shakhnazarov,
Corresponding Member of the Russian Academy of Sciences,
Former assistant to the President of the USSR

The Phenomenon of Russian History

The day after tomorrow a monument will be opened at the grave of Raisa Maksimovna. This, of course, is wonderful. But the book about her is even more important. Because through her, many people will be able to better know who Raisa Maksimovna was, what she thought she left behind. I think that I will not offend the authors if I say that they have taken only the first step. Mikhail Sergeyevich said that he himself was going to write a book about Raisa Maksimovna. That's fine. But society needs more than one book to be written, and which perhaps, others should write, and not Mikhail Sergeyevich Gorbachev. A book about Raisa Maksimovna as a phenomenon of our life, as a phenomenon of Russian life. She was not just the leader's wife, she was the First Lady, as they say. And she coped with this role surprisingly nobly and with great dignity. It is known that the role of the wife of the leader is in our time the only sphere of power that is not regulated by the Constitution. The Americans got out of the situation in their own way – they simply put the President's wife under the public's eyes so that every step was visible, so that everyone could know what she was doing. And Eleanor Roosevelt and Hillary Clinton were somehow chosen along with their husbands. This is how a certain political culture developed. We decided in the exact opposite way – to hide the leaders' wives so that no one knows anything about them at all. And so, this went on until Raisa Maksimovna appeared. But she did not show up alone. Still, Mikhail Sergeyevich led her by hand.

I think we can say that the love story of the Gorbachevs is the greatest novel in our 20th century Russian history. Maybe not only in Russia. Great because it is strong love. Great, because these are two outstanding people. And great also because they both carried out reforms. We do not always talk about this, and we do not always admit it. Of course, only Mikhail Sergeyevich can tell what he consulted with her about, how she helped him. We, the entourage, participated in general discussions. And Raisa Maksimovna was, in this sense, one of the members of our team, of Gorbachev's team. But, of course, she had a special place next to the President, a special opportunity to influence him. And, it seems to me, if she were not Gorbachev's wife, she would still be among his most ardent supporters. As far as I know her, since we talked many times on various topics, the need to budge the hardened system that we had, to update it, to bring freedom – all this was as organic to her as it was to Mikhail Sergeyevich. It was their common cause, the cause of reform. Raisa Maksimovna needs to be understood not just as a woman, as the wife of the President, but as a historical phenomenon. I think this is very important. And if '*Vagrius*' or some other publishing house takes on such a project, then I think we will all welcome it.

Metropolitan of Volokolamsk and Yuryevsky
Pitirim

Path to Eternity

It is especially difficult to speak on such days and hours. Everything that is said is dictated by the heart and living memory. I would like to say something else. About what constitutes the essence of my life for me – faith in the deep reality of the existence of an immortal soul. There are beautiful words in the Bible: "The righteous man leaves, and good deeds follow him." Let me rephrase this expression and say that good deeds go ahead. The Lord Jesus Christ said that God does not have the dead, but only the living – this is the undeniable reality experienced by a person who was in a special, essential closeness to another. I've had a chance to see a lot of people due to my age. There is an ancient Russian custom of parental commemorations several times a year and on Saturdays. So, I want to tell you, Mikhail Sergeyevich, and all those gathered here: material signs are important, but they do not determine the essence of our life. The good deeds of Raisa Maksimovna paved her way to Eternity. She's there. And we will all be together. Thank you.

Maria Nikolaeva Ivashchuk,
Deputy Director of the A. Rublev
Central Museum of Ancient Russian Art

The Second Birth
of the Rublev Museum

Today, it is a great joy and honour for me to give words of gratitude on behalf of all the employees of our museum. Because what was done by Raisa Maksimovna for the Andrei Rublev Museum of Ancient Russian Art is truly invaluable. Before meeting with Raisa Maksimovna, the Rublev Museum was the most ordinary, smallest third-rate museum. You can imagine what a third-rate museum under the jurisdiction of the Moscow City Executive Committee looked like: it occupied only two buildings on the territory of the Spaso-Andronikov Monastery. This museum has always been a museum of a difficult fate. Created in 1947, it has always been a museum that "lived in spite of". They tried to shut it down many times. Many officials did not understand why a museum of icons was needed. And the museum was in such a difficult position until the meeting with Raisa Maksimovna. She came to us for the first time in 1984. She listened very carefully to the director's story, asked the staff how they imagine the life of the museum in the future. She visited us again. And then a miracle happened. There was a decree that the museum was to be assigned the first-rate category, and that it will become subordinate to the Ministry of Culture of the USSR. Moreover, the territory of the entire Spaso-Andronikov Monastery was given as property of the museum. The dream of the museum's first director, its creator, David Ilyich Arsenishvili, has come true. The Museum of Icons – the only Museum of Old Russian Art in our country – has finally received a worthy territory, prospects for the legitimate development of a long life. For us it was a great celebration, a living embodiment of a dream. We have survived to this day. This is all thanks to the invaluable contribution of Raisa Maksimovna. Since then, there have been opportunities for growth, the opening of new exhibitions, wide communication with people. We can talk about the second birth of the Rublev Museum. For this, a deep bow to Raisa Maksimovna. I am very sad that these words are heard after her departure. Mikhail Sergeyevich, it is wonderful that you hear these words of gratitude. Thank you very much from our Russian culture, from us, the museum workers. And I hope that we will meet at the Rublev Museum. We are all waiting for you.

Lyudmila Vasilievna Shaposhnikova,
Director of the International Centre-Museum named after
N. K. Roerich

Breaking Stereotypes...

When a person passes away, each time we try to comprehend what kind of person they were, who they really were. Thinking about Raisa Maksimovna, I want to say that she was a very strong personality. A personality that broke several traditional foundations, which, in general, were no longer needed. The first foundation that she broke were the stereotype of the behaviour of the Soviet leader's wife. She was the first to become the First Lady of the country and was always next to Mikhail Sergeyevich. She behaved like an independent person, fully prepared for this role. And we, looking at her, remembered the wives of the first leaders of our country, who, as it were, remained aloof from real events. Maybe somewhere, in some way they quietly manifested themselves, but the way Raisa Maksimovna entered the public arena, not one of them managed as well as she did. I know that this was not perceived unambiguously. But she still courageously walked her way because she was sure that she was right, and turns out, she really was right. The second moment. I just opened the book and came across a chapter called "The Meaning of our Existence is Culture."

There are very few people in Russia now who truly understand, as Raisa Maksimovna understood it, what culture is and what its significance is in our evolutionary movement. Today it is especially painful to watch how the leaders of our state push culture into the background. And there is no one to come to the rescue and support the culture, as Raisa Maksimovna once did. And this, of course, is the greatest merit of Raisa Maksimovna, especially since she received a philosophical education. Paradoxical, isn't it? But we know how philosophy was taught in our country. There was not much to say about culture. Raisa Maksimovna managed to correct the situation; culture began to be appreciated. But unfortunately, everything has returned to normal, and once again, we no longer have people of this kind at the top. Let's hope that one day, we will.

And the third point. You know our great compatriots: Nicholas Konstantinovich Roerich, Helena Ivanovna Roerich and Svyatoslav Nikolaevich Roerich, their youngest son, a well–known artist and public figure. Svyatoslav Nikolaevich came to us very often. He was received by Mikhail Sergeyevich and Raisa Maksimovna twice – in 1987 and in 1989. Svyatoslav Nikolaevich suffered from inattention to himself. He offered us the enormous cultural heritage of Nicholas Roerich and Helena Ivanovna Roerich. Even before Mikhail Sergeyevich Gorbachev, all this was repulsed by: "Why, what for..." But the people worked abroad for so many years in order to give it to the people of the country disinterestedly, without demanding anything in return. Under the Gorbachevs, the tradition of a coldly official attitude towards our great compatriots came to an end. They were accepted. They were favoured by them. Svyatoslav Nikolaevich told me how pleasant it was and how highly he appreciated Raisa Maksimovna, who had a dialogue with him at the highest level. Our Nicholas Roerich Museum and our International Centre are also one of the cultural achievements of Raisa Maksimovna. She stood at the origins of its creation in the 89th year of the Soviet Roerich Fund. She participated in our organisational group. We were at the Constituent Assembly. She gave us a lot of advice, which later we were able to implement.

Olga Andreevna Kuchkina,
Columnist for Komsomolskaya Pravda,
Poet, Prose Writer, Playwright

Romanticism is Not an Empty Thing

It so happened that Mikhail Sergeyevich and Raisa Maksimovna treated me in a completely special way. It was amazing for me. I did not know that. And I only found out after Raisa Maksimovna was gone. I have been working at Komsomolskaya Pravda for a long time. And involuntarily some of my articles and notes were read by these two people. Fate wanted us to open up to each other through them. I always wanted to talk with Raisa Maksimovna separately about Mikhail Sergeyevich. Moreover, he always interested me primarily as a person, rather than a politician. Nothing came of it. But as it turned out, I had a talk with Mikhail Sergeyevich about Raisa Maksimovna. Sometime after her death. Mikhail Sergeyevich amazed and shocked me. Well, to be honest, when a person is in power, he is visible through the light, but at the same time, we are not very attentive. Still, we are not very fa--sighted, we are inclined to take trifles for the main thing, to find fault, to think generally and to demand God knows what from a person, as if he owes us. And when I met with Mikhail Sergeyevich, it was such an amazing day, he behaved like a child. He needed to throw something out, to speak out. I was there to listen. And I will never forget this conversation, this trust, this sincerity. And for me then everything came together, and everything changed. And it changed in a very important way. In general, we have such an amazing country. As Bunin said: "From this tree – there is both an axe and an icon." He spoke like this about the Russian people. Very often, as if an axe hangs over us. And we only feel this axe. And we can never really make out the icon. At such moments of tragic fractures, everything opens up very clearly, everything is visible. And thank you, Mikhail Sergeyevich, for this love, for the fact that we saw it in reality. And we, the last, perhaps, romantics of the "sixties" and the last romantics of this century, received vital confirmation that our romanticism is not an empty thing, but a very, very real reality. Eternal memory to Raisa Maksimovna.

Tamara Grigoryevna Shumnaya,
Director of the Museum of Contemporary History of Russia

The First Among the First

In 1989, there was a state exhibition in Rome, and many of our museums presented their collections. At this time, Mikhail Sergeyevich and Raisa Maksimovna were on a visit to Italy. How they were met! It was something to behold. We, employees of Moscow museums, ran outside and looked at the huge crowds of people who greeted our leader and his wife. The spectacle was absolutely unforgettable. We were all very worried, because Raisa Maksimovna was supposed to come with us for the first tour... And suddenly there was silence in the exhibition hall. Raisa Maksimovna appeared quickly – to her shop windows, to her stands. She came in a beautiful red blouse, which goes well with her. Next to her are assistants who guide her because the exhibition was huge. I myself led the tour, told her about the exhibits. But there were so many guests, so many Italian friends, and everyone wanted to talk to her, that they pushed her back and didn't let her near the stands, and they just pushed us away. And I, having uttered some phrase about the next exhibit, suddenly found myself so far from Raisa Maksimovna that I had to make considerable efforts to return back to my stand and continue the story. Among this mass of people, she

remained in my memory so light, friendly, attentive and benevolent... When this terrible tragedy happened and Raisa Maksimovna
left so unexpectedly, we at the museum immediately decided to
make an exhibition dedicated to her life and work. When we did
this exhibition, we saw Raisa Maksimovna in a completely different
way. I want to say that now our museum is working on the project
called the "First Ladies of Russia". And in this series, I must say,
Raisa Maksimovna is completely different. She is as bright as a star.
A completely different person.

Vitaly Semenovich Gusenkov,
Assistant to the President of the Soviet Union

A Gift of Fate

Dear Mikhail Sergeyevich, Dear Irina Mikhailovna! Of course, it is difficult for me to speak, because a lot of things in my life are connected with Raisa Maksimovna. More than 12 years, you can say, I worked next to her. These were great years, very significant, very interesting, and for me, of course, it was a gift of fate. I would like to talk about one moment. Last year, NTV made a film about Raisa Maksimovna, which is called "The First 'First Lady'." Naturally, they found out that I worked with Raisa Maksimovna and turned to me. They came to my home, they questioned me for a long time, probably for two hours. They were really interested. They asked: "Who was Raisa Maksimovna's stylist?" I told them that at that time, "Let alone a stylist, the very concept didn't even exist." The concept, like the word, was born in the Yeltsin era. Raisa Maksimovna, if you like, was her own stylist. She paid a lot of attention to everything she had to work on. She very carefully prepared for meetings, trips, she delved into everything herself. There is no doubt that Raisa Maksimovna represented the Soviet Union in the international sphere with great dignity. I am a living witness to this – I basically had to be with her on these foreign trips. She thought and pondered on everything to the smallest detail: what she should say, how she should speak, the nature of her meetings, the circle of interlocutors. I think that such thoroughness, which, probably, was given to her by nature, led to the fact that she had excellent relationships with the spouses of the world's largest leaders. This very well complemented the work that Mikhail Sergeyevich did as General Secretary, as President of the Soviet Union. I think Raisa Maksimovna's contribution in this sense is also huge and invaluable. And once again I want to say that I was very pleased to hear what was said here. I immediately remembered many moments from those 12 years. For example, when Elena Borisovna Vladimirskaya spoke – and I immediately remembered how this check was handed over, how everything was done publicly, in front of everyone, in the House of Friendship. Yes, and much more was remembered of what was said here. Blessed memory of Raisa Maksimovna.

Mikhail Sergeyevich Gorbachev

Getting Back to Normal

My first words of gratitude go to you who are in this hall, firstly, for the memory that you have preserved, for everything that you said on this evening of remembrance. Much of what I heard from you I did not know. Just as I did not know what I heard at the Cultural Foundation during the speeches of friends and comrades in those mournful days of last year. What meetings and discoveries there were, but we simply did not have enough time to tell each other about everything. The President's working regime was such that I returned home at about 10 o'clock during a normal working day, and then every evening, despite mortal fatigue, we went for an hour's walk. We have had this rule for probably around thirty years. Now Irina and I walk with even greater perseverance. After the walk, I go up to my office and work until one, until two in the morning. And I still can't go to bed earlier. Knowing that my assistant Georgy Ostroumov is not sleeping at this time, after one in the morning I can call him when I need to talk. Time has tested us, and everything we are worth. I want to thank you for what you said about Raisa Maksimovna and add on my own behalf that we were very lucky. Olya Kuchkina (we continue to communicate in the Komsomol) was the most beautiful and smartest journalist in our youth. And we (secretaries of the regional committee of the Komsomol), of course, appreciated it. You remained as you were. It's great. She really "rocked" me, for the first time in my life I said too much. It happens. We really protected our world, our home, it was our spiritual, moral fortress, and in all the trials that we went through, it saved us.

I want to thank our young entrepreneurs, they are very close friends to us – Denis Gurinsky and Slava Fedorov, who proposed the idea of creating a Book of Memory of Raisa Maksimovna. I thank the publishing house, which undertook to implement this idea, which has already become a common project. All this is very pleasant. After all, the book is made up of what was said by Raisa Maksimovna and those who knew her, understood her. This is a one-of-a-kind, unique book. Many people took up the pen and wrote something, including those from the Rublev Museum of Ancient Russian Culture, which Raisa Maksimovna loved very much and kept in touch with until the end of her life. I supported her in this. In general, I supported her in everything, she did nothing without consulting me. It's right. But having agreed on the main thing, she was free to do whatever she wanted. She was a very prepared person. She was prepared by life itself. Suffice it to say that Raisa Maksimovna taught two courses for almost 25 years – historical and dialectical materialism. I would like to thank the main initiator of this project, Georgy Ostroumov, who did a lot of preparatory work. I want to say a big thank you to Irishka and her grandchildren. Together they crawled on the floor on their knees for many, many days, spreading out our photo library (and we have a very large one) in order to select the necessary photos.

Almost a year has passed – just short of two days, but our grief has not diminished. The pain doesn't go away. I don't know what will happen next. It's good that Irina and her granddaughters moved in with me and now we all live together. Perhaps this is also a normal human process. Everything that was in the apartment and in the country before, remains so. Irina does not touch the second floor, where I was with Raisa Maksimovna. On the first floor, she already has to do everything herself and she does it well. She got this from her mother. Everything is preserved in Raisa Maksimovna's office: there are folders of an unwritten book. I found there a plan for 33 chapters, and in red ink across the entire sheet is written – "What hurts my heart." She was a very vulnerable person, very sensitive. Those who were members of the Raisa Maksimovna Club know this, they felt it. Indeed, Vitaly Gusenkov is right: she treated everything as if the existence of the world depended on it. In essence and in reality, I feel the same way a lot of the time, and it was the one thing we did not have to sort out. But we found out that all our lives – we figured out questions and even sometimes our relationship. It cannot be said that everything was sweet and sour, no, it was the real life of real people who met when one was 18 and the other 19, and then we lived together for almost 50 years. That's the whole story. We didn't say much about our love for each other. Irina can remember that this topic is not something we talked about often. But no matter what happened, it was clear that we always needed each other, just as we needed our children. After all, Irishka was born contrary to the prohibitions of medicine – Raisa Maksimovna was told she could not have children. So, let's thank her for her own determination...

I have already had to say that simultaneously with Perestroika, a kind of revolution in the social status of women began in our country. By the way, the women's club created in recent years by Raisa Maksimovna began with a discussion of the topic: "Is the voice of a woman heard in Russia?" We know how we hear it. This was followed by other questions about women's participation in public and political life. For example, in the ruling Social Democratic Party of Germany 50 percent of positions are filled by women. The feminine principle in our society and state must be strengthened in all matters. Then we will be a normal society, a normal country. If the issue of old people and children has not been resolved in a country, then this country is sick, it cannot be considered normal. I think it is impossible to talk about the wellbeing and future of the country even when the issue of the position of women in the life of society and the country is not being resolved. After the well-known decisions in the spring of 1985, Raisa Maksimovna asked me: "What should I do, how should I behave now?" I told her: "We will not change anything. I am already 54 years old; you are 53 years old – do we really have to change something? We are already established people; it is time to retire. We will not change anything in our relations." So, we acted – no matter what was said or written.

At the same time, I am now looking at journalists – at Vitaly Tretyakov, our friend from Nezavisimaya Gazeta, at friends from Trud, at Andrey Grachev (one of our family's old friends, he's also writing a book), at Olya Kuchkina (she achieves – "Let's Talk on the Merits"). These are all the luminaries of the press. And I also think about literary horsemanship when they pursue one goal – to smash through everyone and everything. As soon as a squeak from the shell is heard, and they, like literal riders, race away, and before you know it, they have already learned everything. And it's only now that you begin to understand something. You think: "Are you really such a fool, and he is such a genius?" Then it hatches, crawls out of its shell and squeaks – and they already know everything. I think we need to respect each other and be responsible to each other. It is very important. Of course, we are who we are. I will not say that we are bad. We are a very amazing people. We can bear what others cannot bear. And we can envy like no one else, even our friends. But this is a topic that requires a separate discussion. I remember a phrase that Yuri Vladimirovich Andropov once said: "We still need to figure out what country we live in." So, we haven't figured it out yet. And this is the most important thing. We need to take a lot with us from our thousand-year history, but we need to say goodbye to a lot of things forever. We underestimated something, chatted about another thing, trampled it down and forgot, we did not break with what we should have broken with.

But it's too early to draw conclusions. It seems strange to me when people ask: "How would you assess the results of the new

President's activity?" And I got out of the situation when I answered the questions of my one interviewer – a Doctor of Philosophy. I remembered this situation. Once a French delegation arrived in China, and the Premier of the State Council, Zhou Enlai, was asked the question: "How did he evaluate the French Revolution, how it affected the world and, in particular, China." And Zhou Enlai was connected with France, with its culture, he lived and studied there for a while. He thought and said: "You know, it's too early to sum it up…" Now, I want to end where I started, with words of gratitude. And I want to thank you, Lyudmila Aleksandrovna, for coming. I am very glad that you said that you are thinking of Raisa Maksimovna with us, on her memorial day, thinking about very important things, about our life. I would like to convey to you all, to all those present here – and there are many interesting people here – while we see that the President is looking for how to work out the mandate that he received in the elections from the people, and thereby realise the promise. We are all together. We will support him as the people. In the face of the sovereign, the people, all other contracts must be annulled. It is good if we proceed precisely from this, and not from what was under the previous government. I don't want to politicise our evening, but since you, Lyudmila Aleksandrovna, are present here, I'll say this: It's very important for us to maintain understanding between the President and society, that is, understanding between the government and the country, because if this doesn't happen, nothing will happen in our country. And we would very much like, together with the President, to get

425

out of the current state, to embark on a normal track of advancing along the path of democracy, freedom and strengthening mutual understanding. These are the thoughts I wanted to share with you, because this evening is all about mutual understanding. Thank you all so much for being here tonight.

END

Raisa, What Hurts My Heart

REVIEW

Hertfordshire Press's publication of 'What Hurts My Heart' couldn't be more timely, coming hot on the heels of the death of the last Soviet leader Mikhail Gorbachev last month. Translated by xxx, it is a large and remarkable collection of the diaries and letters of Raisa Gorbachev, his wife of half a century, and one of the few Russian first ladies to emerge from the shadows and become almost as well known in the West as her husband.

When the stylish and forceful Raisa died in 1999, former US first lady Nancy Reagan said. "We believe that Raisa was a strong partner with her husband and an important voice in the friendship that our two countries established in the 1980s," Certainly few were better placed than Raisa to give a true insight into the enigmatic Gorbachev and his struggle to both see through the end of the nuclear arms race and the peaceful break up of the Soviet empire.

Some of 'What Hurts My Heart' was published in 1992, as Raisa's memoir 'I Hope'. But this volume contains a whole lot more letters and commentaries never published in English before. They provide a close-up, sharp and often very poignant eyewitness view of some of the major events in world history – the personal and intimate reflections of a woman close to the heart of power, and an absolutely fascinating read for anyone interested one of the most extraordinary figures of the 20th century.

— *John Farndon, writer*

REVIEW

'Raisa – What Hurts My Heart'

So much of the detail and truth of what the Soviet Union was is absent from discourse in the West and in the FSU countries. There are many reasons for this but first and foremost is the sheer weight of the political, military, economic, technological and sporting history in relation to the wider world and the West in particular. There are few examples of something cutting through all of that and providing a glimpse into the deeply personal and enchantingly human history of life in the USSR. *'Raisa - What Hurts My Heart'* is a highly informative and unusually intimate account of perhaps the most famous woman of the USSR – Mrs. Raisa Maksimovna Gorbachaeva, the wife of the most famous president of the USSR, Mr. Mikhail Sergeyevich Gorbachev.

This book is a collection of transcribed interviews, with frequent commentary from the interviewer; and interspersed with letters and published interviews. It is extraordinarily direct, charming and compelling. The nature of life in the USSR is brought out in graphic detail; the hardships, the challenges, the distance between the Party and needs of the people – especially the provincial residents who, despite being regarded as the essence of what it is to be Russian were left short again and again.

Raisa charts her own childhood, her schooling, her university life, including travelling without paying for tickets on the Moscow Metro. She lays out the birth of her romance with fellow student and later husband, Mikhail – he even worked in the summer holidays driving a harvester to pay for their wedding, she borrowed shoes for that auspicious day, and so much more showing the human fragility and endearing nature of people. Raisa's words are replete with references to great literature – she was a polyglot scholar who taught philosophy – the description of her in the writings of Margaret Thatcher is sublime.

The life and experience of Gorbachev himself is presented with so many insightful anecdotes. Perhaps for the first time we can learn about the man himself, his preparation over decades to eventually become General Secretary. We learn about the uniqueness, modernity and humanity with which he approached his service to the USSR and finally as President.

This book is remarkable in a great many ways; it is a succinct overview of aspects of the history of the USSR, it is a first-hand account of events major and minor from an intimate companion and confidante of the man behind nuclear disarmament agreements, Glasnost and Perestroika. And it is a love story between two people who are revealed as kind and thoughtful to all whilst they meet with the notables of many nations and international entities of every kind. It is a unique book, wonderfully uplifting to read and one through which a deeper appreciation of who the Gorbachevs were and what they meant to so many in so many regions of the USSR and wider world can be achieved.

— Afzal R. Amin,
Researcher International Relations: USSR,
Russian and Central Asian Affairs

REVIEW

    This remarkable new book details not just the fascinating life of Russia's leading lady during the late eighties, but also the intricate relationship and love story with Russian President Mikhail Gorbachev. Uniquely told through letters, interviews, diary entries and the memories of the many political and famous people she met (including Margaret Thatcher), this is an unbridled collection of writing. It is raw and compelling, drawing the reader into the heart of this extraordinary woman and allows them to look profoundly into the events of Perestroika and the ultimate dissolution of the USSR.

    The helpful commentary from its author, intertwined with the text, provides insightful context, commentary and captivation. Although, at times, parts may seem an unstructured ramble through someone's hopes and fears, this doesn't detract from the quality of observation and understanding this collection of texts brings. It brings a better perception of what was really like inside the USSR and the events leading up to its dissolution and this is no mean feat given the amount of primary sources to work with. Few have had the privilege of being so close and connected to Raisa Gorbacheva, so readers will join this exclusive club of people who have an appreciation for just what an extraordinary woman she was and what a critical life she led in the role of Russia both at home and abroad. This is a masterpiece of curated writings that will set any reader off to find out more.

Nick Rowan,
OCA magazine Editor-in-Chief